Training for Employment in Western Europe and the United States

Training for Employment in Western Europe and the United States

J.R. Shackleton

with Linda Clarke, Thomas Lange and Siobhan Walsh

Edward Elgar

Published by
Edward Elgar Publishing Limited
Gower House
Croft Road
Aldershot
Hants GU11 3HR
England

Edward Elgar Publishing Company
Old Post Road
Brookfield
Vermont 05036
USA

British Library Cataloguing in Publication Data
Shackleton, J.R.
 Training for Employment in Western Europe and the United States
 I. Title
 331.2592

Library of Congress Cataloguing in Publication Data
Training for employment in Western Europe and the United States / J.R.
 Shackleton with Linda Clarke, Thomas Lange, and Siobhan Walsh.
  p. cm.
 Includes bibliographical references and index.
  1. Labor supply—Effect of education on—Europe. 2. Labor supply—
Effect of education on—United States. 3. Education and state—
Europe. 4. Education and state—United States. I. Shackleton, J.R.
 HD5715.5.E78T7   1995
 331.11\423—dc20   94–34106
                                                                CIP

ISBN 1 85278 863 1

Printed and bound in Great Britain by
Hartnolls Limited, Bodmin, Cornwall

Contents

Figures

Tables

1. Introduction

Concern over the creation and maintenance of labour force skills has never been higher amongst advanced economies. In the economy of the future, UK employers are told by the National Training Task Force, "the firms that have a highly skilled workforce will be the ones which survive and grow" (National Training Task Force 1992). In the United States there is similar official concern that "today's labor force does not meet our current needs, and our needs are increasing as technological change accelerates and foreign competition intensifies" (Commission on Workforce Quality and Labour Market Efficiency 1989). The European Commission calls on member governments to "accept responsibility for providing the education and basic training necessary in order to equip people for working in a technically-challenging environment which demands adaptability and a capacity to develop new skills" (Commission of the European Communities 1991). More dispassionately, the OECD notes a common "re-blossoming of interest in the qualifications and skill of the workforce" across the developed world (Organization for Economic Cooperation and Development 1991).

Such a widespread emphasis on workforce quality no doubt reflects common factors amongst the nations which have been economically dominant in the postwar years, but now face growing uncertainty. They include: rapid technological change as a result of the explosion of computer power and quantum leaps in telecommunications; the apparent end of "full" employment and the perceived threat of a growing "underclass" of the unqualified and possibly unemployable; and the unleashing of new competition from Eastern Europe, Asia and the Pacific. In a world where capital is mobile as never before, and where the nation state seems impotent in the face of economic change, the quality of its workforce seems to be all a country has going for it if it wishes to maintain and improve its living standards into the next century.

Some of this concern is arguably overblown. One of the purposes of this book is to cast a critical eye over some of the analysis and prescription which is being offered by commentators on the education and training systems which are held responsible for creating, sustaining and renewing productive skills.

1

Although educational preparation for the world of work is discussed at
some length, the focus of the book is on training. Two decades ago Mark
Blaug wrote that "we know almost nothing about the economics of
training, its incidence, its costs and its benefits" (Blaug 1972: 199). He
could have added that we knew next to nothing about the politics, the
sociology or the history of training either. This could no longer be asserted
by anybody even vaguely acquainted with the subject. Almost too much is
known, in the sense that the amount of literature on the subject has grown
to colossal proportions, well beyond the ability of one individual to
comprehend and absorb it in its entirety. Some studies concentrate simply
on describing and analysing particular training systems; others attempt
cross-country comparisons. Some discuss training in abstract theoretical
terms; others attempt to use quantitative data to test hypotheses derived
from analytical models. Some attempt an objective approach; others are
unashamedly partisan and have a clear political agenda. This book draws
on all these approaches.

DEFINING TRAINING

We need to begin by considering how to define training and its role in the
economy. It must be said at the outset that there is no common definition
of training, and some lack of clarity, too, about its purpose. Definitions
differ from country to country, but also within a country. In the UK, for
instance, the government-sponsored *Training in Britain* study (Department of Employment 1989) concentrated on "formal, structured and
guided" means of acquiring work-related skills. This meant that general
supervision, basic induction, motivational meetings, attendance at trade
fairs, and so on, were excluded. The Employment Department's annual
publication *Training Statistics*, on the other hand, adopts a wider view:
training is any "intentional intervention to help the individual (or the
organisation) to become competent, or more competent, at work"
(Employment Department 1993: 8). The same source points out that
"there are a number of indistinct boundaries within the training market".

For example, the boundary between training and education, already
alluded to, is a difficult one to draw. Some educational programmes in
school, college or university indisputably provide training for a professional career. However, it can be argued (Blaug 1993) that some general
skills of vocational relevance can be acquired on virtually all educational
courses, whatever the ostensible content – literacy, numeracy, communica-
tions skills of all types.

Similarly, the distinction between work experience and training is unclear. On-the-job experience is very often an important component of formally structured training systems (for example, in the German "dual" system, discussed in Chapter 7). Yet the point at which supervised work experience ends and unsupervised learning-by-doing begins is arbitrary. There is a strong tradition in the USA of seeing job experience, rather than formal programmes, as the paradigm case of employer-provided "training". This tradition, best exemplified in the econometric work of Jacob Mincer (see Chapter 2), no doubt reflects the American experience of extended post-compulsory schooling (often with a strong vocational flavour), frequent job changes, geographical and occupational mobility, and very limited historical reliance on apprenticeship systems.

The tradition in continental Europe is very different. Here long-established and hierarchical systems of education and training place great emphasis on training for a *status*, that of qualified and accredited skilled worker. There is an ideal of a "finished" worker, with a clearly defined set of formally attested skills (often defined largely by other members of the trade) and with rights and prerogatives denied to his or her juniors. The French expression *"formation professionelle"*, often wrongly used in English as a synonym for training, conveys this rather well. The German emphasis on formal apprenticeships under *"meister"*, at low and controlled rates of pay, is well known. Less formal ways of acquiring skills go unrecognized in this tradition, making some indicators of training incidence incommensurable between countries (Commission of the European Communities 1991: 136–7). Commentators in countries like France and Germany also place emphasis on the way in which training relates to other aspects of the labour market, such as pay systems and industrial relations. Furthermore, they tend to assume, unlike many British and American commentators, that training does not simply concern the individual and his or her employer. The government and the "social partners" (organized capital and labour) have important roles to play in defining and validating training.

Given these and other difficulties in defining training, it seems best at the outset to adopt the widest possible definition of training: broadly, any activity which normally tends to promote the acquisition of skills possessing value in the labour market. Such activities may include the acquisition of work experience even if no structured programme of learning exists, so long as it is a reasonable expectation of those undergoing the experience that a learning outcome will occur. This may not be the ideal form of training, and certainly very few human resource management experts would give it the time of day. Since, however, such learning-by-doing is the way in which most people have historically acquired their work skills, it seems unwise to turn up our noses at it.

PLAN OF THE BOOK

This book attempts to synthesize a fair proportion of the literature in the training field, in a way which should be comprehensible to intermediate-level undergraduates (especially in economics or industrial relations), non-specialist postgraduate management students, training practitioners, business people, journalists and civil servants concerned with training issues.

Following this brief introduction, the book is structured into three main parts. Part I is concerned mainly with theory. The human capital theory, predominant in the USA and the UK (though less popular in some parts of Continental Europe) is outlined, discussed and criticized. The approach provides an explanation of many labour market phenomena in terms of rational choices made by individuals, households and firms. However, it points to a range of possible market failures which may require government intervention. Some alternative economic theories of training are also surveyed. A chapter also examines the "political economy" of training: the political context in which training policies are discussed.

Part II consists mainly of a series of "case studies" outlining and commenting on particular education and training systems: those of the USA, the UK, Germany and France. A further chapter spreads the net more widely and makes some broad international comparisons.

In Part III a number of specific issues are looked at in more detail. These chapters (one on education for work, one on training for the unemployed, and one on women and training) develop the economic analysis of training in more detail while drawing on empirical material from many countries.

A concluding chapter draws together the threads of the book.

ACKNOWLEDGEMENTS

The book is one outcome of a project on European training undertaken by the Education, Training and the Labour Market Research Group at the University of Westminster. The project in turn was a component of the University's "Europe in the 21st Century" initiative, partly funded by the former Polytechnics and Colleges Funding Council.

The writing of the book was under the general direction of J.R. Shackleton. Each chapter bears the mark of a number of hands, but Shackleton was largely responsible for Chapters 1, 2, 3, 4, 9, 10 and 13. Siobhan Walsh was the main author of Chapters 5, 6 and 8, and co-wrote much of Chapter 12 with Linda Clarke. Clarke also provided an input into

Chapter 7, together with Thomas Lange. Lange also bears most of the responsibility for Chapter 11.

Thanks are due to Barbara Roweth for her general support, and to Geoffrey Killick for useful comments on draft chapters.

PART I

Theory

2. Training and the Human Capital Model

INTRODUCTION

This book is concerned with examining real-world training experience and policies. However, in order to make sense of the issues which such an investigation throws up, we must locate them in an appropriate theoretical context. Accordingly, in this chapter we outline the dominant theoretical approach to the role of training in the economy – certainly in the UK and the United States. This is the "human capital" model, dating back at least to the time of the founder of systematic economic theory, Adam Smith. In the next chapter some alternative analytical approaches are introduced and examined.

THE HUMAN CAPITAL APPROACH

In his *Wealth of Nations*, first published in 1776, Smith compares the acquisition of skills to the construction of a machine. As with the machine, "much labour and time" is expended, and this must be compensated for by a return on the investment. In order to justify the costs of training (assumed – and we should remember this – to be borne by workers or their families), wages must eventually be higher than those for unskilled labour by a margin which "will replace ... the whole expense ... with at least the ordinary profits of an equally valuable capital" (Smith 1910: 14).

This apparently simple, even banal, observation contains the germ of an analytical approach which has proved extremely fruitful. Yet although the idea of skill acquisition as a form of investment was widely accepted by economists in the nineteenth century, little was made of Smith's point that this leads to an economically rational equilibrium pattern of wage differentials. Writing in 1848, John Stuart Mill, although recognizing the general principle that the rate of return to different types of investment tends to be

9

equalized by the forces of competition, argued that this rule did not apply to investment in skills. The labour market was characterized by non-competing groups of workers (an idea which, as we shall see later, has been revived in modern times): "So complete, indeed, has hitherto been the separation, so strongly marked the line of demarcation, between the different grades of labourers, as to be almost equivalent to an hereditary distinction of caste" (Mill 1909: 393). In such a world there was "a natural monopoly in favour of skilled labourers against the unskilled, which makes the difference of reward exceed ... what is sufficient merely to equalize their advantages" (ibid.: 391).

Similarly Alfred Marshall, though devoting a chapter of his *Principles of Economics* to industrial training (and several others to the factors influencing earnings), rejects the view that the market will equalize the rate of return on investment in training. Investment by young people's families "is limited by the means, the foresight and the unselfishness of ... parents" (Marshall 1920: 466). Investment by employers is not carried "as far as they would have done, if the results of the investment accrued to them in the same way as the results of any improvements they might make in their machinery" (ibid.). What Marshall draws attention to here is that, in a non-slave society, workers in whom investments have been made cannot be forced against their will to continue in a firm's employment: they can take their skills elsewhere. This is again an observation which finds echoes in today's debates.

The modern theory of human capital, therefore, in rediscovering and reinterpreting Adam Smith, owes little to nineteenth- and early twentieth-century economics. Indeed, with the exception of some pioneering work by Milton Friedman and Simon Kuznets (1945), nothing much happened to develop human capital theory until the late 1950s and early 1960s. Then, however, there was a flurry of publications (Mincer 1958, 1962; Schultz 1960, 1961; Becker 1962, 1964) which fundamentally changed the way in which economists thought about skill acquisition and set off an ever-expanding literature on the subject.

The most comprehensive and persuasive early treatment of the modern human capital approach was developed by Gary Becker (Becker 1964). The central argument which Becker put forward is that people spend on themselves in a variety of ways, not only for current gratification but also to secure future benefits. Their expenditure is implicit as well as explicit: an important contribution made by Becker is his analysis of the allocation of time (Becker 1965). Time is the ultimate scarce resource with alternative uses: the accumulation of human capital through education and training has an "opportunity cost" in terms of other uses to which that time can be put.

Resources can be devoted to a variety of forms of investment in human capital. A great strength of Becker's approach is his demonstration that training is not a unique phenomenon. Such activities as spending on health care, school- and college-based education, job search and migration can all be analysed in a similar way: they involve sacrifices today in return for benefits in the future. Moreover, within each of these areas it is recognized that there are various means to any end. As well as global choices (how much to spend in total on training or health care or job search) there are questions as to what type of health care to choose, which way to seek jobs and which mode of training to pursue: there are no rigid "technical" requirements. This is a very important lesson to bear in mind.[1]

THE BASIC MODEL

We start by outlining Becker's basic model of on-the-job training. In this framework a training project can in principle be evaluated in a similar way to an investment in physical capital. That is, if the value of its benefits, suitably discounted, exceeds that of the costs, it makes sense to invest.[2] The starting point is a perfectly competitive market for unskilled labour.

Elementary economic theory tells us that the profit-maximizing firm in this environment will choose to employ labour in any period (t) up to the point where the value of its marginal product (MP) is just equal to the wage rate (W):

$$MP_t = W_t \tag{2.1}$$

However, this well-established proposition is modified by the existence of training, which involves costs. In the simplest case these are opportunity costs – the reduction in workers' productivity while they are undergoing training – but in most cases there are also other more explicit costs such as materials, equipment and trainer time used in the training process.

Training costs, as Adam Smith suggested, can in principle be recouped from labour's higher productivity in the future. Suppose the firm pays the cost of training (including continuing to pay the market wage rate even while productivity is temporarily reduced); it must hope to recoup by getting the benefit of enhanced productivity in future. Its profit-maximizing rule is now, formally speaking, that the sum of the discounted present value[3] of marginal products during and after the training period should just be equal to the discounted present value of wages paid and costs incurred during and after the training period.

Assume for simplicity that training takes place in the initial period ($t = 0$) only, that the explicit training costs (k) are all incurred in this period, that there are n post-training periods over which costs can be recouped, and that i is the relevant discount rate. Ignoring for the moment the implicit (opportunity) cost of training, the profit-maximizing condition can be written as:

$$MP_0 + \sum_{t=1}^{n} \frac{MP_t}{(1+i)^t} = W_0 + k_0 + \sum_{t=1}^{n} \frac{W_t}{(1+i)^t} \qquad (2.2)$$

This expression can be simplified by defining a term G which is equal to the net present value of post-training marginal product minus wages:

$$G = \sum_{t=1}^{n} \frac{MP_t}{(1+i)^t} - \sum_{t=1}^{n} \frac{W_t}{(1+i)^t} \qquad (2.3)$$

We can substitute G into equation (2.2), yielding the following:

$$MP_0 + G = W_0 + k_0 \qquad (2.4)$$

This equation then has to be modified slightly to take account of the opportunity cost of training in terms of temporarily reduced productivity, defined as

$$c_0 = MP_0' - MP_0 \qquad (2.5)$$

where MP_0' is the level of marginal productivity if training had not been undertaken. If we define C as the total costs – explicit (k_0) and implicit (c_0) – we can finally rewrite equation (2.4) as

$$MP_0' + G = W_0 + C \qquad (2.6)$$

This equation plays a key role in Becker's thinking.

GENERAL AND SPECIFIC TRAINING

In order to understand the problem facing policy-makers who wish to encourage skill acquisition, it is necessary to introduce Becker's famous distinction between "general" and "specific" training – itself possibly inspired by Alfred Marshall's discussion of general and specialized abilities (Marshall 1920: 172-3).

General training is that which produces skills which are valuable to more than one employer. These will include quite basic transferable skills such as reading and writing, interpersonal and communication skills – but also higher abilities of a more specialized nature. A qualified electrician possesses general skills; so does an economist, an accountant or a musician. They can expect to find a wide range of employers willing to pay them more than unskilled workers.

By contrast, Becker distinguishes specific training as "training that has no effect on the productivity of trainees that would be useful in other firms" (Becker 1964: 26). Examples he provides include training as an astronaut (valuable to NASA, but not elsewhere), and resources spent familiarizing new employees with a firm – the sort of induction training which is familiar to most employees. We could add examples such as training for a particular company's computing system or stock-control system, or as a tour guide to a particular theme park, or to provide familiarity with an organization's staff appraisal system.

It has to be said that the distinction is not an easy one to maintain, as much training involves elements of the two types. Even something like astronaut training involves, as a side-effect, producing skills which are valuable elsewhere (e.g. as a test pilot or, more prosaically, in public relations: few ex-astronauts have difficulty getting such work). Holding down any sort of a job in one firm may also be a useful indicator to another employer that you possess some valuable attributes – at least, when compared to another job applicant with no such experience. This point is amplified later in the chapter.

Clearly, though, some training is "more general" while other provision is "more specific", and the ambiguity of particular cases shouldn't detract from the principle involved. The distinction is economically relevant because of the implications which it appears to have for the funding of training.

Becker points out that employers have an incentive to fund specific training. Investments in such training enhance the productivity of workers to the particular firm, but not to other employers. As the workers' skills have no enhanced value outside the firm, the employer doesn't need to pay higher wages to prevent them being "poached" by other employers. Workers, on the other hand, will not wish to invest in such training as the skills acquired cannot be taken elsewhere.

The value marginal productivity of specifically skilled labour can therefore exceed the wage rate paid. In terms of equation (2.6) above, the net present value of the post-training marginal product minus wages (G) covers the total cost of training, C, which means that equation (2.6) reduces to:

$$MP_0' = W_0 \qquad (2.7)$$

As the whole of the benefits of investment in specific training can in principle be captured by the firm, such investment is potentially profitable. The worker can be paid the value of his or her marginal productivity outside the firm (i.e. as an unskilled worker) during training, even though his or her productivity within the firm is temporarily reduced[4] to MP_0 as shown by equation (2.5). This is recouped by paying less than the value to the firm of his or her marginal product on completion of training.

By contrast, the benefits of investments in general training are assumed to be much more difficult for employers to capture. Individuals receiving general training have their marginal productivity enhanced in a wide variety of potential employments. In a competitive market they are likely to be enticed elsewhere by employers who are willing to pay for the increased value of their services; alternatively, the employer providing training will have to pay skilled workers more to retain them. In either case, it is argued that it will be unprofitable for employers to provide such training because of their inability to capture the returns on their invest-ment.[5]

This does not, however, mean that firms will provide no general training. What it does mean, as Becker was among the first to point out, is that workers must pay for their training by taking a reduced wage (less than the value of their marginal product as an unskilled worker). In return for incurring this cost, they reap the benefits of training by being paid the value of their enhanced marginal productivity after training is complete. Because their new skills have a value outside the firm, the existing employer must pay the going market rate for skilled labour. This analysis provides an economic rationale for apprenticeship systems and similar practices.

Referring again to equation (2.6), as firms no longer receive the returns on training, $G = 0$. In order for firms to provide general training, it must be made costless to them. This happens when

$$MP_0' = W_0 + C \qquad (2.8)$$

In other words, when the wage in the training period is reduced by C. This, remember, covers both explicit and implicit costs.

These points can be illustrated in a highly stylized diagram such as Figure 2.1. Here it is assumed that training is the only reason why productivity is enhanced over time, and that human capital does not depreciate – assumptions which will shortly be dropped.

In this diagram, unskilled workers receive a constant wage (W_0') equal to the value of their marginal product $MP_0' (= MP_t')$ over the whole time they are employed with the firm. Workers who receive training which imparts specific skills continue to receive the same wage W_0' as the unskilled. In this case, however, the value of their marginal product to the firm does not coincide with the wage they are paid. In period 0 their wage exceeds the

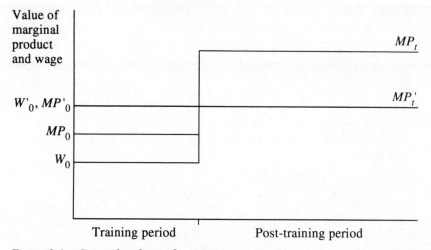

Figure 2.1   General and specific training

value of their marginal product (MP_0); after training their wage is less than the value of their enhanced marginal product, MP_t.

By contrast, those receiving general training initially face a wage which is not only below the value of their marginal product in the "outside" labour market, MP_0', but also below the value of their marginal product as trainees, MP_0. This is because their wage in training (W_0) must, as shown in equation (2.8), be low enough to compensate firms for *all* the costs – explicit and implicit – of providing training. In other words, the trainee effectively pays for the general training received – but he or she also reaps its rewards in the form of higher pay (the value of MP_t) in the future.

SOME QUALIFICATIONS

This is a pregnant insight. Becker's analysis of the different earnings paths likely to be experienced by generally and specifically trained workers has been extremely influential, as has been his discussion of the way in which the market can shift the ultimate burden of training costs. The analysis has further ramifications, such as the (testable) implication of differential unemployment rates between those workers who have had general rather than specific training (Oi 1962). It should be said, though, that the analysis has been challenged on a number of grounds.

One argument, as we have seen, is that the general/specific distinction is difficult to maintain in practice.[6] Another is that the incentives surrounding training and its funding are more complicated than the simple model suggests. Becker himself, for example, points out that there are exceptions to the rule that employees must fund their own general training (Becker 1964: 25). Where employers can prevent trainees leaving immediately on completion of their training, for example, it is possible for them to recoup the costs of their investment. The armed forces are one of the few employers able to do this. In the UK and the USA, as elsewhere, the army, navy and air force provide a large quantity of general training. Since members of the armed forces sign up for long periods, their employers gain the benefits of general skills for a sufficient period to make the investment worthwhile.

Discussion of this issue can, incidentally, be put in the context of the currently fashionable economics of property rights. Different "rules of the game" have the effect of structuring incentives differently. If employers providing training were given an ownership right over human capital, as in a slave-owning society, employer-funded general training would probably be much more common.[7] A less extreme possibility would arise if employers were able to claim a "transfer fee" from employers who enticed workers away on completion of training. Such a suggestion was seriously canvassed in the UK government's February 1992 White Paper *People, Jobs and Opportunity* (Employment Department 1992a), where it was argued that those employees wishing to leave should have to repay the cost of their employer-provided training. The implication is that a transfer market in skills would develop, with "poachers" indirectly compensating "trainers" as the wages of transferees are bid up. This might encourage a higher total amount of training, particularly if a new division of labour between trainers and poachers enabled economies of scale to be exploited, with large firms in effect producing skilled labour for "sale" to smaller non-trainers.[8] However, the experience of professional sports suggests that the restrictions such a system places on employees are unacceptable in modern conditions. And no one country could unilaterally impose such a system of property rights in a world where labour is increasingly internationally mobile.

Some general training may also be funded by employers if there are information imperfections in the labour market (meaning that other employers are not aware of the skills which generally trained workers have acquired). In a discussion of this question, Ziderman and Katz (1990) point out that the UK government's policy to certificate and standardize skill levels within the NVQ framework (see Chapter 6) may actually have the paradoxical result of discouraging employers from financing general training, for such initiatives will make workers' skills more visible to other firms.

In a similar way, if barriers to mobility prevent workers from moving to new employers, Becker points out that general training may be financed by employers. He cites the case of an isolated company town (Becker 1964: 36) where the firm is a monopsonist in the local labour market and in effect general training becomes specific training – an important reminder that these categories are conditional on market conditions.[9] In these circumstances, too, employers will find it possible to retain generally trained workers even if they are paid less than the value of their marginal productivity.

Nor is the pattern of funding of specific training as clear-cut as the simple model suggests. It was assumed that firms would finance specific training because they could recoup the costs of training in terms of higher productivity in the future. However, this depends on workers staying with the firm. While the simple model assumes that the only motive for leaving a firm is to get higher pay elsewhere, in reality workers leave firms for a variety of reasons. Firms with high labour turnover may therefore be reluctant to invest even in specific training. They will certainly try to discriminate against groups of workers who are known (or, perhaps more accurately, believed[10]) to be particularly likely to leave.

This may be too gloomy a view, however, for firms can reduce turnover by offering higher pay to trained workers even though their specific skills have no value in the external labour market. As it stands, this expedient would itself make training unprofitable. However, by "sharing" the benefits of higher productivity with the workforce, the firm may induce employees to "share" the costs by accepting lower pay while in training. Incremental pay scales may be devised which involve a career ladder within a firm. This may be attractive to some workers even if it means initial pay is artificially lowered. Others, however, will not wish to "wait" in this way, preferring higher pay today. In a complex economy with a wide choice of employers, these different preferences can be accommodated. The first group of workers will therefore tend to end up in jobs where training is provided by employers, while the second group will not receive training. Thus human capital theory suggests that the pattern of training provision by employers reflects to some extent the preferences of individual workers. This is a controversial argument, as it can be used (for example) to rationalize the differential access to training experienced by men and women (see Chapter 12).

Another subtlety can be added to the debate by reflecting that Becker's basic model assumes perfect competition in product and factor markets. As Okun (1981) pointed out, the reality may be rather different. If there is imperfect competition in product markets, firms will not be under such great pressure to maximize profits as is implied in Becker's analysis. There is some evidence that firms in more "protected" markets tend to spend more on training. As for the factor market, one possible situation arises where a monopsonist employer faces a "monopoly" of sorts on the part of employees. This might arise where workers are organized in a union. More

generally, in a world of imperfect information, existing workers are a
known quantity to their employers, and possess greater bargaining power
than "outsiders" whose abilities are unknown. In such a situation of
bilateral monopoly, a game-theoretic analysis of the sharing of the costs
and benefits of training may be appropriate, and the conclusions of such an
analysis are by no means obvious and clear-cut (Bosworth *et al.* 1994).

These qualifications notwithstanding, Becker's analysis remains a
powerful one and has served as the basis of considerable further work in
the economics of training.

INDIVIDUAL EARNINGS PROFILES

Individuals undergoing general training will, as we have seen, experience
higher wage levels after training than they did before. Where the costs and
benefits of specific training are shared, for reasons we have just suggested,
this will also be true of individuals receiving this kind of training.

But the transition from one wage level to another is unlikely to be as
abrupt as is depicted in Figure 2.1. One reason for this is that training is
rarely a once-and-for-all event. If instead we imagine a sequence of training
processes, earnings progression will be more gradual. In Figure 2.2 we
illustrate such a case.

For simplicity, assume that an individual receives *general* training in
each successive period. The initial unskilled wage, as in Figure 2.1, is W_0',
corresponding to a marginal product of value MP_0'. However, during

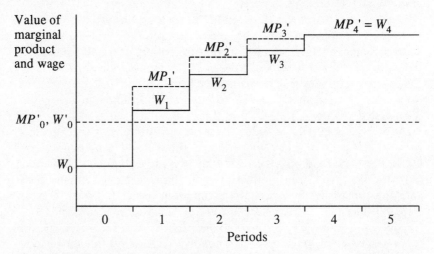

Figure 2.2   Reinvestment in training

period 0 the wage is reduced to W_0 in order to "pay" (i.e. compensate the employer) for the costs of training received during this period. If we further assume that people have a constant working week, whether in training or not, their earnings are equal to $h.W_t$, where h is the (constant) number of hours and W_t is the wage rate received in period t.

At the end of period 0 the first tranche of training is completed, and potential productivity increases to MP'_1. In a perfectly competitive market, the individual can now obtain a wage equivalent to the value of this new higher level of potential marginal productivity. However, the worker chooses instead to invest in further general training, again financed by accepting a lower wage than could be obtained – in this case W_1.

At the end of period 1, productivity has again been enhanced so that the worker could now obtain a wage rate equivalent to the value of MP'_2. Again, however, some of the potential gain is "reinvested" as the worker accepts a wage of W_2. This process of reinvestment continues until period 4, when the worker no longer invests, and settles instead for a wage equal to his or her marginal productivity in all subsequent periods.

Why has investment come to an end? First, because of the law of diminishing returns. Successive increments of training investment will tend to add less and less to the productivity of an individual of fixed inherent ability.[11] Second, because individuals have finite working lives. The more time goes by, the less working time remains for investments in training to pay back their costs. Thus a training investment which would just be "profitable" in period 0, would not be worthwhile by period 4. Thus the human capital model explains the observation that more training tends to be undertaken by younger workers.[12]

With our assumption of a fixed working week, earnings bear a constant relation to wage rates. Earnings will therefore tend to rise with experience, generating an *experience–earnings profile* which is steeper for skilled than unskilled workers. As work experience typically rises with age, this means that we can in turn generate an *age–earnings profile,* such as in Figure 2.3.[13] In this case we have assumed (a) that initial training starts at 20; (b) retirement occurs at 60; (c) employment is continuous; and (d) increments of training occur continuously rather than in discrete periods. Reality is of course much more complicated, but age–earnings profiles of this sort are a standard item in empirical research.

In Figure 2.3 curve Y shows the individual's earnings path over his or her working life. Curve MP shows the individual's potential marginal productivity at each stage.[14] Y_{us}, by contrast, shows what would theoretically have happened to earnings if the worker had remained unskilled.

The area (I + II) between lines MP and Y represents the total training costs (explicit and implicit) incurred during the individual's working life.

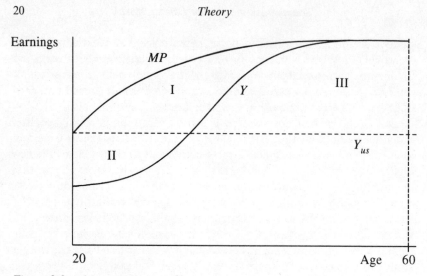

Figure 2.3   *Age–earnings profile*

Area II represents costs paid for by earning less than the unskilled wage, while area I is costs paid for out of the return on earlier human capital investment. Area III represents the gross return on investment.

Although the shape of empirical age–earnings profiles approximate to the concave shape of Y in Figure 2.3, for some groups of workers at least the age–earnings profile turns downwards at some stage before retirement. This is explicable if we recognize that our model of human capital has so far omitted one feature of investment in machinery and equipment: its depreciation over time.[15] In the case of skills there is obviously a sense in which these can become outmoded unless there is continual updating. It is also worth mentioning that, adopting the wider framework of human capital touched on earlier, health status – which clearly has an impact on productivity – may similarly depreciate over time. Just as rising marginal productivity over time pulls up the earnings level, as depicted in Figure 2.3, so can declining marginal productivity pull it down.[16]

SOME IMPLICATIONS

Much of this analysis is owed to the work of Jacob Mincer. Among conclusions which he draws from it is the importance of forgone earnings as a measure of training costs. He argues that firms' records of training expenditures will seriously underestimate the costs of training in an economy as, at best, they can only record the explicit costs of training

(k_0 in equation 2.2 above). In view of the arguments above, the reduction in wages below the value of marginal productivity in the absence of training is the true measure of the cost of on-the-job skill acquisition. His early empirical work – essentially an attempt to estimate areas I and II in Figure 2.3 from a knowledge of age–earnings profiles such as Y – suggested that the real costs of on-the-job training were much higher than had previously been thought, being (for males at least) approximately equal to the costs associated with the formal education system (Mincer 1962).

Another, related, implication is that formal systems of on-the-job training are only part of the picture. Indeed, what contributes to increased productivity is on-the-job *experience* gained with firms. Workers are willing to take reduced pay in order to acquire this experience whether it is accompanied by formal processes of training or not. This surely corresponds to common sense: once beyond the education system, increases in pay tend to be associated with your experience of having performed certain roles rather than your completion of formal courses of training. Of course, such experience can be formally structured, in which case it very clearly meets the definition of training outlined in the previous chapter. It has been argued that Japanese firms place particular emphasis on "job rotation and transfer, multi-task working, participation in quality circles ... [and] zero-defect groups etc." (NEDC/MSC 1984: 49) as well as explicit instruction. But very many firms in all countries allow for and encourage such learning by doing. They are, like Molière's *bourgeois gentilhomme*, who had spoken prose for forty years without knowing it, providing training *whether or not they articulate the fact*.

Work experience is a key element in general training, as is recognized in all education and training courses which involve an element of work placement. This aspect of general training is therefore quite naturally produced alongside – as a joint product with – specific training. However, specific and general training are likely to have different time horizons. Whereas for general training the relevant "pay-back period" extends from the time of the investment until retirement, for specific training it is dependent on the time the worker is expected to stay with the firm. Uncertainty on this question may require a higher equilibrium rate of return than would be the case for general training. Remember that, as we suggested earlier, employers will try to share some of the costs of specific training with workers, and in return offer employees some of the benefits. Evidence that they succeed is indirectly provided by the empirical finding that tenure (the length of time an employee stays with a particular firm) has an independent impact on earnings when educational qualifications, age and years of labour market experience are controlled for (Polachek and

Siebert 1993: ch. 4). Indeed, Mincer and Jovanovic offer the rough estimate that for the USA "50 per cent of lifetime wage growth is due to general (transferable) experience and 25 per cent to firm-specific experience and interfirm mobility" (Mincer and Jovanovic 1981: 21).[17]

In the analyses of Becker, Mincer and other human capital theorists workers pay – albeit implicitly – a very large proportion of the total costs of training, and particularly of general training. This means that the human capital approach places great emphasis on the incentives facing individuals, rather than firms. In this approach there is no presumption that firms "should" or "must" offer training. In the case of specific training, firms will provide it if it is profitable to do so, just as they will invest in a machine – subject to the riskiness of the investment and the cost of borrowing. But general training is a different matter. If individuals are willing to pay, a firm will provide it because this will be costless to itself. But some firms, because of the nature of their technologies or organization, will be better at providing training than others. They will attract employees who are willing to accept lower wages now in order to enhance earnings later. Other firms will have less of a comparative advantage in providing training, and they will draw employees who are attracted by somewhat higher immediate pay but a less steep earnings profile over time.

So firms will specialize in training to a greater or lesser extent depending on their particular circumstances: some "firms", at the other extreme, will specialize entirely in training, producing no other "output". As Becker puts it, "a school can be defined as an institution specialising in the production of training, as distinct from a firm that offers training in conjunction with the production of goods" (Becker 1964: 37). There can be no hard-and-fast rules, therefore, about where training should be provided and who should provide it. Factory schools (employer-provided basic general education) were once common. Changes occur over time in the institutions in which training is provided, as cost structures change. The role of schooling in preparation for employment is discussed in Chapter 10.

MARKET FAILURE?

It should be obvious by now that the human capital model offers a sophisticated analysis of the way in which markets can in principle work to produce an efficient outcome, in training as in other areas. We began by quoting from Adam Smith, the first great believer in free markets. Nevertheless, Smith was also clear-sighted enough to recognize that markets could only work optimally if a series of conditions were met. If they were not, we could have a situation of what we now term "market failure", where it may be appropriate for governments to intervene to remedy matters.

For example, we could note that the ability of individuals to finance an optimal amount of general training is in doubt if the costs of such training are too high to be financed by a reduction in wages during training.[18] In such circumstances they will have to be financed either by the trainee's family or by borrowing. Although in principle it ought to be possible to borrow if the rate of return on investment is greater than the opportunity cost of capital, in practice financial markets do not offer such loans without collateral.

Another set of problems arise if we drop the assumption that the economy is characterized by product and factor markets that are perfectly competitive. If imperfect competition prevails, it is not clear that an optimal level of training will be provided (Bosworth *et al.* 1994). Moreover, in the real world governments intervene even in otherwise competitive markets by taxing individuals and firms. By appropriating part of the returns from investments in training, they thus reduce the incentive to invest. This may provide a rationale for offsetting subsidies to training (Layard *et al.* 1992).

This latter point is an example of a wider principle that markets only work at their best if all relevant costs and benefits can be captured by the explicit or implicit prices which determine firms' and individuals' decisions. This condition is not met if there are *externalities*, which are costs or benefits accruing to other parties. There has recently been an explosion of interest amongst economic theorists in endogenous growth models – where the rate of economy-wide technological progress and the effectiveness with which resources are used are the result of private investment decisions.[19] It has been suggested in particular that there are external effects of human capital on output. That is to say, human capital embodied in a worker raises the productivity of colleagues with whom he or she works, for "human capital accumulation is a *social* activity, involving *groups* of people in a way that has no counterpart in the accumulation of physical capital" (Lucas 1988: 19). To the extent that this is true, the actual level of training in an economy can be below its optimal level as individuals investing in training will be unable to capture all the benefits from their investment. A related line of argument is that increased investment in training, subsidized if necessary, may generate external benefits such as reductions in crime levels and depressive and other illnesses (Organization for Economic Cooperation and Development 1993b: ch. 2).

It need hardly be said that the human capital model depends heavily on the assumption that firms and individuals have full information about all the relevant costs and benefits. For instance, workers undertaking training and firms providing it are assumed to be aware of what the market demand for newly created skills will be for many years ahead. To the extent that the parties involved take a pessimistic view of the future, an economy could settle into a "low-skill equilibrium" (Finegold and Soskice 1988) rather than the "high-skill equilibrium" (with higher productivity and pay) which could have resulted from acting on more optimistic expectations about the future. Other problems arise in the absence of full information if firms or individuals are risk-averse. In addition asymmetric information – where one party knows more than the other – creates the possibility of opportunistic behaviour. For example, firms may find it difficult to persuade workers to share the costs of acquiring specific skills in the manner outlined earlier if workers do not believe that promises of higher wages in the future will be adhered to: again potentially profitable investment in training may be deterred.

Finally, the approach assumes an equilibrium in all markets and, by implication, full employment of all those who wish to work. In a world where a large proportion of the labour force is, for one reason or another, out of work there may be difficulties in assuming that the level of investment in training is optimal.

CONCLUSION

We have outlined here the main features of the human capital approach as it applies to on-the-job training. It represents a powerful attempt to show how a market economy provides training, and leads to some unexpected – and, to many non-economists, possibly incredible – conclusions, of which possibly the most important is that a large part of the cost of training is likely to fall on trainees themselves. This observation, dating back as we have seen to Adam Smith, is all too frequently ignored in policy discussions which are largely devoted to the role of firms and governments.

The human capital approach has the great advantage of seeing training provision in a wider context, explicable using the same methodology as has been applied to a great many other subjects. It develops a useful terminology for discussion of these matters, including the important distinction between "general" and "specific" training. It makes the important point that training is a broad concept, embracing far more than formal instruction, and recognizes that on-the-job experience is a vital element in acquiring skills. It persuasively links a model of training to observed age/experience–earnings profiles.

The model is, however, not without its weaknesses. Some would reject the basic premiss that training provision is the outcome of individual choices, tending rather to stress the wider social context in which training takes place. But even within the human capital framework, it is possible to offer a rationale for government intervention because of the range of potential market failures which economists have distinguished (Centre for Economic Policy Research 1993). However, we shall see that the policies advocated by human capital theorists sometimes differ markedly from what governments do in practice.

In the next chapter we will consider further some of the criticisms which have been made of the human capital model, and go on to discuss some alternative ways of exploring training issues.

NOTES

1. Much discussion of training seems to assume, for example, that particular, clearly defined, combinations of skills are dictated by the "needs" of modern production. But this is too deterministic. Belief in a fixed ratio between inputs and outputs flies in the face of much that we know about the ways in which firms compete by using different combinations of inputs – physical capital such as machinery and buildings, land, skilled and unskilled labour, technical knowledge and so on. See Shackleton (1993) for a fuller exposition of this point.
2. Or, to put it slightly differently, if the projected internal rate of return on a training project exceeds the cost (corrected by an appropriate risk factor), the investment should go ahead.
3. The present value of a sum of money £A to be received t years from now is

$$PV = A/(1 + i)^t$$

   where i is a discount rate measuring the opportunity cost of capital (that is, the rate of return available on the best alternative investment open to the investor).
4. Notice that productivity is not necessarily reduced to zero, as it would be in the case of off-the-job training. Human capital theorists such as Becker and Mincer have always seen on-the-job training as very important, as we shall see later.
5. All this, remember, is in the context of perfect competition. If employers can collude, it is possible that they can reduce the fear of "poaching" by imposing penalties on employers who try to entice workers away from their original employer. As we shall see in later chapters, political systems which permit or encourage certain forms of collusion ("corporatism") may tend to have higher levels of employer-provided training.
6. See Organization for Economic Cooperation and Development (1991: 136–7) for a discussion.
7. Human capital theory can in fact yield some interesting insights about slavery. Fogel and Engerman (1974) claim that skill levels amongst blacks fell in the post-Civil War southern United States precisely because of the dramatic change in property rights consequent on the abolition of slavery. Blacks were either unwilling or unable to invest as much in human capital acquisition as slaveowners had done.
8. It can be argued that this outcome would not be dissimilar to the effect of a levy-grant system of funding training (see Chapter 4).

9. See Pollard (1965: ch. 5) for a discussion of the development of factory villages in the United Kingdom. This source also makes the interesting point that "training" involves not only the aquisition of "skills" but also the imparting of appropriate attitudes to work discipline – an observation that is still highly pertinent today.

10. Mistaken beliefs may be difficult to distinguish from prejudice or discrimination. If women are thought more likely to leave than men, they will receive less employer-provided training. See Chapter 12.

11. In this sort of framework, each period involves a choice whether or not to invest in further training: individuals weigh up the marginal cost of investment against the present value of marginal gains. See Ben-Porath (1967) for a fully worked-out model on these lines.

12. The amount of (formal) training received varies considerably from group to group within the population – by age, sex, occupation, industry, size of firm, etc. Most of these variations can be accounted for within the kind of framework developed here. See, for example, Greenhalgh and Mavrotas (1994).

13. Adapted from Ziderman (1978: 29).

14. Note that this is *potential* productivity. Remember that as long as training continues, *actual* productivity falls below its potential, as illustrated in Figure 2.1.

15. See Becker (1964: ch. 7, s. II).

16. We should also remember that in practice preferences alter as individuals get older. Another reason for age–earnings profiles to turn down is that older workers may switch to less-demanding (and therefore less-well-paid) jobs.

17. Interfirm mobility can have both positive and negative effects on earnings depending on, for example, the reason for separating from the previous employer.

18. Or, as Polachek and Siebert (1993: 90–1) argue, if minimum wage or other labour market regulation prevents wages from falling to the level where training would be costless to the firm.

19. See Crafts (1992 and 1993) for an overview of this literature.

3. Criticisms of the Human Capital Interpretation of Training and Some Alternatives

INTRODUCTION

The human capital model which we have just outlined is an extension of "neoclassical" economics, which had become the orthodoxy amongst economists by the second half of the twentieth century.[1] This approach does not appeal to everyone, as it focuses on the implications for competitive equilibrium in labour markets of rational choice by individuals who are assumed to possess a high degree of information about present costs and future benefits. Such a view of real-world labour markets seems to many people to be counterintuitive.

In this chapter, therefore, we consider some of the criticisms which have been made of the human capital model in its application to training, and then go on to consider other explanations of the pattern of skill acquisition.

SOME PROBLEMS WITH THE HUMAN CAPITAL MODEL

There is a wealth of evidence that those with better educational qualifications and more on-the-job training tend to have higher earnings on average than those without these advantages.[2] In this very broad sense, the human capital model is consonant with reality. However, so are a number of other models. And there are other aspects of human capital theory which raise doubts about its explanatory power.

One example is the question of variations in marginal rates of return to different types of education and training. Many studies have attempted to calculate the *internal rate of return* on human capital investments. In terms of the model sketched in the previous chapter, the internal rate of return is that discount rate which sets the present value of the costs associated with an investment in training just equal to the present value of the costs.

In principle, in a perfectly competitive economy with rapid dissemination of information, the marginal rate of return on all types of investment (human and physical) should tend to be equalized. If not – for example, if training to become a plumber carried a much higher rate of return than training to be a carpenter – we would expect to see the market "correcting" this disequilibrium. As knowledge of the disparity spread, there would be an increase in the numbers seeking training as plumbers and a decrease in those looking for training in carpentry. Eventually the larger supply of trained plumbers would depress their wage rate, while the shortage of carpenters would force their wages up. The final result would be an equalization of the rate of return to both kinds of training.

The problem is that, although the rates of return on different types of education and training are usually found to be positive, they display little tendency to be equal at the margin. Psacharopoulos (1985), for example, reports private rates of return in the UK to secondary education of 11 per cent, and to higher education of 23 per cent on the basis of 1978 data. For the USA he finds rates of return (from 1976 data) of 11 per cent and 5.3 per cent respectively. Polachek and Siebert (1993), using 1972 data for the USA and the UK, report rates of return on labour market experience (a proxy for general training) of only around 2–3 per cent, but rates of return on job tenure (picking up specific training) which are significantly higher.

An implication of these variations is that wage differentials in the United States and the United Kingdom seem to be greater than are necessary to compensate for differential training costs. This is the point, made by John Stuart Mill, which we noted in the last chapter. Of course, various explanations can be offered for this. Mill's explanation involved the hypothesis of non-competing groups: we shall explore modern versions of this idea later in the chapter. However, another answer is to argue that there are non-pecuniary rewards associated with particular jobs – a point going back once again to Adam Smith.

If jobs employing some types of skills are inherently more unpleasant than others (they involve facing cold and danger on a North Sea oil rig rather than sitting in a safe, comfortable office, for example), they will tend to carry a wage premium. For a given cost of training, other things being equal, they will therefore display a higher equilibrium rate of return. There is definitely something in this: empirical work (Marin and Psacharopoulos 1982) has provided suggestive evidence that there is an equilibrium risk premium for dangerous jobs. However, risk is only one factor which influences equilibrium rates of return, and few datasets provide sufficient information to enable us to uncover all possible sources of "net advantage" from different types of work.

Moreover, the position is further complicated if we recognize that people have different tastes, and therefore different assessments of the non-pecuniary aspects of jobs. What is an attractive job to one person is unattractive to another. Continuing the comparison we have just suggested, some individuals – call them "outdoor types" – may find office jobs unappealing. If tastes differ, whether or not non-pecuniary disadvantages of jobs will carry a premium will depend on the *demand* for relevant skills as well as their supply costs. If the demand for workers on North Sea oil rigs is less than the number of outdoor types, there is no reason for such work to carry a premium (and thus display a higher equilibrium rate of return on a given training cost). However, if the demand exceeds the supply of outdoor types, equilibrium wages will rise and with them the apparent rate of return on training. This is illustrated in Figure 3.1.

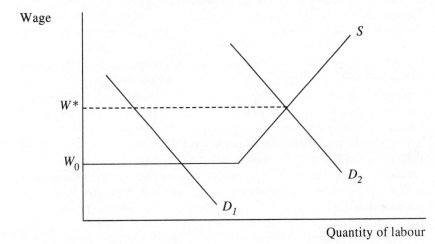

Figure 3.1   Compensating differential

In this diagram, the supply curve shows the wage at which a given quantity of labour will be supplied. It has a flat section, where workers are willing to work in the North Sea for a wage W_0 which covers their transfer earnings (what they could obtain elsewhere; this includes a normal return on their investment in training for this job). As the curve turns upwards, extra labour can only be attracted by paying a higher wage, including a premium to compensate "indoor types" for the rigours of the job. Whether such a premium has in fact to be paid clearly depends on the location of the demand curve. If the curve is D_1, no premium need be paid; if it is D_2, the "compensating differential" necessary to attract labour is $(W^* - W_0)$.

These and similar complications suggest that the attractive simplicity of the human capital model outlined in the previous chapter is illusory. Indeed, it has led some commentators, for example Mark Blaug (1975, 1980), to suggest that the theory is inherently irrefutable as so many qualifications have to be made when it is exposed to empirical examination;[3] in this case, critics may reasonably doubt its usefulness.

TRAINING AND PRODUCTIVITY

Another criticism of the model concerns the benefits which are supposed to flow from training. As we saw in the last chapter, in the human capital model the higher earnings typically following completion of training are the result of enhanced productivity. But some critics have argued that much training does not create productivity gains in any direct sense, but rather provides a means by which employers and employees try to mitigate the effects of imperfect information in the labour market.[4]

Firms are typically faced with a range of job applicants about whose productivity little can be directly known in advance. In this context, initial training of workers, for instance, sometimes provides a way of "screening" potential candidates for permanent posts within firms. It provides a relatively cheap means by which employers can observe workers in action without necessarily being committed to a permanent contract. There seems little doubt that this is one use to which employers have put the government-sponsored Youth Training programme in the UK, for example. In a rather similar way, employers may use previous training and vocational qualifications as a way of sorting out shortlisted candidates from a large field of applicants.

In the literature on the economics of education and training this analysis is described as the *sorting–screening hypothesis*. It is argued that employers' decisions to hire workers do not rely on "any cognitive development or psycho-motor skills" (Organization for Economic Cooperation and Development 1989) but on aptitudes and attitudes which can be revealed by responses to training and education.

In this view, successful completion of training may be a good predictor of employment success and high earnings, but the process of training need not have imparted significant new skills. Brown (1991) notes that "attitude", including willingness to obey orders, being punctual, having a good attendance record, being able to work with others, and so on, is often the key to successful employment. Maybe training cannot impart these characteristics,[5] but successful completion of training certainly attests to their possession. It is rational, therefore, for individuals to seek training in order to "signal" to employers that they are worth employing (Chapman 1993: ch. 5). The implications of this analysis are discussed further in Chapter 11 of this book.

It is worth asking at this stage just what evidence exists to link training with productivity. In fact, there is surprisingly little. One approach involves the use of macroeconomic production functions to estimate the significance of human capital formation in different countries' economic growth. The idea is to calculate the "Solow residual",[6] the amount that remains after subtracting from a country's rate of GDP growth those elements which can be explained by increased quantities of inputs of physical capital and labour. This residual has been shown to be correlated with measures of educational achievement (Denison 1967), and from this it has been inferred that human capital more generally plays an important role in economic growth. If training augments human capital, it will therefore lead to increased economic growth.[7]

The argument is plausible, but suffers from some weaknesses. For one thing, studies[8] using this method suggest that there are diminishing returns to educational achievement, with most of the benefits coming from the attainment of universal primary and secondary education: developed countries like those with which we are concerned in this book have probably already exhausted the bulk of the benefits to be expected from educational attainment.[9] For another, there is the possibility of reverse causation. Richer countries can afford to spend more on education, which remains in part a consumption good as well as an investment. It is also important to emphasize that, because of the shortage of comparable international data covering on-the-job training (see Chapter 9), there has been no attempt to incorporate wider measures of human capital into these studies. We therefore have to take on faith the belief that vocational training produces the same sort of macroeconomic effects as formal education. In fact it is more problematic than that. Even if we had comparable data on training, we know from microeconomic studies (reviewed in later chapters) that training and education interact: those individuals with more education get more training. While survey data could in principle help us to separate out the effects of education and training at the level of the individual, this cannot be done at the macro level. And at the micro level, as we shall see, alternative explanations are available.

Another approach to quantifying the direct productivity benefits from training is found in the very substantial research programme conducted at the UK's National Institute for Economic and Social Research over the last decade.[10] A common procedure which they have adopted is to take

matched plants in the UK and other countries which display different levels
of productivity – almost always, incidentally, with the British plants being
those which are less productive. These productivity differentials are shown
to be associated with differences in the skill qualifications of the workforce –
in particular with middle-range craft skills. Descriptive accounts of plant
practices are then used to tease out the ways in which less-skilled workforces are thought to be less flexible and less effective than they could be.

A typical example of the method is provided by a NIESR study of the
Netherlands,[11] where similar engineering plants are shown to be 30–40 per
cent more productive than in Britain. Where only 40 per cent of British
workers in these plants possess craft qualifications, the equivalent figure for
the Dutch plants is around 80 per cent. The National Institute team argues
that the range of skills encompassed in the Dutch workers' training makes it
possible to switch workers between processes much more easily.

This type of approach is interesting and imaginative, and has the benefit
of getting down to nitty-gritty details of how skills are deployed in practice.
But it does have some problems. One is the inability to control adequately
for differences in the amount, age, composition and layout of capital
equipment: although this is scrupulously attempted by the team, it is an
almost impossible task. Another is the concentration on formal qualifications as an index of training, a simplification on which the analysis
developed in Chapter 2 casts some doubt.

And finally there is the interpretative burden placed on the observed
correlation between high qualification levels and labour productivity.
Correlation does not necessarily imply causation, and there is a distinct
possibility that the underlying cause of both high commitment to training
and higher productivity may lie elsewhere, for example in the different
managerial cultures in the two countries.[12]

All in all, then, despite the attractions of the National Institute's
approach, "it is difficult to avoid the feeling that this is a research
programme with a predetermined outcome" (Chapman 1993: 114).

ALTERNATIVE EXPLANATIONS OF EARNINGS PROFILES

In the last chapter we briefly commented on experience–earnings and
age–earnings profiles, which are typically concave. Those investing more
in training have steeper profiles. It has been suggested that, rather than
enhanced skill levels accounting for the shape of these profiles, other
factors may be at work. One motive (Becker and Stigler 1974; Lazear
1979, 1981) may be the prevention of shirking at work.

In this view, employers find it difficult and costly to monitor worker effort. They therefore seek ways in which they can motivate staff to perform effectively. One such method is to "defer payment" to workers by paying them less than their marginal productivity early in their career and paying them more in later years. In effect, as Addison (1989) puts it, "the deferred payment acts as a performance bond". Workers know that if they are caught shirking they will lose their jobs and their deferred pay, and are thus encouraged to work hard.

These and other models suggest other reasons for observed earnings profiles[13] than those offered by the human capital model. In principle, as Mincer noted, such alternative models could be tested against the human capital version. If it could be shown that earnings growth was largely independent of productivity growth, the human capital model would look very shaky (Mincer 1974).

Tests, as so often in economics, have not thus far been conclusive. Medoff and Abraham assert that "no one has ever provided evidence which demonstrates that experience–earnings differentials can in fact be explained by experience–productivity differentials" (Medoff and Abraham 1981: 187). In their own work they found no statistically significant correlation between wage growth and performance rankings among professional and managerial employees in a small number of US corporations. However, more recently, James N. Brown, using data from the US Panel Survey on Income Dynamics, was able to track individuals over time and relate their receipt of training to wage growth. He concludes that "the data indicate a strong contemporaneous link between training and wage growth ... the most reasonable inference ... is that wages increase with tenure primarily because productivity increases with tenure" (Brown, 1989: 990).

LABOUR MARKET SEGMENTATION

So there are differences of opinion over the validity of the human capital model. What other approaches to labour market analysis is it possible to take, and what have they got to say about training? Most of the developed alternatives can be classed under the general heading of labour market segmentation (LMS). The three distinctive features of this type of analysis, according to McNabb and Ryan (1990) are (a) that there can often be different job rewards for workers of comparable abilities; (b) product markets as well as labour markets have an impact on wages and other job rewards; (c) tastes and attitudes are endogenous – in other words there are "virtuous" and "vicious" circles in the labour market, positive and negative feedback which reinforces segmentation.

The LMS approach "typically eschews the equilibrium analysis associated with neoclassical economics" (Taubman and Wachter 1986: 1186). Instead of the returns to training being equalized at the margin, great disparities can continue to exist. The approach, therefore, follows the tradition of J.S. Mill[14] rather than that of Adam Smith. It sees labour markets as being split into a number of non-competing groups of workers, "Balkanized" as Clark Kerr, one of the earliest modern writers in this field, put it (Kerr 1954). In the simplest version of this model, we hypothesize a *dual labour market*, the main features of which are illustrated in Figure 3.2. One group of workers has jobs which carry high wages, pleasant working conditions, employment security, pensions and other benefits, a career ladder and significant opportunities for training. They constitute the *primary* labour market. The other group (in the *secondary* market) has low wages, unpleasant working conditions, little job security, few benefits or perks, little prospect of promotion and limited training.[15]

How individuals fall into one or other group may depend on pre-market segmentation – differential access to formal schooling, family background, personal influence in obtaining an opening to good jobs and so on. Once individuals enter the labour market, however, a feature of this type of model is "negative feedback" (Taubman and Wachter 1986: 1185)[15] which reinforces the disadvantages of those in poor jobs. Declining morale, poor skills, periods of unemployment, and so forth, make it less likely that they will ever progress to good jobs. "Positive feedback", however, entrenches the position of the primary group which establishes a good employment record, and enhances its skills through training and experience. This in turn leads to higher pay and promotion.

The model can be fleshed out in different ways for different purposes. It can be used to draw attention to the disadvantaged position of women in relation to men (see Chapter 12), ethnic minorities to ethnic majorities, part-time to full-time workers or disparities between other observable sub-groups in the labour market.

The approach is essentially descriptive, though it does describe a *process* by which inequality is maintained, rather than simply a static picture. Its proponents see variations in income and other features of jobs as the result of institutional forces rather than the outcome of individual choice (as in the human capital model). It thus shifts the focus of our attention to a different problematic, and in particular (as we shall see later) to a different range of policy issues and instruments. In the hands of some LMS writers, the human capital approach is seen as apologetic, offering an "efficiency" rationale for labour market inequality. Thus the dual labour market hypothesis tends to form part of a larger critique of market institutions: in more extreme versions this may be associated with a Marxian analysis of inequality under capitalism (Bowles and Gintis 1975).

Primary	Secondary
Good educational background	Poor educational background
Formally qualified workers	Few formal qualifications
Stable employment record	Unstable employment record
Long job tenure	High turnover
Significant job responsibilities	Few job responsibilities
Pleasant working conditions	Poor working conditions
Good pay	Poor pay
Company pensions and other benefits	No company pensions
Promotion prospects	No promotion prospects
Unionized workforce	Low unionization
Significant training provided	Little training provided

Figure 3.2   The dual labour market: some stylized features

However, even neoclassical economists sometimes argue that in practice a degree of segmentation can occur. Thus Becker (1957) has written on the economics of discrimination and has acknowledged that the market for human capital can be treated as segmented in some respects (Becker 1967: 102), while Patrick Minford, the influential British macroeconomist, has seen trade unions as exercising a malign influence on the economy by segmenting the workforce and preventing the UK labour market working effectively (Minford *et al.* 1983).

It would be wrong to caricature the dual labour market approach. Nobody is suggesting that the economy is completely and rigidly dichotomized. As numerous commentators (for example, Cain 1976) have pointed out, attempts to classify the whole economy into just two "segments" are doomed. For instance, such "strict duality" would seem to imply, amongst other things, a bimodal earnings distribution – and the distribution of earnings is unimodal. So defenders of the LMS approach argue that the dual labour market model is simply "a heuristic convenience, a vivid but essentially arbitrary way of conveying the wider notion of segmentation" (McNabb and Ryan 1990: 154). Subsequent models have elaborated on the basic idea of duality, but recognized that in reality labour markets can be segmented in a variety of ways – by race, gender, age and so on (Chapman 1993).

THE "JOB COMPETITION" MODEL

One approach which builds on the idea of labour market dualism is the Job Competition model (Thurow and Lucas 1972). In this approach it is asserted that the neoclassical view of the labour market can be characterized as one of "wage competition": that is, changes in wages are the manifestation of competition. An alternative is to think about competition for *jobs*. The idea is that there are "good" jobs and "bad" jobs available. Good jobs feature, among other things, access to training. Individuals "queue" for these jobs, with their place in the queue determined by their personal characteristics, including family background, formal education and previous labour market experience, which indicate trainability to the employer. "In marginal productivity terms, marginal products are associated with jobs and not with individuals. The operative problem is to pick and train workers so that they can generate the desired marginal product of the job in question with the least investment in training costs" (Thurow and Lucas 1972: 21).

Wages in the primary sector are downwardly rigid, being determined by what "good" firms are willing to pay as a result of social custom and (mainly technologically determined) productivity. They are largely uninfluenced by short-run demand and supply conditions in the labour market. However, it is worth noting here that conditions in the *product market* seem to have an impact on wages in a way which would not be predicted from the human capital model: there is evidence of a "moderately strong and consistent" association between pay and "product market concentration ratios, capital–labour ratios, firm size and access to government contracts in a variety of advanced economies" (McNabb and Ryan 1990: 165). More generally, firms faced with stable product demand create "primary" conditions of employment, while those which face unstable demand operate in the secondary segments of the market, so it is not size *per se* which is the determining factor, as is sometimes assumed.

Although education, training and job experience are associated with earnings, as in the human capital approach, it cannot be inferred from positive rates of return to education and training for the individual that the *social*[16] return is synonymous with the *private* return involved. For enhanced training and education of job applicants only improves their position in relation to other applicants: it does not add to the supply of "good" jobs. As access to pre-entry qualification is based on social stratification, substituting one group of labour market entrants for another in the good jobs would presumably have little impact on productivity. An implication of this is that, although there will be an overall correlation between earning and completed education and training, there will be many individuals (women, ethnic minorities) in the secondary labour market who "are capable of performing well in primary jobs but the rationing of access to good jobs denies them the opportunity to do so" (McNabb and Ryan 1990: 157). Within the secondary sector, their qualifications are not particularly relevant and they will be underemployed.[17]

The policy conclusion drawn from this is that attempting to raise incomes of disadvantaged workers through improving access to education and training ("supply-side" policies) is likely to be unsuccessful. Instead it is necessary to alter the demand for labour or the structure of job opportunities. This might be done, it is claimed, by the government continually running the economy at close to the capacity level of output, offering guaranteed jobs at a minimum wage and pursuing anti-discrimination programmes and quotas to ensure equitable access to jobs.[18]

These policies would typically be rejected by human capital theorists. They tend to assume that there is a "natural" or "non-accelerating inflation" rate of unemployment determined by supply-side factors, and that attempts to run the economy at higher levels of utilization would simply accelerate inflation.[19] The use of minimum wage laws and quotas might discourage employment. And Polachek and Siebert (1993: 90–1) argue that minimum wage and anti-discrimination legislation reduce the amount of training provided. This is because they prevent wages from falling to the level at which training becomes effectively costless to the employer, as explained in the previous chapter.

INTERNAL LABOUR MARKETS

The Job Competition model is one of several approaches which emphasize that the labour market is "structured" rather than "structureless". In traditional neoclassical theory, firms are shadowy institutions whose internal workings are obscure,[20] subordinate to impersonal market forces.

By contrast, segmented labour market theorists argue that large firms in particular have an important influence on how labour is hired and fired, and work experience and training are organized (Blaug 1993: 23).

A key element is the *internal labour market* (ILM). This concept, dating back to the work of Kerr (1954) and Dunlop (1957), has received most attention in the work of Doeringer and Piore. They define the ILM as "an administrative unit, such as a manufacturing plant, within which the pricing and allocation of labour is governed by a set of administrative rules and procedures" (Doeringer and Piore 1980 : 107). The ILM is contrasted with the structureless secondary labour market which resembles the neo-classical model, where wages are determined by demand and supply (Wachter and Wright 1990; Siebert and Addison 1991).

The two types of markets are connected via "ports of entry" (Kerr 1954) into the ILM. These are usually at a fairly low level of the organization. Once inside the firm, employees are protected from outside competition. They have a high degree of job security, and promotions are largely from within the firm, a career ladder is present, and typically workers remain with the firm for long periods. There may be an incremental pay system, with higher pay based on seniority.

Kerr and other early writers drew attention to the way in which unions played a role in entrenching internal labour markets, using their bargaining power to enforce work allocation rules on employers and controlling ports of entry by such mechanisms as the pre-entry closed shop. However Doeringer and Piore tend to stress more fundamental factors which lead to the development of internal labour markets even in the absence of unions. Two which are of particular relevance here are skill-specificity (which is alleged to be of growing importance over time) and the importance of on-the-job training.

Skill specificity has two effects in their analysis. As in Becker's approach, the more specific the skill, the larger the proportion of the cost of training which will have to be paid by the employer, other things being equal. Second, the more specific the skill, the higher the absolute cost of training because it is unlikely that employers will be able to exploit economies of scale in the training process. Both these effects mean employers will wish to minimize labour turnover in order to obtain a return on their investment. The promotion of an internal labour market makes staying with the firm attractive (we have already suggested how the tenure–earnings relationship can be manipulated to this end).

Another factor favouring the development of ILMs is the importance in many fields of employment of on-the-job training. Doeringer and Piore argue that this is frequently informal, with the process being described as "osmosis", "exposure" or "experience". This is, as we have seen, also the view associated with Mincer, although he draws rather different conclusions. Even the formal element of training, according to Doeringer and Piore, "often involves little more than a systematic rotation of the trainee through enough job classifications to ensure exposure to the full complement of tasks" which workers are expected to perform (Doeringer and Piore 1980: 113). Workers learn from watching other workers, or asking them advice on problems encountered: no formal classroom-based training system, however sophisticated, can substitute entirely for this.

Yet what is involved is that existing workers must "share" their skills with trainees who are in principle their rivals. Why should they do this? As Williamson has put it:

> The success of on-the-job training is plainly conditional on the information disclosure attitudes of incumbent employees. Both individually and as a group, incumbents are in possession of a valuable resource (knowledge) and can be expected to fully and candidly reveal it only in exchange for value   (Williamson 1980: 151)

This "value" is manifested in the job security, seniority rules, promotion prospects and other privileges associated with the internal labour market: the ILM is seen as a profit-maximizing response by firms to the need to secure worker co-operation in the transmission of skills. It should be borne in mind, however, that ILMs are also often found in the public sector, where the influence of unions seems likely to play a role.

We can see, therefore, a number of reasons why internal labour markets can exist. However, there are a number of questions which can be asked. Much of the literature seems to imply that ILMs are more developed than in the past, with labour markets becoming more structured over time. Yet it is known that many of the characteristics of ILMs were found in the "factory villages" of the nineteenth century, and can be found today in the dual labour markets of the Third World. Moreover, there appear to be significant differences between the extent of the ILM phenomenon in developed countries such as the UK, the USA and Japan (Collier and Knight 1985), despite access to the same technology and similar levels of human capital.

Furthermore, there are variations in the incidence of ILMs over the business cycle (Sengenberger 1981). And there is some evidence of a secular movement away from internal labour markets: there has been a substantial growth in what the EC calls "atypical" employment in Europe – short-term contracts, part-time work, outwork, telework, and so on (Meulders 1992). This is partly stimulated by changes in government policy (in the UK, for instance, there has been a big shift towards "contracting out" of government services and deregulation of the labour market), partly by the slimming down of private-sector firms and their increasing reliance on outsourcing in the more competitive environment of the Single Market, and partly by the changing demography of the workforce. So any simple view that the internal labour market is an inevitable response to a particular stage of economic development seems debatable.

ASSESSMENT

How do we assess the rival claims of the human capital and segmented labour market approaches? On the one hand, we have the view that (despite the evidence of some frictions) the labour market is essentially competitive and that its outcomes, including the provision of training, depend ultimately on the choices made by individuals seeking to do the best they can, given their endowments. On the other, there is the view that the labour market is characterized by non-competing groups, and that outcomes are often arbitrary, unfair and inefficient.

An obvious problem is that some known facts about labour market outcomes are capable of being interpreted as evidence for both approaches. For example, the existence of internal labour markets can be rationalized by human capital theorists as a means by which the finance of specific training is facilitated, and the ILM is seen simply as a superficial description of an underlying competitive market process in action.[21] The evidence on the tenure–earnings relationship, as we have seen, can also be interpreted in more than one way. In part the problem arises because of the different methodological approaches. Mainstream economics, of which human capital theory forms a part, makes use of a combination of deductive reasoning from first principles involving individual utility maximization (Robbins 1932) coupled with testing of predicted outcomes, rather than assumptions (Friedman 1953). It therefore has little time for detailed qualitative descriptions of institutions, preferring to concentrate on a limited number of key economic decision variables which can be rendered in quantitative or quasi-quantitative terms. On the principle of Occam's Razor, simplified models are preferred to complicated ones, and the benefits of descriptive realism have to be offset against the costs in tractability and generality which it imposes.

Labour market segmentation approaches certainly offer us a more immediately appealing description of the labour market. But given the methodological approach just outlined, it is not surprising that conventional economics has seen LMS approaches as "sketchy, vague, and diverse if not internally conflicting. Description, narratives, and taxonomies crowd out model development" (Cain 1976: 1221). Cain and others have tried to pin the theories down to testable propositions, and have claimed that the evidence largely refutes LMS propositions. One test we have already noted in relation to the dual labour market hypothesis: the distribution of earnings and other job rewards is unimodal rather than bimodal. But, as we have seen, this is only evidence against the most naive of models.

Another way to pin the approach down is to try to demarcate primary and secondary sectors in an objective manner. One method picks up on the view that in the secondary labour market earnings tend not to be associated with education and training. At a very broad level of generalization, there are doubts about this proposition. For example, there is evidence that the rate of return on education for women is higher than that for men (Sapsford and Tzannatos 1993: 92), even though women are more likely to be in the secondary labour market. A supporter of the dualism hypothesis, Paul Osterman, attempted a more rigorous examination of the question.

Osterman classified a sample of male workers into primary and second-ary segments according to their occupational characteristics, and estimated separate earnings functions for each segment. He found that the "human capital market holds up well for upper tier workers, but has little explan-atory power for workers in the secondary labour market" (Osterman 1975: 520); accordingly, labour market dualism was inferred. This piece of work attracted considerable criticism, mainly for "truncation bias" (Cain 1976: 1246–7). The point here is that the coefficients on education and experience will be downwardly biased if the classification of workers into segments is implicitly based on the same sort of factors as earnings. Thus workers in the secondary sector with good education and experience will tend to move from the secondary to the primary sector rather than increase their earnings within the secondary sector; the data will therefore be truncated as those in the secondary sector with a good educational background will only be a subset of those who started out in the secondary sector. This problem is a common one in attempting to distinguish labour market segments, and it is one of the reasons that leads Taubman and Wachter to the conclusion that the labour market segmentation hypothesis "has not generated a testable empirical hypothesis for identifying demarcation boundaries for segmen-ted labour markets" (Taubman and Wachter 1986: 1198).

Another approach to testing the LMS case is to examine data for occupational mobility: a high level of mobility tends to argue against a strong belief in labour market segmentation. In a well-known study, Mayhew and Rosewell (1979) used data on 10,000 male workers in the UK, examining their lifetime mobility between occupational statuses. They found considerable mobility at every point in the occupational distribution. There were some men who moved very substantial distances up and down the occupational scale, but a large proportion of men experienced some mobility from any particular point in the scale. Similar results have been found in the United States, with the proviso that there is little downward mobility for the very top occupational groups, and that the lowest 5 per cent of black males show very low levels of movement (McNabb and Ryan 1990: 173).

Although it appears that we can reject extreme versions of the labour market segmentation hypothesis, this does not completely dispose of the LMS challenge. As Ryan (1981: 18) puts it, "segmentation is clearly a matter of degree – you can have more or less of it". Asking whether the labour market is segmented or competitive requires a judgement akin to that of deciding whether a glass is half empty or half full. Ultimately it comes down to a statement of belief on the part of the observer. Human capital theorists, because their theorizing is part of the wider neoclassical analysis which has applications across the whole range of economic behaviour – indeed, beyond, into the fields of the new social economics associated with Gary Becker and his followers (Shackleton, 1981) – see the labour market as fundamentally competitive, as they have been taught to. Although some institutional rigidities and problems may be accepted and identified, they are not fundamental to our understanding. The LMS theorists, on the other hand, fundamentally reject this view and see institutions as the determining factor.

TRAINING, REGULATION AND THE WAGE FORM

Another body of literature concerned with institutions and structures in the labour market grows out of the Marxian tradition of emphasizing the "social relations" of production – power, authority and class in the productive process (Dobb 1938) – and represents a critique of the pure market relations modelled in neoclassical theory.

This view, particularly influential in France and Germany, sees human capital analysis as inadequate because it treats skilled labour as a commodity like any other, in a timeless, ahistorical world. Differences between the role of training at particular stages of economic development, and in different institutional and cultural contexts, are ignored.

Thus Méhaut (1993: 2), for example, focuses on the way in which the labour market at any particular time "is made up of a set of institutions, rules and social relationships". In this he follows the French "Regulation" school, which aims to analyse the historical development of capitalist economies (Boyer 1986) by constructing a theory of its institutions. It is claimed that there is an organic link between the dominant method of capital accumulation and the wage-earning relationship. And

> "five components ... characterise the historical configurations of the relationships between capital and labour: the means of production and the form taken by the social and technical division of labour; the ways in which wage earners are mobilised and attached to the firm; the determinants of direct or indirect wage income; and lastly, the wage-earner's way of life, which is more or less linked to the acquisition of goods and the use of non market collective services. (Boyer 1986; quoted in translation in Méhaut 1993: 3)

This school emphasizes that the training arrangements in force in the 1950s and 1960s were a product of a particular form of wage-earning relationship associated with "Taylorist" factory organisation (based on scientific management, hierarchical structures and the division of labour), full employment and a welfare state where many tasks necessary to the maintenance of capitalism (education, social security, and so on) were socialized. In the 1990s, in the "post-Fordist" era, where old factory and employment structures are breaking down, new arrangements are necessary.

A rather different emphasis is placed by the "Aix group" (Maurice *et al.* 1986; Rose 1985). In their view, categorisation into stages of historical development is difficult to sustain. More important, perhaps, are differences between national patterns of the wage-earning relationship.

One key to understanding the nature of such arrangements lies in the analysis of the *wage form*, "understood as the qualitative aspect of the wage relation, relating to all forms of payment – wages, salaries, incomes, bonuses, allowances, insurances and benefits – their respective methods of negotiation and determination" (Clarke 1992). Different wage forms imply "particular means of reproducing and developing skilled labour" (ibid.: 2), that is, different forms of training provision.

For example, Clarke contrasts the "regulated" wage form obtaining in the Federal Republic of Germany (where nearly every aspect of the employment relation, including training, is dealt with in the framework of negotiations between "social partners" – employers and unions – backed up by the force of law) with the "deregulated" form in the UK where negotiation is narrowly focused on wages and lacks legal backing. In the UK the narrow focus on pay means that the unions failed to control and regulate apprenticeship training and that there is no "right" to training as there is in Germany. We shall have more to say on the role of unions in influencing training provision in subsequent chapters.

In some fields, such as construction, the "deregulated wage form" found in the UK has become debased into a form of self-employment. This is because self-employed workers enjoy a range of tax advantages that are denied to directly employed workers. Workers in such a system have little investment in permanent relationships with contractors, and it is argued that one of the consequences is a suboptimal level of training. By contrast with Germany there has been a fragmentation of skills; workers often receive training only in proprietary processes specific to one employer. The lack of general skills is, it is asserted, a prime reason for low productivity in the British construction industry. The point may have wider application; it is a common element in the criticisms of British training made by the National Institute of Economic and Social Research, referred to earlier.

Given the tradition from which this type of analysis emerges, it is not clear how far it has, or is intended to have, an immediate policy relevance. It may be taken to imply that a government-led (or social partner-led) attempt to regulate the wage form should be instituted if training provision is to be improved. However, this is likely to prove difficult if not impossible (Clarke *et al.* 1994). It is perhaps better read as part of a critique of the ideological significance attached to human capital theory as a justification for inequality of income under capitalism.

CONCLUSION

The implications of different theoretical approaches for our understanding of training have been contrasted in these last two chapters. For human capital theorists, training is a crucial means by which productivity is enhanced. It can take a variety of forms, but its provision is the result of a partnership between workers and firms, with workers bearing a large proportion of the costs and making many of the crucial decisions through job choices. For LMS theorists training may not be associated directly with productivity increments and is primarily brought about by the decisions of employers, who may not be willing to finance an appropriate level of training to generate sufficiently rapid economic growth or, importantly, to offer all members of the workforce equal chances of improving their skills and living standards. For writers influenced by the Marxian tradition, the discussion of training provision cannot be detached from a wider consideration of the workings of labour markets under advanced capitalism.

In the next chapter we build on this theoretical survey to discuss some general aspects of government policy towards training. This in turn leads in subsequent chapters to the examination of particular national experiences and policies.

NOTES

1. For an overview of the development of neoclassical thought since the nineteenth century, see Backhouse (1985). Labour economics was one of the last areas of economics to fall to the neoclassical paradigm. "Institutionalist" approaches to the labour market (which minimized the role of individual choice in favour of a detailed study of firms, unions, collective bargaining and legal regulation) remained powerful until the late 1950s in the United States and the UK. In continental Europe such approaches still exercise a strong appeal, as we indicate later in the chapter.
2. See, for example, Polachek and Siebert (1993: chs 3 and 4).
3. With respect to human capital theory, Blaug (1980: 238) writes: "its rate-of-return calculations repeatedly turn up significant differences in the yields of investment in different types of human capital, but its explanation of the distribution of earnings nevertheless goes on blithely assuming that all rates of return to human capital formation are equalized at the margin. Worse still is the persistent resort to ad hoc auxiliary assumptions to account for every perverse result, culminating in a certain tendency to mindlessly grind out the same calculation with new sets of data, which are typically signs of degeneration in a scientific research program."
4. Another view (Blaug 1972: 194) is that training is a "fringe benefit", part of the compensation package. There may be indirect productivity benefits if, as a consequence, workers are motivated to work harder or be more flexible.
5. Although this is debatable; many government training schemes for the disadvantaged attempt to do precisely this. And, in a rather different context, Rainbird and McGuire (1993) report that a great deal of formal firm-provided training in the UK is currently linked to changing corporate cultures and the promotion of quality care objectives.
6. Originally put forward in Solow (1957).
7. As we noted in the last chapter, the new theories of economic growth associated with economists like Robert Lucas suggest that there are externalities associated with investment in human capital. This implies that different mathematical and econometric specification of models is required from that used by the earlier theorists. So far little significant empirical work has appeared using Lucas-style models.
8. For a review of some of the earlier studies in this field see Psacharapoulos (1973).
9. A simple back-of-the-envelope calculation, incidentally, may also serve to deflate some of the claims for the macroeconomic efficacy of increased investment in training. A standard result in growth theory is that an increase in the growth rate of an economy (Δg) is equal to the marginal social rate of return (r) multiplied by the change in the ratio of investment to GDP (I/Y):

$$(\Delta g) = r \, \Delta \, (I/Y)$$

   A country which raised its investment in training from 5% of GDP to 10%, and which faced a marginal social rate of return on training of 5%, would therefore experience a rise in its growth rate of just 0.25%, other things being equal.
10. A good introduction to this ongoing programme is National Institute for Economic and Social Research (1990). This brings together 15 of the studies the National Institute conducted in the 1980s.
11. Mason *et al.* (1992).
12. In this context it is worth reporting the finding of the recent study by the McKinsey Global Institute, *Manufacturing Productivity*, which looked at labour productivity differentials in nine industries in Japan, the USA and Germany: it found that differences in the basic skills of workers did not seem to matter, as most of the things which determine productivity came down to managerial choices. The study also found that the degree of competition in a market was an important element in determining productivity levels, as was the amount of direct foreign investment occurring (*The Economist* 1993b).

13. There are various models generating the same shape for experience–earnings profiles. They include one concentrating on reducing labour turnover (Salop and Salop 1976) and another relating to job-matching (Jovanovic 1979).

14. Other writers who made notable contributions to the subject include J.E. Cairnes, F.Y. Edgeworth, Millicent Fawcett (whose pioneering discussion of women as a non-competing group has recently been disinterred by Pujol 1992) and the American institutional writers W.C. Mitchell and Henry Commons.

15. "Learning-by-doing in the secondary sector is thus equivalent to negative general training where individuals are 'scarred' by working" (Taubman and Wachter 1986: 1185).

16. The social rate of return reflects the discounted present value of the costs and benefits to *society* rather than to the private individual or firm financing training. There can be a difference between social and private rates of return for a variety of reasons. For instance, there may be direct or indirect cost subsidies, or some of the benefits may be taxed away. Another possibility touched on in the previous chapter is that there may be externalities involved. For a further discussion of the social rate of return, see Chapter 10.

17. In a recent study, 40% of a sample of American male workers reported themselves as "over-educated" for the jobs they performed (Sicherman 1991). This question is discussed further in subsequent chapters.

18. For further discussion in the context of women's role in the labour market, see Chapter 12.

19. See Chapter 11.

20. However, this deficiency has been attacked from a number of directions in recent years. For a useful introduction, see Ricketts (1987) or Williamson (1985).

21. The ILM is seen by labour market segmentation theorists as involving the substitution of arbitrary rules (formal and informal) concerning the allocation, training and remuneration of employees for those of the market. Human capital theorists tend to retort that, however superficially important these rules seem to be, the ILM largely behaves "as if" market forces predominate. To the extent that ILMs do cause the economy to diverge from optimal outcomes in relation to training and employment, this may be blamed on the influence of unions (which tend to be stronger in ILMs than in the external labour market), or on government regulations which fall more heavily on such firms (Taubman and Wachter 1986: 1188–95).

4.   The Political Economy of Training

INTRODUCTION

In this chapter we review the arguments used to justify state intervention in the provision of training, and the types of policies which are advocated. We point out some of the unintended consequences of government intervention, showing how the provision of state support for training programmes may sometimes produce perverse results.

We then go on, drawing on public choice theory, to discuss the way in which policies are likely to be determined in practice, recognizing the influence which interest groups may exercise in the shaping of government intervention.

These general observations serve as a background from which we discuss the experience of a number of particular countries in Part II.

WHY INTERVENE?

In the two preceding chapters we have discussed the ways in which training has been theorized by economists of different persuasions. Very broadly speaking, human capital theorists (who tend to adhere to mainstream neoclassical views of the generally benign influences of competition and the market) have stressed the ways in which the free choices of individuals and firms generate acceptable levels of training. Their analysis tends to discount the commonly expressed fear of "poaching", the belief (as we saw in Chapter 2) that firms are likely to underprovide general training because they are worried about trainees being enticed away by other employers when their training is complete.[1] In the human capital framework such fear seems exaggerated because general training is largely self-funded. Specific training, on the other hand, is rarely seen as a problem because it is assumed that firms can capture the returns on such training to compensate for its costs.

However, human capital theorists concede, as we have seen, that there may be circumstances when the market fails. These may arise for example as the result of inadequacies in financial markets which prevent individuals borrowing enough to finance their own general training, distortions arising from imperfect competition, the existence of externalities, information problems or the lack of sufficient aggregate demand in the economy. If the existence of problems of this sort can be demonstrated, human capital theorists can justify some government intervention to promote higher levels of training, or to change the content of training, or to alter the distribution of training between individuals.

Critics of the human capital approach vary in their conclusions. Some fear that "credentalism" may lead to resources being wasted as individuals strive to obtain qualifications which add little to productivity although they improve their standing in a queue for career jobs: such qualifications are simply a positional good. Others argue with the inferences drawn from phenomena such as experience–earnings profiles, claiming that they do not reflect productivity enhancement but rather responses to problems such as shirking at work. The optimality or otherwise of such arrangements then have to be discussed on different grounds, such as the general desirability of interfirm mobility.

Economists adopting the labour market segmentation framework, although normally accepting that (in some rather loose sense) training is a "good thing", tend to see it as a feature of a "good job". Enhanced productivity from those receiving training is seen as being associated with investment in newer technology, or as part of a management philosophy favouring improved quality throughout the organization. The context is the need to secure a competitive edge in a world where product differentiation is far more important than neoclassical theorists normally suggest. Here training is only one aspect of a wider emphasis on human resource management (which includes, for example, restructuring of payments systems, appraisal schemes, job enhancement, quality circles, promotion, grievance procedures, pension arrangements, collective bargaining (or its absence) and so on). Méhaut (1993) is one of many who speak of the movement from "Fordist" management principles towards the "learning organization".

Rather than freely chosen, and substantially self-financed, training of individuals being seen as the key simultaneously to personal advancement and productivity growth, as in the human capital framework, the emphasis here is on the need to encourage industry to increase the provision of "good jobs" which – almost as a byproduct – produce good training. The neoclassical emphasis on equilibrium is rejected. Instead, the need continually to improve economic performance and promote "virtuous circles" of skill acquisition, productivity gains and quality improvements is stressed.[2] This is to be achieved through maintenance of a high level of capacity utilization, training subsidies and labour market regulation.

Some radical critics of the human capital approach, however, see training in a more sinister light: as a deliberate means by which labour market segmentation is reinforced as part of a "divide and rule" strategy for lowering wage costs. The untrained are seen in the modern context as a permanently excluded group, a sort of "reserve army" which is used to act as a threat to more favoured groups of workers, to keep down inflationary wage demands and other forms of worker self-assertiveness. In such a framework training may be seen as artificially underprovided, and the demand is for greater training provision as part of an across-the-board assault on economic and social inequality. It is seen as an entitlement, almost a feature of welfare provision, rather than as an investment which should be justified on narrow rate of return analysis.

In all these approaches, then, there is room for significant intervention by government. Even after more than a decade of privatization and deregulation in other spheres, it is rare to find a commentator who advocates leaving training completely to market forces.

FORMS OF INTERVENTION

Intervention can take three forms: direct production of training by government agencies, funding, and regulation. We shall see in Part II of this book some of the variations which can occur under these headings in different countries; here we simply sketch some common features.

There is a long history of *direct provision* of training by the state. In a sense, the free-at-the-point-of-use compulsory education (typically ten or eleven years) which all developed countries now provide for their children is part of the "training system" of a country.[3] It provides a substitute for the voluntary private provision by the Church, charitable trusts and firms which was used in the past (and indeed is still available today). State schools aim to provide the basic general skills of literacy and numeracy, together with some introduction to a range of academic disciplines and work-relevant studies. In many countries, secondary education provides explicit vocationally orientated curricula for at least a section of the school population (more "academic" children are often educated separately). Beyond the minimum school-leaving age, which varies from 14 to 17 amongst developed countries, voluntary further and higher education facilities are often provided by governments at low or zero direct cost to the individual. In many cases grants or loans subsidize some of the maintenance costs of students in higher education; there may also be some financial support for those in further education.

In addition to the formal education system, governments have for a long time also directly provided training for particular groups such as demobilized servicemen and women, the unemployed, the disabled and others who may otherwise find it hard to obtain training. Such provision has increased substantially in the postwar period, and in the 1970s and 1980s in particular.

A feature of recent years in some countries has been the replacement of direct provision (government-owned colleges and training centres) by *funding* of training provided by outside agencies. This can be direct funding, where the government contracts with employers, colleges or other training providers to train individuals. There is also increased interest (for example, in the UK, Germany, France and the USA) in providing vouchers or credits to individuals who can then shop around amongst competing providers. This type of "arm's-length" provision is increasingly favoured because of the perceived problems of motivating trainers who are permanent employees of the government.

Funding can also be provided indirectly through subsidies such as tax concessions to firms who provide training, or to individuals who undergo training. And governments are also, of course, major employers in their own right. As such they naturally provide training of all descriptions. Evidence from a variety of countries indicates that government employees typically receive more training than their counterparts in the private sector. Indeed, in many areas government training arguably distorts or reduces the provision of private-sector training by making much of it redundant. For example, the air forces of countries like the USA, the UK, France and Germany provide a large proportion of the trained pilots working in the civil aviation sectors of these and other countries. Government-run hospitals typically provide internships for junior doctors who then practise in the private medical sector. Government legal departments often provide a major source of corporate lawyers, and so on.

Governments also influence the provision of training through *regulation* of the economy. They can do this deliberately by requiring that only appropriately qualified and registered personnel practise a trade or profession. Such requirements are almost universal for higher professions such as law and medicine. In some countries, such as Germany, a much wider range of occupations are regulated in this way. The justification often offered is that of protecting the public against malpractice.

Legislation may also require employers to give training or day-release education facilities for young people, or to spend a given percentage of turnover, wage bill or some other appropriate quantity on training. It may require or permit levies on employers for industry-based training. Less obviously, governments may create a "need" for training as a result of regulations intended for some other purpose, for example health and safety or tax law. On the other hand, it has been argued that regulations may sometimes have the reverse effect of reducing the provision of training. One example, as we have seen, may be labour market legislation – minimum wage or equal opportunity laws – which means that wages cannot fall to the level where individuals can finance their training through reduced pay (Polachek and Siebert 1993: 89–91).

The term "government" is often used rather loosely when discussing policy. The way in which actual rather than theoretical governments operate varies from context to context. In some countries, power is concentrated in the hands of central government. Here provision, funding and regulation of training are, in principle at least, capable of being considered as a coherent whole. In other cases, however, there is a separation of powers between federal, state and local or regional governments. Here the picture becomes more complicated. Within the European Union, this complexity is increased by the growth of interest of the Commission in education and training matters. A number of initiatives such as FORCE (*Formation Continue en Europe*, an action programme to promote continuing vocational training), have been developed. The Social Charter of Fundamental Workers' Rights, the forerunner to the Maastricht Treaty's Social Chapter, proposed vocational training facilities for individuals during working time. Although the proposals were modified, and the UK is anyway exempt from the Social Chapter, it is likely in the medium term that some EU-wide developments in training policy will emerge via a different route. For instance, a proposed directive on "atypical" workers, requiring improved access to vocational training for temporary and part-time employees, has been justified in terms of the Single European Act's competition provisions (Addison and Siebert 1993).[4]

Much also depends on political cultures. In some countries, "winner-takes-all" is the rule and training policy can have a strong party flavour. In others, the electoral system is such as to favour collaboration or coalition between parties, and policy may have a more consensual flavour. It is clear, for example, that the postwar German political system has placed a much higher value on neocorporatist compromise and accommodation of special interests than has, say, Britain or the United States. As Streeck and his collaborators put it, there is in Germany a "well-established tradition of consensus politics based . . . on centrist coalition governments, a strong role of the Lander at the Federal level, and an elaborate body of constitutional law" (Streeck *et al.* 1987: 2). Similarly, the role of interest groups may be accorded greater or lesser legitimacy. In a number of European countries, emphasis is placed on the role of the social partners (organized employers[5] and organized employees) who may be given a privileged position in influencing training policy (Henley and Tsakalotos 1992; CEDEFOP

Table 4.1   Calmfors and Driffill's ranking of centralization

Country	Ranking
Austria	1
Norway	2
Sweden	3
Denmark	4
Finland	5
Germany	6
Netherlands	7
Belgium	8
New Zealand	9
Australia	10
France	11
UK	12
Italy	13
Japan	14
Switzerland	15
USA	16
Canada	17

Source: Calmfors and Driffill (1988).

1990b). They may even be granted the power to organize and administer training levies in particular industries. In other countries – notably the USA and the UK – governments are very much less sympathetic to neocorporatism of this kind.

One indicator of corporatism[6] – the degree of centralization of collective bargaining – has been put forward by Calmfors and Driffill (1988). Their ranking of leading industrial countries is shown in Table 4.1. Calmfors and Driffill, and also Freeman (1988), have claimed to find a significant relation between similar indicators and macroeconomic performance, with those at the extremes of the ranking tending to perform better than those in the middle. Their ranking may also serve as an acceptable rough guide to the degree of involvement of the social partners in training policy, for centralization of collective bargaining tends to be associated with a wider role for unions and employers associations. With this in mind, we examined the relation between Calmfors and Driffill's centralization ranking and a country's ranking in terms of public expenditure on active labour market policies (mainly training), using data from the Organization for Economic

Cooperation and Development (1993b). We found a rank correlation coefficient of 0.57, significant at the 95 per cent level of confidence. This broadly supports the hypothesis that a country where economic interest groups are well-organized will be one where governments play a relatively important role in funding training.

GOVERNMENT FAILURE?

We outlined earlier the way in which government intervention was often felt to be an appropriate response to the perceived deficiencies of the market. It is important to bear in mind, however, that there are potential "government failures" to set alongside "market failures". Governments usually only have at their disposal a selection of rather blunt instruments, and attempting to use them may itself create considerable inefficiencies. In this section we indicate some of the problems which can arise with two popular forms of intervention: levy systems to finance training, and government-funded retraining schemes for the unemployed.

Levy schemes for financing industry training are frequently advocated. Such a system used to operate widely in the UK,[7] and its revival has been advocated by the Labour Party amongst others. Something similar operates in France,[8] and was advocated for the USA by Bill Clinton when on the Presidential trail. The idea is that some level of spending – say 1 per cent of the wage bill – should be spent on training. Those who spend less have to pay a net levy. One obvious problem is the difficulty of defining training expenditure, given the wide range of activities which can improve productivity and earnings prospects (Commission on Workforce Quality and Labor Market Efficiency 1989: 17). But there are more fundamental problems when trying to determine an appropriate level at which to set the levy.

Economically rational firms will, even with the strongest commitment to the promotion of training, want to spend differing proportions of their revenue on training.[9] The appropriate level of spending for a firm will depend on a variety of factors relating to its business. Such factors will include the stage of the product or process cycle (when new products or processes are introduced, the need for training will be greater than at later stages of the cycle), the technology employed, the sector (employers in service industries, with more employees dealing directly with the public, are likely to require continual training inputs), the scale of the enterprise (there are economies of scale in training) and the degree of competition (both foreign and domestic). Spending requirements will also depend on the nature of the workforce: its age structure, its previous levels of education and training and the nature of the occupation in which

Table 4.2 Standard occupational classifications and training requirements, UK

Major group	General nature of qualifications, training and experience for occupations in group	% of working men, 1989	% of working women, 1989
1. Managers and administrators	A significant amount of knowledge and experience of the production processes, administrative procedures or service requirements associated with the efficient functioning of organizations and businesses	16.5	8.0
2. Professional occupations	A degree or equivalent qualification, with some occupations requiring post-graduate qualifications and/or a formal period of experience-related training	9.3	7.1
3. Associate professional and technical	An associated high-level vocational qualification, often involving a substantial period of full-time training or further study. Some additional task-related training is usually provided through a formal period of induction	8.1	11.3
4. Clerical and secretarial occupations	A good standard of general education. Certain occupations will require further additional vocational training to a well-defined standard (e.g. typing or shorthand)	7.2	28.6
5. Craft and related occupations	A substantial period of training, often provided by means of a work-based training programme	25.1	4.0

54

Table 4.2 *Standard occupational classifications and training requirements, UK – continued*

Major group	General nature of qualifications, training and experience for occupations in group	% of working men, 1989	% of working women, 1989
6. Personal and protective service occupations	A good standard of general education. Certain occupations will require further additional vocational training, often provided by means of a work-based training programme	4.6	8.3
7. Sales occupations	A general education and a programme of work-based training related to sales procedures. Some occupations require additional specific technical knowledge but are included in this major group because the primary task involves selling	5.2	11.4
8. Plant and machine operatives	The knowledge and experience necessary to operate vehicles and other mobile and stationary machinery, to operate and monitor industrial plant and equipment, to assemble products from component parts according to strict rules and procedures and subject assembled parts to routine tests. Most occupations in this major group will specify a minimum standard of competence that must be attained for satisfactory performance of the associated tasks and will have an associated period of formal experience-related training	12.9	5.3

Table 4.2 Standard occupational classifications and training requirements, UK – continued

Major group	General nature of qualifications, training and experience for occupations in group	% of working men, 1989	% of working women, 1989
9. Other occupations	The knowledge and experience necessary to perform mostly simple and routine tasks involving the use of hand-held tools and in some cases requiring a degree of physical effort. Most occupations in the major group require no formal educational qualifications but will usually have an associated short period of formal experience-related training. All non-managerial agricultural occupations are also included in this group, primarily because of the difficulty of distinguishing between those occupations which require only a limited knowledge of agricultural techniques, animal husbandry, etc., and those which require specific training and experience in these areas.	11.1[a]	16.0[a]

Note: [a] Includes unknown.
Sources: Office of Population Censuses and Surveys; *Employment Gazette.*

56

individual workers are engaged. Some indication of the training requirements of broad occupational groupings is given in Table 4.2: the descriptions are those of the UK's Office of Population Censuses and Surveys. It
also gives an indication of the proportions of the British workforce in these
categories.

The way in which a given amount of spending on training is deployed
will vary, too. Thus while firms, industries and sectors display different
training *density* (average numbers of days of training per employee), there
are also different ways in which these figures can be arrived at. Short spells
of training can be provided for a large proportion of the workforce (high
incidence) or longer spells for a smaller proportion of employees (high

Table 4.3   *Measuring training levels in an industry: Great Britain, 1986–7*

Density		Incidence		Intensity	
Industry	*Days/ Employee*	*Industry*	*%*	*Industry*	*Days/ Trainee*
Health	17.6	Health	78	Construction	23.8
Education	9.6	Retail	68	Health	22.5
Central govt	8.5	Extract/		Elect. eng.	18.2
Retail	8.3	energy	64	Mech. eng .	17.7
Finance/		Education	64	Metal goods	15.9
bus. serv.	8.0	Central		Finance/	
Elect. eng.	7.3	govt	59	bus. serv.	15.5
Extract./		Finance/		Education	15.0
energy	7.0	bus. serv.	52	Text./clothg	14.5
Mech. eng.	6.3	Mfr min./		Central govt	14.3
Catering	6.3	chem.	48	Catering	13.9
Metal goods	6.2	Catering	45	Retail	12.3
Construction	5.8	Local govt	45	Wholesale	12.2
Mfr min./		Transpt/		Other process	11.8
chem.	5.1	commn	40	Local govt	10.9
Local govt	4.9	Elect. eng.	40	Extract/energy	10.9
Wholesale	4.1	Metal gds	39	Mfr min./chem.	10.7
Other process	4.0	Mech. eng.	36	Transpt/commn	9.8
Transpt/commn	3.9	Other process	34		
Text./clothg	3.8	Wholesale	34		
		Txt./clothg	26		
		Constructn	24		

Source: Department of Employment (1989)

intensity). It is clear that there will be differences in the pattern depending on the nature of the job.

Table 4.3 neatly illustrates this point, as it shows that industries are ranked differently on the three indicators. In retailing, for example, 68 per cent of the workforce receives some training, on average 12.3 days. By contrast, in construction only 24 per cent undergo training, but they are trained for 23.8 days. Clearly there is a rationale for this in the type of work employees perform. In retailing, employees deal constantly with the public and need to be updated on rapidly changing product lines, customer care and company policy; there is also a relatively high turnover of staff, meaning that a sizeable proportion of staff in any period are new to the job and undergoing induction training. In construction change is less rapid, but there are craft skills which take considerable time to acquire.

Because of the different requirements of different industries and occupational fields, there is no one level of training provision which is appropriate for all firms. Critics of levy systems argue that the requirement to spend an arbitrary amount on training encourages wasteful spending (up to the required percentage, firms' expenditures are in a sense "free" and thus may not always be put to the most sensible use). They claim that in practice it amounts to a tax on small firms (larger firms would normally spend more than the required amount on training anyway) and thus tends to reduce competition.

Another very common form of intervention – almost universal in the 1980s and 1990s – is the government training or retraining scheme for unemployed workers. Other chapters discuss such schemes in more detail: here we just make two general points.

The first point concerns the incentive problems involved in running schemes. Awareness of the need to motivate trainers usually means that governments judge the effectiveness of schemes by reference to performance indicators such as the cost per trainee, number of qualifications achieved, and numbers of trainees who achieve jobs at the end of courses. Such indicators can lead administrators to go for the cheapest rather than the most appropriate forms of training (training for retailing, say, rather than engineering), and the lowest rather than the highest qualifications (as these will almost certainly have higher success rates). Where trainers can select their trainees, this also encourages "creaming" – choosing those individuals most likely to become employed because of their age, gender, ethnicity, education, previous experience or motivation (Anderson *et al.* 1993). Since many of these people would, given time, probably find jobs anyway, the "value added" by training may be rather limited – and the hard core of difficult-to-place unemployed will find their position in any job queue worsened.

It is worth noting, too, that there are known to be very substantial *displacement effects* from government-sponsored training schemes. These involve reductions in employment of one group of workers when employment is made available to others. It has been suggested, for example, that retraining schemes for the long-term unemployed in East Germany are simply fitting some of the long-term unemployed for jobs that would have gone to the short-term unemployed, who will now become long-term

(a) *Short run*

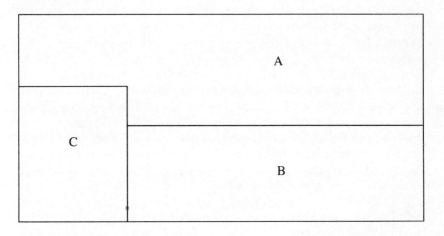

(b) *Long run*

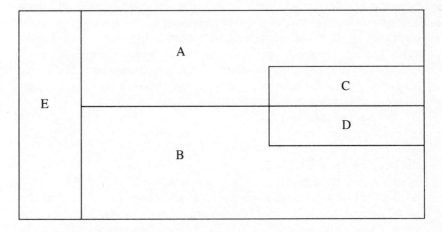

Figure 4.1   Displacement effects of training schemes

unemployed in turn; and there is little net employment gain (Lange 1993a). Studies of the UK's Youth Training Scheme (now renamed Youth Training) have also shown high displacement rates (Deakin and Pratten 1987; Chapman and Tooze 1987; Begg *et al.* 1991).[10] The principles involved can be illustrated by reference to Figure 4.1. The argument shows, incidentally, how the true success rates of such schemes are likely to be overstated.

Suppose a scheme is instituted to give 100,000 otherwise unemployed workers a twelve-month training course with employers. It has two functions: in the short run to reduce official unemployment figures, and in the longer term to improve workers' chances of permanent employment by making them more attractive to employers. The short-term consequences of the scheme can be illustrated by part (a) of the diagram. Of the 100,000 trainees (areas A + B + C), a proportion (C) would have been recruited anyway; firms now simply get their costs subsidized. This is known in the literature as *deadweight loss*. Another proportion (B) will take the place of other people who would have been recruited by employers in the absence of the scheme; this is known as the *substitution effect*.[11] The net reduction in unemployment is therefore only A. Indeed, it may be even less than this if the prospect of getting on to the scheme increases the number of those looking for jobs ("economically active").

The longer-term results are illustrated in part (b). Over the duration of the course a proportion (E) will drop out: we assume that they return to unemployed status.[12] The area A + C indicates those who obtain jobs, the area B + D representing those who remain unemployed after completing the course. However, it is likely that, if the course had not existed, a proportion of the 100,000 would have found jobs anyway within the space of a year. Some of those are among the successful trainees (C); some are among the unsuccessful (D). This latter group would have been better off not attending the course. Overall the real "success rate", on these assumptions, is given by A − D, not, as might superficially be supposed, by A + C. As A + C can be obtained fairly easily, while C and D are not separately observable,[13] it is not surprising that the real success of measures of this sort is often exaggerated.

PUBLIC CHOICE

It is certainly not intended to suggest that all policy interventions in this area are doomed to failure, but these examples show how policies may have unintended outcomes which detract from their effectiveness, and in some cases may produce "successes" which are illusory.[14] This approach sees the danger of government failure lying in the inability of policy-makers fully to grasp the complexities of the problems with which they are grappling. Policy-makers are acting in good faith, attempting to promote the public interest, but are incompetent.

A rather different view of the role of policy-makers is taken by economists associated with the "public choice" school.[15] Public choice theory assumes that individuals maximize utility within the political sphere as well as within the economy. It hypothesizes a "political market" in which policies are the outcome of demand and supply forces. On the one hand, policies are "demanded" by groups of voters, producers and interest groups which will benefit from their enactment. On the other, policies are "supplied" by politicians and bureaucrats, in exchange for votes, campaign contributions or, in the case of bureaucrats, budget appropriations.

Power in the political market place is unevenly spread. On the demand side, consumers have little power because it is costly to organize and express their diffuse interests. The demand for policy intervention thus tends to be concentrated among producer groups with particular interests in common – for example, farmers, trade unions, professional organizations, firms in the same industry – who are individually prepared to contribute to the cost of lobbying in expectation of increased profits or other income. On the supply side, politicians will tend to concede those policies which appear to offer the greatest political advantage in terms of securing or retaining power.

Public choice analysis, though not universally accepted, has been applied to an increasing range of policy issues. It can offer a plausible explanation of the pattern of government intervention and economic regulation in parliamentary democracies. The ostensible rationale for government policies is increasingly seen, in this framework, as only part of the picture – and it is looked on with some suspicion. It has been argued by some that there is a systematic tendency for oversupply of intervention – a real "government failure" (Stigler 1971). Is this scepticism justified in relation to training policy?

Certainly, many interest groups stand to gain from government regulation and/or funding of training. Unions, for example, are typically strongly in favour of increased formal training provision. Regulation and insistence on formal qualifications can be used, as we have suggested, to reduce competition in the labour market. Historically European and American unions have defended trained labour against "dilution" by the unskilled. Wherever possible they tend to press for higher entry qualifications to jobs, a policy enhancing "rents" (returns in excess of the earnings which they could obtain elsewhere) to existing workers.[16] However, the ability of unions to secure influence over training policy varies from country to country. For example, British unions have in the past been riven by demarcation and interunion rivalry. Postwar German unions, to take a very different example, were organized exclusively on industrial lines and have faced less of a problem: their influence has been correspondingly greater.

Employers also hope to gain from government intervention in training. Public funding, as we have seen, often substitutes for training which firms would otherwise finance themselves. And employers who provide general training may often support industry levies or compulsion in order to equalize the burden of training costs which other firms would otherwise avoid. In this light, the support of the UK's Confederation of British Industry (the main employers' association) for compulsory training for young workers is explicable (Confederation of British Industry 1993). The CBI's pressure group activity has been successful in a number of directions; for example, the National Advisory Council for Education and Training Targets was set up in March 1993 as a result of its initiative. The Council monitors progress towards meeting the CBI's targets for the year 2000. These targets are now government policy too.

Then there is the growing body of professional "trainers" – a term which embraces private- and public-sector organizations and individuals drawing their incomes from providing training and preaching the "need" for investment in human capital. Academics, in both their roles as educators and as researchers, have generally welcomed with open arms enhanced public investment in training. And we have already seen evidence of classic interest group activity in bodies such as the new British Training and Enterprise Councils (see Chapter 6). First set up as a more efficient means of delivering training policies determined by central government, they have now established themselves as a strong political interest in their own right, calling for increased government spending in a way which goes far beyond what civil servants would have been permitted to do when they were running training schemes. In Germany, unions and employers' associations, much more powerful than in the UK, are themselves significant providers of training services, and this helps feed the demand for further training. In France Chambers of Commerce are similarly important training providers.

Finally, the attractiveness of intervention in training to politicians is easy to discern – particularly in recent years when higher unemployment has coincided with loss of faith in demand management and where nationally based industrial policies are seen as increasingly irrelevant. The need to be seen to be "doing something" which can be presented as improving long-term competitiveness as well as alleviating short-term problems is a powerful one.

The gist of this analysis, then, is that in examining the policies adopted towards training, we need to bear in mind the particular interests which policies may serve. Rather than assuming that policy-makers are merely passive interpreters of the public interest (whatever that may be), we should look carefully at the coalition of pressure groups united behind particular initiatives. It may be that some of the undesired results of government intervention are underemphasized by those promoting their own interests.

CONCLUSIONS

In this chapter we have set the scene for the next part of the book. Part II examines vocational education and training policies in a range of countries. We have outlined the rationale for government intervention in terms of various sorts of market failure – the inability of an unregulated labour market to produce an optimal level of training. However, we have also pointed to the dangers of "government failure", in particular the apparently unintended adverse consequences of policies designed to enhance and expand training provision. Finally, we have hinted that some of these adverse consequences may be played down in public debate as a result of coalitions of special interests which stand to gain from increased training provision.

NOTES

1. The poaching issue can be dramatized by setting it up as a one-period, two-firm prisoners' dilemma game where the Nash equilibrium (the position to which each firm is led by assuming that the other will make its best move) involves no firm supplying training (Chapman 1993: ch. 9). Whether this outcome would be chosen with repeated plays over time, however, seems dubious.
2. The much-vaunted Total Quality Management movement places great emphasis on continuing training of this sort.
3. This is not to imply that this is, or should be, the only function of compulsory education. For an interesting analysis of why compulsory education developed, see West (1971).
4. European Union policies on training are discussed further in Chapter 9.
5. Colin Crouch has written that "success in vocational education and training . . . depends on . . . strong collective organisations of employers" (Crouch 1992: 33).
6. Defined as "the extent of inter-union and inter-employer cooperation in wage bargaining with the other side" (Calmfors and Driffill 1988: 17).
7. The UK's Industrial Training Act of 1964 made provision for tripartite Industrial Training Boards (ITBs) to manage the system of grants and levies. By May 1966, 7.5 million workers were in industries covered by them. They were strongly criticized by small firms, which paid the levy and had to deal with a large amount of paperwork, but were often unable to claim back grants as they could not spare workers for the off-the-job training favoured by the ITBs. The levy system survives on a statutory basis in construction in the UK, and on a voluntary basis in engineering construction.

8. Firms are required to spend 1.1% of their wage bill on continuing training, and 0.5% on initial training – or else pay these same percentages into a government-administered training fund. See Chapter 8.
9. Even if we bear in mind that much of the cost of training may ultimately fall on the employee, as suggested earlier.
10. See also Organization for Economic Cooperation and Development (1993b: ch. 2) for estimates of displacement effects from a number of other countries.
11. Displacement effects in some schemes can be substantial. In one study of the UK Youth Training Scheme (Begg *et al.* 1991) the deadweight loss was estimated at 71% and the substitution effect at 9%.
12. Although other possibilities exist. They may get jobs, or they may withdraw from the labour force.
13. They could in principle be estimated, but sophisticated econometric techniques and access to a considerable amount of data about the trainees would be required.
14. Indeed, there has even been a suggestion in some studies that the real effect of some schemes is negative, as they can actually *reduce* individuals' chances of getting jobs as a result of "stigmatizing" job-seekers (Organization for Economic Cooperation and Development 1993b: 64).
15. James Buchanan, Gordon Tullock and Anthony Downs were key early figures in this school. Seminal works include Buchanan and Tullock (1962); Downs (1957); Stigler (1971); and Buchanan *et al.* (1980).
16. For a brief discussion of the attitude of unions towards training, see Chapman (1993: 60–1).

PART II

International Comparisons

5. Vocational Education and Training in the USA: A Patchwork

INTRODUCTION

> The American training 'system' ... is not a system, but a patchwork of programmes targeted at different clients, financed in different ways, provided by different sources, and designed for different purposes. (Berryman 1991)

Discussion of vocational education and training in the United States is complicated by its extensive decentralization, with several layers of funding and responsibility, and different numbers and types of organizations involved catering for huge numbers of individuals; in 1991 61.2 million people were enrolled in schools or colleges (National Center for Education Statistics 1992b).

In the USA, most initial vocational preparation is undertaken in educational institutions. Each state is responsible for its own system of education and, using federal, state and local monies, funds are allocated to the various educational establishments according to local criteria. Schools and colleges in turn develop their own systems of provision and curricula. The federal government has a relatively minor role to play in education, dealing with legislative matters, funding for specific groups and initiatives, and giving some financial assistance to students at college. This makes it difficult to discuss "the American system" since it will differ from state to state and between institutions. Cantor (1989) describes the American system as being made up of fifty unique educational systems – a different one for each state.

Training of employees is very much the responsibility of individual firms, with little regulation and no extensive apprenticeship system or reliance on formal qualifications. However, despite widespread commitment to the free enterprise ethic, government still plays a significant role in funding and providing training and retraining for various disadvantaged groups.

In this chapter we outline vocational education and training provision in the United States, and comment on some of its strengths and weaknesses.

ELEMENTARY AND SECONDARY EDUCATION

Educational funding comes from various sources, but spending is largely financed by local taxation and the state budget; in 1989–90 elementary and secondary schools received 47 per cent of their budget from state funds, 46.5 per cent from local sources and only 6 per cent from the federal government (National Center for Education Statistics 1992b). Most federal funds are aimed at specific groups of people and initiatives. Administration is often devolved to the local level, transferring the responsibility for running schools, hiring staff and determination of curricula to school districts, although states can direct districts to follow policies.

Compulsory education varies from state to state but in most it amounts to at least ten years, starting at either six or seven. Elementary schools cover the first six to eight years of education: they provide a broad general education, although there is no national curriculum. It is necessary to complete elementary school to progress to secondary education in high school.

High schools are largely non-selective, like the comprehensive system in the United Kingdom. Again the curriculum is individual to each school, but generally involves study of prescribed "core" subjects and additional optional courses, culminating in the attainment of a *high school diploma*, enabling students to continue to higher education. High school diplomas say little about the level of achievement, however, and students are often required to sit an additional assessment test, or to have a detailed report from school, in order to be admitted to particular universities.

Participation rates are high, with the vast majority of 14–17-year-olds enrolled in high school. For example in 1990 95.6 per cent of 16-year-olds, 89.5 per cent of 17-year-olds and 64.4 per cent of 18-year-olds were in schools (National Center for Education Statistics 1992a). Table 5.1 shows that 82 per cent of 25–64-year-olds had completed secondary education in 1989. Educational attainment has increased in recent years, so the proportion of 25–34-year-olds who were high school graduates was as high as 87 per cent in the same year.

Despite these figures – very impressive by international standards – concern has been expressed about high school dropouts, who constituted 12.5 per cent of 16–24 year olds in 1991 (National Center for Education Statistics 1992b). Such individuals have poor employment and training

Table 5.1 Percentage of population who have completed secondary and higher education in the US and other large industrial nations, 1989

Country	25–64 years old Both sexes		25–34 years old Both sexes		Male		Female	
	Secondary	Higher	Secondary	Higher	Secondary	Higher	Secondary	Higher
US	82.0	23.4	86.6	24.2	85.7	24.9	87.4	23.5
Japan	69.7	13.3	90.6	22.9	89.3	34.2	91.8	11.5
Germany	78.4	10.2	91.5	11.8	94.5	13.3	88.2	10.3
UK	64.5	9.2	76.7	11.2	79.7	12.8	73.7	9.5
France	48.1	7.0	63.0	7.6	65.6	8.1	60.4	7.1
Italy	25.7	5.7	41.1	6.7	40.9	6.9	41.2	6.5
Canada	71.4	15.1	83.5	16.1	82.1	16.9	84.8	15.2

Source: Reproduced in National Center for Education Statistics (1992a).

prospects. The aggregate figure also masks wide variations between areas. Many inner-city schools, for example, have disproportionately high numbers of dropouts, up to 50 per cent in some cases (*The Economist* 1992a). Consequently various incentives have been developed involving business-school partnerships to encourage higher participation and standards. Schemes include offers of free pizzas and hamburgers for improved grades, scholarships and job offers for good academic performance, equipment donations, monthly allowances to encourage potential dropouts to remain in school and so on.[1] In another imaginative initiative, in 1988 West Virginia became the first state to prevent high school dropouts receiving drivers licences: the idea has spread quickly to other states. Such experimental initiatives, whether public or private, are easier to develop in the United States than in countries such as the United Kingdom, Germany and France, where education is more tightly controlled.

THE VOCATIONAL ELEMENT OF HIGH SCHOOL EDUCATION

Each state is legally required to establish a Board of Vocational Education to prepare a five-year plan and supervise the system of vocational education in state institutions, and the federal government allocates money for particular elements of the plan. According to Cantor (1989), federal funding of vocational education was substantial during the 1960s and 1970s. However, throughout the 1980s, following the election of Ronald Reagan as President, federal funding fell significantly and in the late 1980s only accounted for about one-eighth of public expenditure on vocational education.

School programmes typically contain elements of academic, technical and vocational subjects, although a limited number of institutions specialize in vocational courses, 225 in 1987 (ibid.). Most vocational high school education therefore involves students opting for particular units as part of their general high school diploma. Academic study has traditionally carried more status than vocational education and consequently, as elsewhere, schools in the United States have often been criticized for providing poor preparation for work. However, in recent years students have opted for vocational courses in increasing numbers, as Table 5.2 demonstrates. Vocational education may be of a general nature (typing, business or craft courses), or more occupationally specific (computer programming, motor mechanics or nursing). Such courses provide basic entry-level skills, although they are typically not separately certificated. Even students doing

Table 5.2   Types of course taken by high school graduates, 1969 and 1987 (%)

| | Academic | | Vocational | | Personal use | |
	1969	1987	1969	1987	1969	1987
Total	73.0	68.5	18.0	19.7	9.0	11.8
Gender						
Male	74.2	67.3	16.6	20.2	9.1	12.5
Female	72.1	69.6	19.1	19.3	8.8	11.1
Race						
White	75.1	68.5	16.7	20.0	8.1	11.5
Black	65.6	67.5	22.9	20.4	11.4	12.2
Hispanic	61.9	66.7	23.3	19.2	14.8	14.1
Asian, Pacific Is.	68.2	74.1	16.7	12.5	15.2	13.3

Source: Reproduced in National Center for Education Statistics (1992a)

an academic programme, preparing for college or university can (and do) take a significant number of vocational units.

Table 5.2 also shows that the proportions of vocational to other courses taken vary by gender and by race. In 1987 men took a slightly greater proportion of vocational units than women, reversing the situation in 1969. Those of Asian/Pacific Islands origin are the most likely to follow an academic programme. Blacks are slightly more likely to opt for vocational courses than other races, and Hispanics are more likely to take courses for personal use. There was a marked decrease in the proportion of academic courses taken by whites between 1969 and 1987, whilst the proportion has increased for other races.

Much recent debate in the United States has involved critical comment on elementary and secondary education. Concern has concentrated on the quality of basic education, drawing attention to poor standards of literacy and numeracy. For example, both the National Commission on Excellence in Education and the Education Commission of the States' National Task Force on Education for Economic Growth criticized deficiencies in compulsory education, concluding that they would create serious problems for the future workforce (*Education Week* 1993). The Commission on Workforce Quality and Labor Market Efficiency (1989) reported that between 20m and 40m American adults had literacy problems and half of all 18 year olds had not developed basic language, mathematics and analytical skills.[2] It was also found that in 1988 employers had to allocate between $240 and $260m to basic literacy skills training for employees, giving substance to their criticisms of the system (*Education Week* 1993). Consequently the Bush Administration established *America 2000*, setting national education goals to be achieved by the year 2000. These are largely related to basic skills and educational attainment levels (US Department of Education 1991).

POST-COMPULSORY EDUCATION

Individuals wishing to remain in education after high school have several options: higher education, apprenticeships or various "second-chance" programmes for the disadvantaged. In full-time higher education individuals can either pursue a two-year *associate degree* or a four-year *degree* course. Other post-compulsory education tends to focus on particular skills, to raise basic levels of education or promote personal development.

In 1991–2, 9,983 institutions offered post-secondary education (National Center for Education Statistics 1992b). They included universities, community colleges, Regional Occupation Centers and Programs, correspondence schools and private colleges. Universities and private colleges offer degrees, masters' degrees, PhDs, advanced professional degrees and vocational and professional qualifications (courses for which can last up to a further seven years). Community colleges provide education and training up to and including the associate degree.

Numbers involved in post-compulsory education have for many years been high by comparison with other countries. Participation continued to rise over the last decade, especially for non-traditional college-goers such as women, part-timers and older people. In 1970 part-timers made up 32 per cent of college students; by the 1990s the proportion had risen to an estimated 43 per cent with projections of 45 per cent by 1997 (National Center for Education Statistics 1992b).

In 1990 60 per cent of high school graduates (58 per cent of males and 62 per cent of females) enrolled in college, up from 47 per cent in 1973. One-fifth of high school graduates joined two-year colleges and two-fifths enrolled in four-year colleges (Perelman 1990). However, it should be borne in mind that many of these will have dropped out subsequently.

A slightly larger proportion of men than women is enrolled in higher education amongst 16–24-year olds, with the reverse being the case for ages 25–34. Table 5.3 illustrates how much of the growth in the numbers in higher education has been the result of the enrolment of women increasing at a faster rate than that of men. The percentage of men aged 25–34 who are in higher education has fallen since 1973; this is probably the result of the end of conscription, which delayed entry to college for some males.

Table 5.3 Percentage of high school graduates aged 16–34 years enrolled in college, by sex, age and type of college: selected years, 1973–90 (%)

	Male high school graduates				Female high school graduates			
	16–24 years old		25–34 years old		16–24 years old		25–34 years old	
	2-year	4-year	2-year	4-year	2-year	4-year	2-year	4-year
1973	9.4	22.2	3.1	2.9	6.7	17.3	2.0	1.2
1977	8.7	23.9	3.2	3.5	8.1	19.6	2.9	2.5
1980	8.8	22.1	2.3	2.6	9.0	19.6	3.1	2.5
1983	9.2	23.0	2.7	2.8	9.4	19.6	2.9	2.6
1985	8.6	24.2	2.1	2.7	9.4	21.4	3.3	2.6
1987	9.5	26.1	2.0	2.7	10.1	21.8	2.6	2.7
1990	10.7	27.0	1.9	2.7	10.7	25.1	3.3	3.2

Source: Reproduced in National Center for Education Statistics (1992a).

VOCATIONAL POST-SECONDARY EDUCATION

Whereas 94 per cent of the budget of elementary and secondary schools comes from government at one level or another, only 30 per cent of the finances of higher education institutions derive directly from federal, state or local government. The majority of students pay tuition fees, and firms pay for a variety of customized courses for their employees, with government also paying for courses for its employees or for groups on special programmes.

Although universities, as in other developed countries, play a major role in preparing people for work, there are two types of higher education institutions providing vocational preparation which have no exact counterparts existing on a similar scale in other countries. These are the community colleges and private vocational colleges.

Community colleges[3] have accounted for an increasing proportion of higher education and, in 1991–2 some 1,444 were in operation (National Center for Education Statistics 1992b). In addition to associate degrees they provide courses for adults requiring basic and continuing education, services for local industry and businesses (such as "start-up" courses for new firms), short work-related courses, and non-certificated "personal development" courses. Vocational certificates are awarded for part-time and full-time courses and colleges often provide the training element in the JTPA (Job Training Partnership Act) and apprenticeship programmes, which we shall discuss later. Some high school students can study full-time vocational courses at community colleges or Regional Occupation Centers to complete their diplomas, or can spend up to half the week in college, continuing their general education at school for the remainder.

The associate degrees which are taught at community colleges are two-year courses. They can be taken either as a qualification in their own right or to form the first two years of a bachelor's degree. Students can transfer to universities once they have obtained their associate degree, with advanced standing based on the credits they have already accumulated. About 43 per cent of all degree students begin in community colleges, and over 40 per cent of associate degree enrollees transfer to other institutions to a bachelor's degree programme (Her Majesty's Inspectorate/ Department of Education and Science 1990).

Associate degrees can be academic or vocational in nature, broadly categorized as liberal arts programmes, academic sciences or technical/ vocational in orientation. A number of core general subjects must be completed to transfer to a full degree. However, transferability varies between states and institutions, a problem associated with lack of national standards or curricula.

Other courses at community colleges include vocational certificates and diplomas to prepare individuals for the labour market, either for initial entry or retraining for a new career. Such courses are approximately the equivalent of NVQ levels I–III in the UK (see Chapter 6) and are generally shorter versions of associate degrees, lasting about a year. They tend to be more narrowly specialized, without the element of general education.

Adult Education Diplomas and Certificates of Completion are awarded to adults who undertake continuing education at community colleges, generally in the evening but also during the day and at weekends. Like high school diplomas, these do not accurately measure individual attainment levels. Many courses are of a relatively low standard, ranging in length from just a few hours up to a year.

Although community colleges provide a valuable way of providing post-school education in the local community, they have (like American higher education institutions in general) been criticized for their high drop out rates and the wide variation in the quality of courses, since no national certification exists.

In addition to the publicly controlled community colleges, there is a large private sector in American tertiary education. Private colleges are primarily vocational, tending not to provide general education, but rather to develop skills in particular occupational areas. Diplomas and certificates are awarded. It is not unusual for a school to provide courses related to just one subject area such as business-only courses (many colleges concentrate on awarding Masters of Business Administration, for example). Private colleges often have close links with employers, with the aim of ensuring that they are supplying students with the skills industry requires.

There was a dramatic rise in the proportion of students attending these institutions over the 1980s. This has provoked controversy over their cost and quality. In 1988 there were over 4,000 colleges registered with various accrediting associations such as the National Association of Trade and Technical Schools (NATTS). About 1.6 million students were enrolled, representing 15 per cent of post-secondary enrolment (Perelman 1990), compared with only 9 per cent in 1981 (NEDC/MSC 1984).

The MBA and business education industry generally boomed over the 1980s. By 1990, 700 business schools awarded about 75,000 MBAs, far more per head of population than in any other nation, and it has been estimated that investment in business education amounted to at least $6 billion a year when shorter courses for business managers and executives are included (Haynes 1991). Some have indeed argued that general business education has gone too far: potential managers are highly qualified but may not be able to relate theory to any real experience. Their education is largely self-funded, and is thus predominantly general, while firms may prefer further training to be more specific, related to their own processes, goals and corporate culture.

Some critics have argued that resources are seriously misallocated in vocational education, in that the United States has simultaneously the largest proportion of the workforce with degrees in any major developed country,[4] while also having a large proportion of the workforce with very limited levels of educational attainment (Gapper 1992).

EMPLOYER-PROVIDED TRAINING

Vocational education and training in the US has traditionally been school- and college-based but pressure has been growing for greater employer involvement. For example, there is renewed interest in the apprenticeship system, following its reported successes in Germany. During his presidential campaign, Bill Clinton promised to ensure that all firms would spend the equivalent of 1.5 per cent of their payroll costs on training. He has subsequently abandoned this commitment, which was unpopular with employers, but his administration continues to press for an expansion of employer investment in skills, including a planned revival of apprenticeships (*The Economist* 1994).

What is the current picture on employer-provided training? A major problem with discussing this issue is the lack of comprehensive national data. Firms are not required to collect information on training activities and few questions in national surveys concern training. Relevant information is available only in the form of *ad hoc* studies based on particular data sets, and is largely based on individuals' self-assessed experiences (Bishop 1991; Blanchflower and Lynch 1992; Lynch 1991 and 1993; Buechtemann *et al.* 1993; Lillard and Tan 1986; Mincer 1991; Tan *et al.* 1991).

The most widely quoted estimate of employer spending for the mid-1980s was that firms spent about $30 billion each year on the formal training of their employees, or around $263 per worker (Hilton 1991). However, this estimate only covers off-the-job training. On-the-job training is less well recorded and estimates range from $90 billion to $180 billion in the late 1980s (Pines and Carnevale 1991). Mincer (1991), employing the methodology briefly outlined in Chapter 2, adds opportunity costs to direct costs. Not surprisingly, he puts total annual expenditure on training in the USA considerably higher, at between $240 billion and $330 billion.

Some of the most useful up-to-date information on training comes from the answers to questions asked in a supplement to the January 1991 *Current Population Survey* (CPS), not least because they replicate supplementary questions attached to the January 1983 CPS allowing direct comparisons to be made. Individuals were asked what training was necessary for their present job and what training they had undertaken whilst in their present job.[5]

Patterns of training in 1991 were similar to those of 1983, as Table 5.4 demonstrates. In 1991 nearly 65.3 million people, or 57 per cent of workers employed, said they required skills training to do their job, an increase of only 2 per cent since 1983. Proportions requiring training for their present job increased with age to 44 and then declined. In all age groups, except 16–19, the main source of training was "school" (which, in the American usage, includes college and university), followed by informal on-the-job training. 16–19 year olds were more likely to have received on-the-job training than others, probably because they would have left the education system with the minimum qualifications and required some basic entry-level work preparation that others receive by staying at college beyond the minimum leaving age. The lower figures for older age groups, as suggested in Chapter 2, will reflect time in the workforce (as past experience can to some extent reduce the need for formal training), the shorter pay-off period to further training investment, and the tendency of older employees to take less-demanding jobs as they near retirement.

The proportions of men and women said to need training were virtually equal, but there are differences in the sources of training. Women were more likely than men to receive their training from the education system, whereas men were almost equally as likely to be trained on-the-job as at school and were more likely to receive any other form of training than women.[6] Whilst in 1991 whites were still more likely to have received any training than other races, the disparities had narrowed since 1983. Whites were at least as likely to have received any type of training as blacks or Hispanics. Along with blacks and "other races", they would probably have received it at "school", whilst Hispanics relied more on training at work. More educated individuals were more likely to complete training for their job, and to receive it at school. Not surprisingly, those with a high school diploma or less were more likely to have received on-the-job training than other forms.

Above-average numbers of people in professional, technical, skilled and managerial occupations required training, with large numbers receiving their training at school. On the other hand unskilled occupations with routine functions, such as services, machine operators, cleaners, sales and clerical workers, required less than average numbers to take qualifying training, and were most likely to be trained on-the-job.

A third of all trainees received the training necessary to enter their jobs from school, with more than half of these at four-year colleges.[7] Informal on-the-job training, although the second most popular source of required training, was actually reported more frequently than the education system

Table 5.4   Workers who needed training to qualify for their jobs, by age, sex, race and source of training, 1983 and 1991 CPS data (%)

| | % employed needing training | | Source of training, 1991[a] | | | | | |
	1983	1991	School	Formal company	Informal on-the-job	Armed forces	Correspondence course	Other
Age								
total 16+	55	57	33	12	27	2	1	7
16–19	25	26	8	4	16	(b)	(b)	4
20–24	47	46	25	8	23	1	(b)	5
25–34	62	60	36	13	30	1	1	8
35–44	62	63	38	14	30	2	1	8
45–54	57	60	34	14	28	3	2	8
55–64	52	53	28	10	24	3	1	7
65 +	41	44	23	6	17	2	2	9
Gender								
Male	56	57	31	14	29	4	2	9
Female	54	56	35	9	25	(b)	1	6
Race								
White	57	58	34	12	28	2	1	8
Black	44	47	24	12	20	2	1	5
Other[c]	54	58	37	11	23	2	1	8
Hispanic[d]	43	41	17	8	20	1	1	6

Notes
[a] total percentages may exceed 100 as some workers identified more than one source of training
[b] negligible
[c] includes Asians/Pacific Islanders, American Indians, Eskimos and all other races
[d] Hispanics can be from any race
Source: Amirault (1992).

in eight out of twelve occupations, with higher than average proportions of the workforce citing it in executive, administrative and managerial occupations (37 per cent), precision, production, craft and repair (36 per cent), technicians and related support occupations (31 per cent) and administrative support (30 per cent).

Formal company training does not seem to be a significant source of training, according to the CPS employee responses, but this may reflect peoples' perceptions of their need for training in order to get their present job. Only 12 per cent of workers obtained their required training on formal company programmes. Consequently they may be likely to undertake this training themselves rather than rely on a firm to hire them and then train them. Of course, individuals' perceptions of what qualifications they require to do their job are not necessarily accurate: some people could be "overeducated" for their job. Also many jobs have a minimum qualification requirement so individuals will not apply until they have this basic level of education or training. The numbers of firms giving formal training or on-the-job training may possibly give a more reliable estimate of numbers who required training in order to satisfy job requirements than individuals' subjective assessments. Table 5.5 shows training actually received by respondents since taking up their current job. 41 per cent of CPS respondents said they had undergone training since starting their present job, up from 35 per cent in 1983.

PATTERNS OF PROVISION

Table 5.5 describes similar patterns to those of Table 5.4. Training incidence increases with age up to a peak in the 35–44 age group before decreasing, and all age groups experienced an increase in training from the 1983 levels, except the 16–19-year-old group, where incidence remained constant.

Employers have increasingly sponsored both qualifying training and continuing training whilst in the job. Formal company training is a more important source of continuing training than other sources for all age groups, except the 16–24 group where informal on-the-job training is more important.

Several other studies have confirmed the picture shown in Table 5.5, which indicates that the pattern of employer-provided training by age in the United States is significantly different from that in other countries, such as the United Kingdom and Germany. For example, Tan *et al.* (1991) found that only 12 per cent of American young people received any formal training within their first year in the labour market (in contrast to 30–40 per cent even of non-apprentices in Britain and Germany). The US figure is low mainly because more Americans will have received job-related vocational training or education in a full-time education institution, thus reducing the need for entry-level training.

Table 5.5   Workers who had continuing training whilst in their job, by age, gender and source of training, 1983 and 1991 CPS (%)

	% trained in job		Source of training[a]			
	1983	1991	School	Formal company	Informal on-the-job	Other
Age						
Total 16+	35	41	14	16	15	7
16–19	18	18	3	3	13	1
20–24	28	31	8	9	14	3
25–34	39	41	13	16	15	7
35–44	41	48	17	19	17	9
45–54	38	46	17	18	16	9
55–64	31	37	12	13	13	7
65+	19	25	8	7	8	6
Gender						
Male	35	40	12	17	15	8
Female	34	41	15	14	15	7
Race						
White	36	42	14	16	15	8
Black	28	34	10	13	14	4
Other races[b]	32	38	11	16	13	6
Hispanic[c]	23	28	7	10	12	3
Education						
High school & less	26	29	6	11	13	4
Some college	41	46	16	19	17	7
College graduate	54	61	27	22	17	14

Notes
[a] total percentages may exceed 100 as some workers identified more than one source of training
[b] includes Asians/Pacific Islanders, American Indians, Eskimos and all other races
[c] Hispanics can be from any race
Source: Amirault (1992).

Table 5.5 shows that the proportions of men and women trained were again similar, and again women have to rely more on schools for their training than do men, with males more likely to receive formal company training. Lillard and Tan (1986) found that more men than women receive company or managerial training. This applies even to women who have not had a career break; women who have taken career breaks receive little further training.

The CPS data also show that whites are most likely to receive training, with Hispanics least likely. Formal company training is the most important source of training for white and "other race" employees, whilst on-the-job training predominates for blacks and Hispanics. Whilst all races experienced increases in training since 1983, the relative positions remained virtually the same.

Previous education affects the training received, so that the higher the level of previous education the more likely individuals are to receive further training. Of college graduates, 61 per cent updated their skills in 1991, as compared with only 29 per cent of those educated up to high school level.

Tan *et al.* (1991) have also emphasized the disparity in levels of most types of training received which is associated with differential educational attainment. High school dropouts are least likely to receive training for various interrelated reasons: they are more likely to be black or Hispanic (groups which have less chance of being trained); they are less likely to be in jobs which attract a lot of training; and they are more likely to have periods of unemployment, thus failing to build up as much work experience as high school and college graduates.

Table 5.6 shows that workers in particular industries and occupations attract more training than others, ranging from 67 per cent among professional speciality workers to 6 per cent in private household occupations. As expected, professional and skilled occupations have above-average proportions of people updating their skills, since they are likely frequently to have to absorb recent changes in technology and practice. Formal company programmes will probably be the major source of updating, although in the case of the professional speciality group (doctors, lawyers, accountants, and so on) "school" is more important.

A smaller than average proportion of individuals in lower-skilled occupations receive continuing training. In several of these occupations informal on-the-job training is the most frequent source: examples include services, machine operators, cleaners and labourers. School tends not to be used for training in less-skilled occupations. Only 2 per cent of transportation workers and 1 per cent of cleaners and labourers received continuing training at educational institutions, whereas 20 per cent of

Table 5.6   *Workers who had continuing training whilst in their job, by occu-*
            pation, 1983 and 1991 CPS (%)

| | % trained in job | | Source of training | | | |
Occupation	1983	1991	School	Formal company	Informal on-the-job	Other
Exec./admin./ managerial	47	53	18	25	18	12
Professional speciality	61	67	20	20	17	15
Technical & related	52	59	7	26	22	9
Sales	32	35	12	16	15	6
Clerical/admin. support	32	40	12	16	16	4
Private household	3	6	2	—	1	3
Services	25	29	7	9	13	5
Farming/fishing/ forestry	16	21	7	3	7	7
Craft & related	35	38	9	17	16	4
Machine operators etc.	22	25	4	8	15	2
Transportation	18	25	2	10	11	3
Cleaners, labourers etc.	14	15	1	5	9	1

Source: Amirault (1992).

those in professional speciality and 18 per cent in executive, administrative and managerial occupations were trained there.

Several commentators, for example Tan *et al.* (1991) and Mincer (1991), have found that workers in industries subject to frequent technological progress are more likely to receive employer-provided training. This tends to take the form of in-house training to enable the technology to be fully utilized; the appropriate training is not available in the external market because of time lags for innovations to filter outside the original firm. High-technology industries may employ already well-educated personnel, further increasing the likelihood of receiving training from the firm.

Another factor relevant to training incidence is the size of the firm. It is known that the distribution of training by firms is highly skewed. It is claimed by Bernstein (1993) that more than half of training expenditure comes from less than 10 per cent of all US companies. Another estimate suggests that $27 billion was invested by 15,000 employers, approximately 0.5 per cent of all employers, and only 100–200 firms allocate more than 2 per cent of payroll on formal training (National Center on Education and the Economy 1990).

It is widely assumed that the likelihood of training increases with the size of firm. This hypothesis is supported by evidence from the literature, although Bishop (1991) also found very small firms (up to ten employees) provided more training than medium-sized firms. He reasons that in very small firms there are fewer opportunities to achieve divisions of labour so employees must be taught wider-ranging skills, and the opportunity cost of informal training is lower as there will be more slack time during which training can be scheduled.

To summarize the position: employer-provided training tends to be focused on white-collar, better-educated, established workers as opposed to blue-collar, non-college-educated new entrants to the labour force. Generally it has been shown that men are more likely to be trained than women, whites than non-whites, more experienced workers than new young workers and large firms are more likely to train people than small firms.

LABOUR UNIONS AND THE APPRENTICESHIP SYSTEM

Another influence on training provision is labour unions. Despite their weakness by comparison with their European counterparts, American unions have often played a role in encouraging training. Unions frequently sponsor their members to undertake vocational courses at either community colleges or one of the several union colleges where craft level education and training is available for a variety of occupations. There have also been developments in the training field involving agreements between employers and unions. Some collective agreements include joint provision of training funds for the employees by the employer and the union, whilst others include the union running trust funds for training and retraining paid for by employers. For example, two-thirds of apprentices' training is financed by both the employer and the union (Her Majesty's Inspectorate/Department of Education and Science 1990): indeed Gospel (1993) claims that the survival of apprenticeship[8] in the United States (albeit on a very small scale) is mainly the result of union influence in such industries as construction. In 1989 joint training programmes were valued at over $300 million, covering more than 700,000 workers (Carnevale and Goldstein 1990).

A formal apprenticeship lasts for three to four years and during that time trainees must complete at least 2,000 hours of on-the-job experience and 144 hours per year off-the-job training in vocational schools or community colleges (Carnevale and Goldstein 1990). The quality of training is highly regarded but covers only a small proportion of the workforce and a limited number of occupations in construction and manufacturing; in 1989 approximately 263,000 people nationwide were apprentices, compared with 1.7 million in West Germany (Gapper 1992). According to Buechtemann *et al.* (1993) the proportion of apprenticeships fell over the 1980s so that apprentices now account for less than 2 per cent of school leavers and less than 0.2 per cent of the workforce.

There has been renewed interest in the apprenticeship system and the Labor Department is looking at the possibility of expanding the existing system by developing pilot schemes in six US cities, with a view to broader coverage of occupations and industries and to opening apprenticeships to all young adults. President Clinton has called for an extension of the apprenticeship system to allow any high school graduates not wishing to progress to college the opportunity to complete an apprenticeship.

The United States, like many advanced nations, is concerned about shortages of intermediate skills. Those not attending college have been referred to as the "forgotten half" of the workforce; many recent initiatives have concentrated on them. At present the average apprentice is 23 years old or more and has had some previous work experience or education (Hilton 1991) and so these new proposals would not only expand the system but would change its focus to become a major source of initial training for school-leavers.

The foundations for Clinton's new apprenticeship have been laid, with $270 million allocated in the 1994 fiscal year and plans to spend $1.2 billion over five years on the scheme (Del Valle 1993). The money is aimed at financing the creation of links between states/school districts and individuals and employers, establishing at least 100,000 trainee positions with employers, and creating a national skills accreditation and standards board with representatives from industry, education, labour and government. Guidelines would be set for combined on-the-job training and classroom education, enabling study to be transferable to college degrees, and developing a system of certification for reaching each standard. An attempt is being made to develop a flexible system, learning from the problems of apprenticeships in Germany, so individuals are not labelled for life when they embark upon an apprenticeship and can change occupations relatively easily.

GOVERNMENT AND TRAINING IN THE UNITED STATES

Mention of this initiative serves as a reminder that, despite there being a stronger predisposition to the free enterprise ethic in the United States than in many European economies, there is nevertheless a substantial commitment of government funds to vocational training as well as education. These funds take a variety of forms and are used in many different ways. At the end of 1993 there were 150 federal programmes alone (*The Economist* 1994).

Historically, one major area of funding has been veterans' benefits. Because of the significantly larger scale of the peacetime military in the US compared with European countries, this source of funding has been consistently more important than elsewhere. Since the 1944 GI Bill the federal government has subsidized education and training for those who have served in the armed forces. Such subsidies are available for two- and four-year college attendance (veterans' benefits are the largest single federal programme of student aid), vocational and technical schools, correspondence courses, apprenticeships and various other activities. Their attractiveness as a recruiting device has led the individual services to add "kickers" to federal funding, which became less generous for a spell after the mid-1970s (although the position was largely restored by the Montgomery GI Bill of 1985). The sums of money available to individuals are substantial, a fairly typical entitlement having a discounted present value of nearly $18,000 in 1986 (Angrist 1993). A sample of veterans aged 30–54 in 1987 indicated that about 60 per cent had received some aid from the Veterans Administration (ibid.: 641–2).

Second, many federally funded programmes have been developed to assist the unemployed, particularly those suffering from various forms of labour market disadvantage – ethnic minorities, single mothers, the disabled, and so on. Early examples occurred under Roosevelt's New Deal of the 1930s, but there was renewed activism after the Manpower Development and Training Act of 1962. A whole range of programmes grew up in the 1960s and early 1970s. The Comprehensive Employment and Training Act (CETA) was passed in 1973 to bring together all training and employment measures for funding purposes. By the early 1980s the total budget for CETA programmes was over $8 billion, and places in training and temporary subsidized employment were provided for nearly 3 million people – a scale of operation comparable with that in Europe (Hughes and Perlman 1984).

Although CETA had some successes, under Ronald Reagan's Presidency there was a switch of emphasis. The Job Training Partnership Act of 1982 was intended to concentrate resources on the most difficult to employ of the disadvantaged, while also seeking to achieve higher success rates amongst trainees and those in job placements – to some extent a conflict of objectives. The Reagan and Bush administrations also saw the CETA programmes as too heavily influenced by the public sector and over-centralized. As a consequence, under JTPA there has been a devolution of responsibility to the state, and within states to service delivery areas. JTPA scheme headings are listed in Table 5.7, while the 1989 budgets and numbers of participants are given in Table 5.8.

No public service jobs are available under JTPA, leading to a much greater reliance on the private sector for programme "success". Within the service delivery areas, programmes are administered by Private Industry Councils (PICs) with strong business representation – a source of inspiration for the TECs which were later developed in the UK (see Chapter 6). PICs are given performance targets and rewarded for keeping cost per trainee low and job placement rates high. This has led to accusations that they tend to "cream" by choosing trainees who are more likely to succeed, despite the rhetoric of aiding the most disadvantaged. There is some evidence that this is the case. Anderson *et al.* (1993), in a study of Tennessee, find that the 71 per cent placement success rate in certain programmes would fall to 62 per cent if participants were selected randomly from those eligible. Such creaming is likely so long as the programmes can only cater for a minority of those eligible. For example, Title IIA schemes were only able to cater for about 6 per cent of the theoretically eligible population in the 1980s.

Creaming is not the only charge raised against the JTPA. The operation of JTPA schemes was investigated by the Labor Department's Inspector General and the General Accounting Office, both concluding that JTPA funds had been misused in several ways (Garland 1992). For example, wage subsidies were used to hire individuals who would have been hired anyway; states had used funds to attract inward investors from other states; some individuals not eligible for schemes had received training; some private training agencies had received money for placing trainees in non-existent jobs, and some trainees have been "trained" for longer than necessary in order to continue receiving the wage subsidy.

Apart from complaints about these irregularities, there have been criticisms that placements are too short, badly paid and generally lead to secondary labour market jobs. It is also claimed that public funds often

Table 5.7   Job Training Partnership Act and related schemes

JTPA Title II-A: Training Services for Economically Disadvantaged Youths and Adults
Eligibility requirements for this program are based on official measures of poverty and recipients of welfare payments. In 1987–8 approximately half the participants were minorities and over a quarter were high school dropouts (Perelman 1990).

JTPA Title II-B: Summer Youth Employment and Training Program
This program provides assistance to disadvantaged 16–21 year olds in getting part-time, minimum-wage work in the summer, offering remedial and basic education, classroom and on-the-job training and supportive services. On 1 July 1993 a new youth training program was introduced, under II-C, available all year and not just in the summer.

JTPA Title III: Employment Training for Dislocated Workers
Services are given to dislocated workers, understood to be workers who lose their jobs and are unlikely to be able to return to their previous occupation or industry. With this budget individual states must match Federal funding determined by an unemployment rate formula and in addition to employment and training services, under this program individuals are given relocation and pre-lay-off assistance.

JTPA Title IV
Under this program several social groups are provided with training and employment services:
(a) Native Americans: Employment and training services are financed for the special needs of Indians, native Alaskans and native Hawaiians, who may face significant barriers to employment.
(b) Migrant and seasonal farmworkers: Competitive grants are awarded every two years to non-profit organizations and state/local government agencies to administer the training and employment services for those facing seasonal unemployment and technological displacement.
(c) Job Training Corps: An initiative to cater specifically for the academic and vocational training needs of under-privileged young people, generally between the ages of 16 and 21. Free accredited residential courses and facilities are offered and a "basic wage" every fortnight plus some savings given to them at the end of the course (HMI/DES 1990).
(d) Veterans Employment and Training Services (VETS): This budget supplements existing veteran programmes administered by the Federal Department of Veterans' Affairs.

Table 5.7   Job Training Partnership Act and related schemes – continued

Recent additions to JTPA have led to the creation of **Title V**, Jobs for
Employable Dependent Individuals (JEDI) Incentive Bonus Program,
and **Title VI**, which enables states to establish Human Resources
Investment Councils

Opportunities Industrialization Centers were set up in 1964 for local,
community vocational skills training institutions. They are funded by
the private sector to provide programmes and to offer some free training
for the disadvantaged and to prepare some students for the General
Education Diploma.

The Federal government also provides monies to fund other employment and training initiatives, not included in the JTPA. The *Senior
Community Service Employment Program* subsidizes part-time employment and training for over-54-year-olds. Individuals on the scheme generally receive the minimum wage for work in the community such as
assistance in schools and hospitals. The *Job Opportunities and Basic Skills
Program (JOBS)*, part of the 1988 Family Support Act, targets needy
women with dependent children with education, training, and child- and
health-care assistance.

Other schemes provide employment and training services for handi-
capped people (*Vocational Rehabilitation*), refugees (*Refugee Resettlement
Program*) and workers dislocated or whose hours and wages are cut as a
result of foreign competition (*Trade Adjustment Assistance*).

---

merely substitute private provision that would have occurred anyway, as
suggested in the previous chapter, and that employers often use the training
grant as a wage subsidy, giving only a minimum level of training (*The
Economist* 1991). Thus the type of placement or quality of training and
outcome are of secondary importance to obtaining a positive outcome and
thereby securing some future funding.

The General Accounting Office study found that over 40 per cent of on-
the-job training under JTPA was in low-skill occupations such as machine
operator, labourer or dishwasher, and concluded that much of this training
lasted too long, on average more than double the recommended length.[9]
Since JTPA funding pays the training firm half the trainee's wages throughout the training period, the longer the reported training period the more
money the employer receives. Furthermore it was found that about 85 per
cent of this long-term training, where it exceeded the guidelines, was being
given to relatively well-prepared individuals, who could be expected to be
trained in the recommended time.

It should be emphasized, incidentally, that training subsidies are not only provided by the federal government. The individual states also play a significant role. Because of the difficulties of securing Congressional

Table 5.8   Summary of US government-funded training programmes

Programme	1989 budgets ($m)	Participants 1987 (thousands)
JTPA Title II-A: Economically disadvantaged adults and youths	1,788	1,094
Title II-B: Summer Youth Program	709	640
Title III: Dislocated workers	284	183
Title IVa: Native American Programs	59	33
Title IVb: Migrant/seasonal farmworkers	69	47
Title IVc: Job Corps	742	104
Title IVd: VETS	10	n/a
Post-secondary vocational education (1988)	355.3	n/a[a]
Senior Community Service Employment Program	344	100
Vocational rehabilitation	1,668	917
Trade adjustment assistance[b] (1988)	54.3	13
Refugee Resettlement Program[c] (1987)	47.2	n/a
Training for food stamp recipients	116	n/a
Targeted jobs tax credit (1988)	240	598

Notes
[a] Participation figures not reliable but could amount to 4m; from Perelman (1990).
[b] Training element, not including TRA benefits; figures cited in Perelman (1990).
[c] Perelman (1990).
Source: Reproduced in Levitan and Gallo (1990).

approval for programmes at the national level, it is sometimes possible for a wider range of programmes to be implemented by the states individually. For example, 46 states had implemented various forms of subsidy to firms to upgrade the skills of their existing employees by 1989 (Holzer *et al.* 1993).

Both the decentralization of federal schemes and the possibility of independent state funding in the USA has encouraged a culture of experimentation. In some cases this has taken the form of deliberate controlled experiments of a kind rarely seen in Europe (Organization for Economic Cooperation and Development 1993b: 53–67). One example of this is the National Supported Work experiment, which operated from 1975 to 1979. This provided sheltered work experience (mainly in construction for males, and in service occupations for females) where stress was gradually increased until private-sector workplace norms were reached, whereupon the participants attempted to achieve "real" employment. Eligible individuals were randomly assigned to the programme or to a control group. The programme seems to have achieved satisfactory outcomes for some groups of trainees, notably lone mothers (Couch 1992). Another such controlled experiment was the Youth Entitlement Program, which gave job guarantees for disadvantaged youths who agreed to complete high school (Ferber and Hirsch 1982: ch. 6). In addition to formally controlled experiments of this kind, variations which necessarily occur in programme implementation over the vast geographical distances and very different socioeconomic structures of the United States provide a "natural experiment" which researchers can often exploit.

CONCLUSIONS

The United States has a more fluid society than that of most European countries. It has one of the highest levels of job mobility in the OECD: only 35 per cent of male workers in their late thirties have been employed by their current employer for more than ten years, whereas the equivalent figure for Germany is 58 per cent (Gapper 1992). It is perhaps not surprising, therefore, that emphasis is placed on the acquisition of general vocational training in schools and colleges rather than in employment. The American educational "system" has substantial plus points in its favour: its flexibility, its openness and the high level of participation in post-compulsory education. Nevertheless, questions can legitimately be asked about the quality of the output of some of its schools and colleges; and the lack of common standards and transferable qualifications seriously reduces the benefits which students obtain from it.

Employer-provided training in the US follows a fairly predictable pattern, broadly in line with the implications of human capital theory. The incidence of training has been increasing significantly in recent years, though critics will still charge that the average level of provision is inadequate. They will point to the way in which minority groups receive low levels of training which perpetuate labour market disadvantage, as suggested in Chapter 3.

We have seen that, despite the rhetoric of free market liberalism, American governments have in practice for many years funded large amounts of training and retraining for disadvantaged groups. In some cases schemes have provided vivid examples of the possibility of "government failures" of the kind sketched in Chapter 4. One advantage of the decentralized nature of government training delivery in the USA, however, is the possibility of controlled experimentation. This may mean that the US is less likely to produce catastrophically bad training schemes than it would if it had a more centralized system.

NOTES

1. Privately funded initiatives come from individuals as well as companies. The reported $500 million offered by former Ambassador Walter Annenburg at the end of 1993 to assist inner-city schools is only the latest in a long history of substantial acts of educational philanthropy in the United States.
2. See, for further discussion, US Departments of Education and Labor (1988) and Kirsch *et al.* (1992).
3. There are a variety of names used in the US, such as technical college, city college, technical institute and junior college. The term community college is used to refer to all such establishments providing post-secondary education up to associate degree level.
4. There are suggestions (Buechtemann *et al.* 1993) that significant proportions of the US workforce are overqualified for the work they perform. The issue of overqualification is discussed in Chapter 10.
5. Details of the CPS results can be found in United States Department of Labor (1992) and Amirault (1992). The supplementary questions to both the 1983 and the 1991 CPS concerning training were: "Did you need specific skills or training to obtain your current (last) job?"; and "Since you obtained your present job, did you take any training to improve your skills?". If respondents said yes to either they were asked to identify sources, financing, length of training and whether or not they completed the training. Individuals could choose from various categories for their sources of training: high school/post-secondary school; formal company programme; informal on-the-job training, or experience from previous jobs; the Armed forces; correspondence courses; and informal training from a friend, relative or other experience unrelated to work. School programmes identified as sources included high school vocational programmes, post-high school vocational programmes, community college programmes and four-year or longer college programmes.
6. See Chapter 12.
7. Blanchflower and Lynch (1992) emphasize that training at work rarely leads to formal qualifications in the United States. They also find, however, in line with evidence elsewhere, that the higher the existing qualifications of the worker the more likely he or

she is to receive training at work. Thus there is an incentive for individuals to build up their stock of education at college as a means of securing further training at work; the employer cannot be relied on to "train up" unqualified workers.

8. "In the colonial period, the US inherited from Britain a system of craft apprenticeships which were the main formal method of training for manual workers well into the nineteenth century ... by the early twentieth century the traditional occupational apprenticeship had declined in most areas other than construction, printing and shipbuilding and in some metal working trades in a few large urban centres" (Gospel 1993: 8). Elbaum (1991) has conjectured that because of the high level of geographical mobility in the United States employers were unable to enforce apprenticeship rules. Gospel (1993) has also drawn attention to the continuing influx of skilled labour from abroad, the development of labour-saving technologies and the weakness of unions as factors contributing to the decline of apprenticeships in the American context.

9. The US Department of Labor has published guidelines for the appropriate length of training required for all occupations.

6. Training and Education in the United Kingdom: A System in Transition

INTRODUCTION

The UK is widely criticized for a lack of commitment to producing a skilled and educated workforce.[1] Apparent deficiencies in education and training are held to be crucial to the explanation of the UK's relatively slow rate of economic growth.

Despite the difficulties of making international comparisons in education and training (see Chapter 9), participation rates of young people in post-compulsory education are often used as indicators of this national inadequacy. For example, Table 6.1 seems to show the UK lagging behind

Table 6.1   Full-time education participation rates and proportion of GDP spent on education, selected countries

Average participation rate 16–19 year olds (% of age cohort)[a]	%	Education expenditure as percentage of GDP, 1988 (rank order)[b]
Belgium	83.2	4
Germany	80.4	3
Denmark	79.0	1
Holland	76.7	2
France	72.2	5
Spain	50.5	6
Italy	47.3	7
UK	35.6	8

Notes
[a] Taken from figures published by the Royal Society in May 1991
[b] Taken from an OECD survey, 1992
Source: Reproduced in Betts (1993)

other major European countries in terms of numbers in education and government expenditure on education as a percentage of GDP.

As in the United States, but in marked contrast to Germany and France, training in the United Kingdom is largely unregulated. Employers are not normally obliged to provide training for any employees, and such training as is provided need not lead to formal qualifications. It is still possible (though less so than in the past) to progress at work without certificates to attest skills.

In this chapter we examine the system of education and training in the United Kingdom. First, we look at initial preparation for employment, emphasizing the vocational elements of compulsory and post-compulsory education. We then examine employer-provided training at work, and finally look at government-funded training and its policy context. We note the ways in which the UK government is attempting to instil a new commitment to the provision of training in the minds of British employers and employees.

EDUCATIONAL PREPARATION FOR WORK

Until recently, vocational and academic education tended to be provided by different institutions in the UK. Technical schools were established in the 1944 Education Act to deliver practical education, although Ainley and Corney (1990) suggest that they were under-funded and neglected by the government from the start. Even at their peak they only catered for about 4 per cent of the secondary school population. Eventually technical schools were incorporated into the comprehensive school system, where students of all abilities have been taught a largely academic curriculum in the same school. Such vocational education as comprehensive schools have provided has been concentrated on academic low-achievers.

Until the late 1980s, therefore, vocational education has frequently not been available to the whole ability range of students in schools, and has in effect been treated as less important than the study of traditional academic subjects. As a result large numbers of the population never received any vocational education in the school system. To fill this gap, the main providers of technical education for many years have been further education colleges, and one of the most common modes of attendance has been evening classes.

During the 1980s the UK government and business people have called for higher levels of educational attainment and more work-related education in schools. Employers have expressed concern about education being "an inadequate and inappropriate preparation for entry into work" (Noah and Eckstein 1988). The main complaints have concerned poor attitudes to work and discipline, poor basic education, and a limited understanding of the working environment. Numerous reforms were made to the education system over the 1980s to introduce more work-relevant education and raise the profile of vocational qualifications.

Education is compulsory in the UK between the ages of 5^2 and 16, with the majority of students attending state-funded schools. Only a small minority attends privately financed schools. Students are mostly taught the same subjects up to the age of 14. At this age they start two-year courses in chosen subjects, culminating in examinations and other forms of assessment for GCSE (General Certificate of Secondary Education) qualifications. School curricula have traditionally varied between local education authorities and schools. However, a national curriculum was introduced in 1989, and is to be fully operational by 1997. It requires that at least nine subjects, including English, mathematics, science and technology, be taught to specified standards between the ages of 5 and 16. In addition it is intended that a modern language be taught to all 11–16 year olds. The aim of introducing the national curriculum was to ensure that all students receive a broad and balanced education to nationally defined standards.

Another development of the late 1980s was the Technical and Vocational Educational Initiative, which sought to provide general and technical education, work experience and an understanding of the needs of business for young people in schools. It was intended to attract more young people to remain in education at 16, even if they did not wish to proceed to higher education. In 1991–2, 65 per cent of 14–18-year-olds still in education were to be involved in the initiative (Shackleton 1992).

At 16, students can leave school to enter the labour market or can remain in full-time education. Several types of institution provide post-compulsory education, including schools, sixth-form colleges, further education colleges, adult education centres and City Technology Colleges. Of students in full-time post-compulsory education 60 per cent opt for schools and sixth-form colleges and 40 per cent for further education colleges[3] (Department for Education 1993d).

The numbers of young people remaining in full-time education are increasing. In 1991–2 nearly 58 per cent of 16–17-year-olds in England attended full-time post-compulsory education compared with 35 per cent in 1979–80 (Department for Education 1993b). A recent Youth Cohort Study, which looked at students aged 16–17 years in 1991, found that of those seeking qualifications, 34 per cent were aiming for academic qualifications, 25 per cent were working for vocational qualifications and 15 per cent were working towards both (Drew *et al.* 1991).

The standard academic programme between the ages of 16 and 18 has for many years been a two-year General Certificate of Education Advanced Level course.[4] Up to four (but more commonly two or three) A Levels are completed, the traditional prerequisite for higher education. A significant proportion of 16-year-olds also spend their first year completing more GCSEs, transferring to A Levels in their second year.

Various one- and two-year vocational programmes can be taken in post-compulsory education. The main awarding bodies are the Business and Technician Education Council (BTEC), City and Guilds and the Royal Society of Arts (RSA), as well as numerous professional bodies. BTEC diplomas and City and Guilds courses cover occupationally specific and more general vocational studies at the craft and technician level. RSA courses largely cover commercial, secretarial and public administration fields.

In the 1980s the system of vocational qualifications, and in particular the huge array of validating bodies, was criticized for the confusion they created for workers and employers (Cantor 1989). To deal with this problem, the government established the National Council for Vocational Qualifications (NCVQ) in 1986. Its remit was to develop a coherent system of vocational qualifications and thus enable a clear understanding of the level of any course and its equivalent. The outcome has been the development of National Vocational Qualifications (NVQs). NVQs are based on national standards, to convey levels of competence and skill and the ability of individuals to perform activities in employment (Thompson 1989). NVQs relate to the outcome of courses, not the particular course. Therefore each NVQ may apply to many different courses and certificates.

A tier system of NVQs, covering different areas of work, has been established, with five levels. Level One corresponds to qualifications (of less than GCSE standard) designed to give the student basic skills and competence in routine, repetitive tasks. At the upper end of the skill hierarchy, Level Five NVQs cover professional and higher and middle management occupations, broadly the equivalent of post-graduate qualifications. Awards are still made by bodies such as BTEC, RSA and professional organizations (such as accountancy and other business-related qualifications) but their standards are assessed by the NCVQ, and awarded a "kitemark" if qualifications reach an appropriate level.

In addition the NCVQ has pioneered new approaches to assessing pre-existing competences; people who have informally acquired skills through work or other experience can now have them certificated. Although the system is not without its dangers (Prais 1989), it has attracted interest even amongst German experts from a very different training culture.[5]

The development of NVQs is thus aimed not only at accrediting individuals' skills according to common standards: it is also intended that NVQs will help remove the stigma from vocational qualifications, encouraging more people to pursue them, and raise the overall attainment level of the workforce (Thompson 1989). Accordingly NVQs are a central feature of the National Education and Training Targets, originally promoted by the Confederation of British Industry and other pressure groups, but now officially adopted as government policy. These targets include, for example, 80 per cent of young people achieving NVQ Level Two or equivalent by 1997, with 50 per cent reaching Level Three by 2000.[6]

A recent related innovation in the education of 16–18-year-olds is the introduction of General National Vocational Qualifications (GNVQs). GNVQs were announced by the government in the 1991 White Paper *Education and Training for the 21st Century*. They are an attempt to bridge the divide between vocational and academic qualifications, by offering alternatives to academic studies. A pilot scheme was launched in September 1992 across 106 schools and further education colleges covering nearly 9,000 students in England, Wales and Northern Ireland (National Council for Vocational Qualifications 1993).

GNVQs are available at three levels: Foundation, Intermediate and Advanced, taught in schools and further education colleges.[7] Foundation and Intermediate GNVQs, studied full-time over a year, are the equivalent of four or five GCSEs, grades D–G and A–C respectively. Advanced GNVQs, intended as a vocational alternative to two A Levels, take two years of full-time study. The aim is to give a broad-based vocational education, retaining some element of general education, and enabling students to combine vocational and academic education if they wish. GNVQs can be taken in conjunction with academic A Levels or GCSEs or on their own (Department for Education 1993a). It is anticipated that GNVQs will prepare students either directly for employment or for higher education. As part of their promotion they have been given the alternative title of "vocational A Levels".

GNVQs are currently available in five subject areas: Manufacturing, Leisure and Tourism, Business Studies, Art and Design, and Health and Social Care. New GNVQs were piloted from September 1993 in Science, Built Environment, and Hospitality and Catering, and the range was further extended in 1994. All GNVQs cover general core subjects of Communication, Application of Number, and Information Technology.

The development of GNVQs is a further element in the UK government's policy of trying to increase the participation of 16–18-year-olds in full-time education by improving the status of vocational qualifications. Despite the government impetus behind them, however, there is concern

that GNVQs may still be seen as inferior to their academic equivalents and
may not be fully accepted by employers and higher education institutions
(Tysome 1993). Some commentators (Prais 1989; Smithers 1993) feel that
both NVQs and GNVQs are inferior to their continental equivalents
because they do not test knowledge and understanding as well as competence; do not involve rigorously objective examinations; and do not
sufficiently emphasize literacy and numeracy. In the case of GNVQs a
complaint from schools and colleges has been that there is no formal
syllabus to teach to, and teachers and lecturers fear high failure rates.
These are, however, still very early days, and it is far too soon to write off
these new qualifications.

QUALIFICATIONS

While the current qualification system is in such a state of flux, it is
perhaps appropriate to indicate the base from which the UK is starting. It
is well known that a larger proportion of the British workforce has no
significant formal qualifications than is the case in many other developed
countries. Table 6.2 gives a snapshot of the qualifications of those of
working age in 1992. It can be seen that women tend to have fewer and
lower-level qualifications than men. This difference in attainment
increases with age. Among 20–24-year-old women 5.3 per cent have
degrees in comparison to 5.7 per cent of men, whilst in the 45–59 year age
group 3.9 per cent of females and 7.1 per cent males have degrees. A
similar pattern emerges for women and men holding no qualifications.
For the age group 20–24, fewer women than men have no qualifications

Table 6.2   Highest qualification held for people of working age, by sex,
           1992 (%)

Highest qualification	All	Men	Women
Degree or equivalent	9.7	12.0	7.1
HE below degree level	6.9	5.8	8.1
GCE A Level or equivalent	26.6	35.2	17.1
GCE O Level or equivalent	18.5	13.5	23.9
Other qualification	10.3	8.8	12.0
No qualification	27.9	24.4	31.6
Don't know/no reply	0.2	0.2	0.1

Source: Labour Force Survey, Spring 1992 (Employment Department 1993).

(16.3 per cent and 17.2 per cent respectively); in the older age group (45 +) 53.4 per cent of women have no qualifications whilst only 44.2 per cent of men are in this position.

This pattern is almost certainly a mixture of lifecycle effects and long-term trends for the workforce as a whole. Young women have greater access to and success in the education system nowadays, and thus they fare better in relation to their male contemporaries than their mothers or grand-mothers did. However, men may add to their qualifications throughout their working life to a rather greater extent than women. If the former effect is dominant, we could expect the proportions of women concentrated in low-level occupations to decline in the future, as more recent generations of better-qualified women progress. If the latter effect dominates, however, it suggests that moves towards greater labour market equality may not be all that pronounced.[8]

Women and men tend to take different routes in post-16 education, in terms of type of activity and subjects studied. Men are more likely to continue to higher education (although the proportion of women doing so has risen very rapidly in recent years), and to complete first and higher degrees. They are also, however, more likely to enter employment on completion of compulsory education than are women. Young females tend to be more likely to enter further education and study non-advanced vocational courses, and more of them enrol for part-time courses, often in the evenings. Again, such courses are generally less advanced than those undertaken by men (Clarke 1991). For example, many more women than men study for RSA/Pitman exams; by contrast men are more strongly represented among those achieving City and Guilds qualifications (see Table 6.3).

What we can call "gender subjects" appear at all levels of education in the UK: at school girls study modern languages, biology and the arts but

Table 6.3   *Vocational qualifications obtained since the end of the fifth year by young people reaching minimum school-leaving age in the academic year 1987–8, by gender and activity, Spring 1991 (%)*

Activity	All	Males	Females
City & Guilds	44	59	29
RSA, Pitmans	21	5	36
BTEC	26	28	24
All others	12	8	15

Source: Youth Cohort Study, Cohort 4, sweep 3 (Employment Department 1992b).

more boys study physics, chemistry and geography; in further education girls concentrate on the arts, business studies, secretarial and health-related courses whilst boys have a greater propensity to study science, engineering and maths. Later, in higher education, women are under-represented in engineering and the sciences and over-represented in the arts and some social sciences. Inevitably subject choice will be a problem for women, given its implications for occupational choice and given restrictions which the government has placed on the expansion of higher education places in the arts and social sciences.

OTHER EDUCATIONAL REFORMS

In addition to the reforms already outlined, it is worth mentioning one or two other important developments. For example, the expansion of higher education in the UK has been very rapid in the last decade, with the age-specific participation rate of young people now around 30 per cent, double that of a decade ago. Although this is still somewhat low by the standards of countries such as the United States, Japan or Germany, the shorter length of degree courses (and consequently lower dropout rates) means that the output of graduates now compares reasonably favourably with other developed countries (Organization for Economic Cooperation and Development 1993a). This expansion has been achieved cheaply, as high rates of productivity increase have been achieved: one estimate is that productivity rose 20 per cent over the five years 1988–93 (Edwards 1993). It has been associated with changes in institutional status, as the old polytechnics (which historically emphasized vocational higher education in such subjects as engineering and business studies) were first detached from the control of local education authorities and then given fully fledged university status. It is these former polytechnics which have grown most rapidly. Between 1975 and 1991 their student numbers rose by over 50 per cent, while the old universities' student population rose by a third (Cave and Weale 1992). Credit accumulation schemes and modularization of courses have been introduced with the ostensible rationale of increasing flexibility and student choice expansion. As UK higher education has expanded, the numbers of "non-traditional" students recruited have risen disproportionately. These include mature students (especially female "returners") and part-timers; both of these groups have been particularly common in the former polytechnic sector.[9] Many mature students will not have entered via the A Level route. Rather, they have been admitted on the basis of other qualifications. Often they will have taken part in specially designed "Access" courses;

increasingly, too, they have been admitted on the basis of relevant work experience rather than examination results.[10]

These initiatives are paralleled lower down the educational system, where a variety of efforts have been made to stimulate educational achievement and links with the world of work. In addition to developments noted earlier we should mention national records of achievement, employment compacts and City Technology Colleges. National records of achievement are being introduced to provide school leavers with a standardized record of what they have achieved in addition to examination results. Employment compacts have been developed in urban priority areas: employers agree targets with young people over such matters as improvements in attendance and attainment, in return for the promise of a job or training.[11] City Technology Colleges, specializing in high-tech subjects, though modelled to some extent on the old technical schools (Ainley 1990), were introduced in the late 1980s. Run by non-profit-making charities rather than local government, they concentrate on mathematics, science and technology and maintain close links with industry, giving pupils early work experience.[12]

EMPLOYER-PROVIDED TRAINING: WHO GETS IT?

The preparation which young people receive for work in the UK education system is, therefore, in a state of rapid change. Some of the complaints made by critics are being addressed. What of the other element of the indictment, that employer-provided training is inadequate?

According to the authoritative and detailed *Training in Britain* study, employers sponsored 42 per cent of the training provided in the year 1986–7, making this group the principal sponsor of training (Department of Employment 1989). The Labour Force Survey also asks individuals to report who pays for their training. In 1992 just over 70 per cent of those who had received some off-the-job training had their fees paid by their employer, and about 15 per cent funded themselves (Employment Department 1993).

Looking at the pattern of training provision by employers in the UK, we can see that there are wide variations in individuals' access to such training. The main sources to which we refer are the major *Training in Britain* study undertaken for the Training Agency in 1986–7 (Department of Employment 1989) and the annual and quarterly Labour Force Survey (LFS), details of which are given regularly in the *Employment Gazette*.[13] From the available data we can infer that different sectors and firms provide training for different reasons to different types of employees. This is reflected in the level and type of training and associated expenditure.

Table 6.4   Employees[a] of working age receiving job-related training in the four weeks before the survey, by industry and type of training, 1992

Industry division	Type of training received, percentages			
	On-the-job only	Off-the-job only	Both on- & off-the-job	Any training
All employees	4.0	8.6	1.9	14.5
Agriculture, forestry, fishing	—	—	—	6.1
Energy and water supply	5.3	10.3	2.8	18.4
Extraction and manufacturing	4.1	8.0	2.1	14.3
Engineering, metal goods and vehicles	3.4	7.2	1.8	12.4
Other manufacturing	2.3	4.2	0.8	7.3
Construction	2.0	7.8	2.1	11.8
Distribution, hotels and catering; repairs	2.7	6.7	1.3	10.7
Transport, communication	3.6	7.6	1.4	12.6
Banking, finance and insurance, etc.	4.9	10.0	2.1	17.0
Other services	5.7	11.3	2.7	19.7

Note:
[a] Employees are those in employment, excluding the unemployed and those on government training schemes.

As suggested in Chapter 4, firms, industries and sectors display different levels of training, and a firm can spread a given amount of resources in different ways. As a result simple comparisons may disguise differences in the length and type of training received. As indicated previously, a high *density* (high average number of days of training per employee) could be the result of short spells of training provided for a large proportion of the workforce (high *incidence*), or longer spells for a smaller proportion of employees (high *intensity*). It is clear that there will be differences in the pattern depending on the nature of the job (see Table 6.4). For example, within the private sector, training in manufacturing tends to be given to a lower proportion of the workforce but for longer periods than in the service industries. Differences in incidence and intensity can be seen in more detail at the industry level. For instance, extraction and mineral/chemicals gave training to the highest proportions of their workforces, providing 64 per cent and 48 per cent, respectively, of their employees with training in 1986–7. In this sector lower than average proportions of employees were given training by the process, construction and textile/clothing industries.

In 1986–7 within the services sector, retail and financial services trained the greatest proportion of their workforces (68 per cent and 52 per cent of their employees respectively), with the wholesale and transport/communication industries the least (34 per cent and 40 per cent). These differences can be related, at least in part, to the different business strategies pursued in these areas.

The 1992 Labour Force Survey data also show variations between industries which broadly correspond to this analysis. More employees received training, on average, in the services sector. "Other manufacturing" trained the lowest proportion of the workforce in the manufacturing industries and construction also trained a lower than average proportion. "Other services", including education, medical and other health services, trained the greatest proportion of employees, with almost one-fifth receiving some form of training. Banking, finance and insurance also trained a significantly greater than average proportion of their workers.

Broadly speaking, in 1986–7 the public sector provided high levels of training both in terms of the proportion of workforce covered and the number of days' training each trainee received. The manufacturing industries tended to train a low proportion of their workforce but provided each trainee with an above-average amount of training days. The private service sector provided an above-average proportion of its employees with training, but length of training was less than in the other two sectors. In all industries employees are apparently more likely to receive off-the-job training,[14] and a relatively small proportion receive both on- and off-the-job training.

Within manufacturing, firms respond to the need to be more competitive by introducing new technology and production processes, creating the need for intensive periods of formal training. New technology may also require training to satisfy stringent safety requirements. The existence of legislation was cited by about a third of all respondents in the *Training in Britain* study as a reason for enhanced training. In manufacturing about half of the firms gave this as a major influence, reflecting the greater importance of health and safety legislation within this sector.

In the services sector, firms tend to react to increased competition by different strategies, for example product diversification, increased emphasis on customer care and more competitive pricing strategies, following rationalization. Thus the impetus to training provision in these industries comes from changes in product and service areas. Skill requirements are part of a continuing process of improving customer care, as service industries tend to be characterized by a high degree of customer contact, and so training of a large proportion of the workforce to keep these skills up to scratch is vital for their economic success.

Within both sectors it might be expected that industries facing most competition provide the highest levels of training.[15] The motivation to train most frequently cited in the *Training in Britain* survey was the need to improve competitiveness. Thus one would expect retail and financial services, say, to be more active trainers than those industries in less-competitive markets and with more homogeneous products, such as the transport/communication and construction industries (diversification being particularly important in financial services following deregulation in the 1980s).

There is a slight increase in the proportion of employees trained with increasing size of firm: 25 per cent of small firms (10–24 employees) did not train at all in 1986–7, whereas all large firms (1,000 + employees) provided some training (the proportion of non-trainers declines steadily with increasing size).

There are also differences in training provision in the UK in terms of the types of workers who receive training. For instance, younger workers receive more training than older workers. This clearly fits the predictions of the human capital model. On the one hand, young workers generally have lower levels of existing skills and experience than older workers; on the other hand, they have longer expected working lives remaining in which to recover the cost of the investment in their training.

Overall, according to the Spring 1992 LFS, 13.5 per cent of employees of working age received job-related training in the four-week period prior to the survey. A slightly greater proportion of women than men received training: 14.2 per cent as opposed to 12.9 per cent. This represents increases in the proportions of both sexes being trained since 1984, with the proportion growing faster for women.

Although the proportion receiving training falls with increasing age for both sexes, the fall is sharper for men than for women, as Table 6.5 demonstrates. The figures for women in the later age brackets are probably boosted by the existence of women returners and provision is likely to be characterized by short induction courses for these women as opposed to career development training. Career development schemes have formal or informal age limits, and are often run on a full-time basis which will exclude women returners and part-timers.

According to *Training in Britain*, women receive training of a shorter duration than men. In 1986–7, 86 per cent of male trainees but only 73 per cent of women received training of a duration of more than three days. Similarly, Table 6.6 shows how young male workers not only receive more

Table 6.5 People in Great Britain of working age receiving job-related training during the previous four weeks, by age and sex, 1992 (%)

Age	All	Males	Females
16–19	25.8	28.5	22.8
20–24	17.5	17.0	18.1
25–29	15.0	15.1	15.0
30–39	13.5	12.9	14.4
40–49	12.0	11.0	13.2
50–59	7.5	7.1	8.0
60–64	3.1	3.1	—
Total	13.5	12.9	14.2

Source: As Table 6.4.

Table 6.6 Experience of training for young workers reaching the minimum school-leaving age in the academic year 1987–8, by gender, at February 1990 (%)

	All	Men	Women
On-the-job training	77	81	73
Off-the-job training:			
college	26	32	18
training centre	17	14	20
> 1 location	6	8	4
Duration:			
induction (1/2 days)	9	5	15
up to 4 wks	10	9	13
1–11 months	7	7	8
1 year, < 2	6	6	7
2 years, < 3	19	17	21
3 years, < 4	9	11	6
4 years or more	13	20	2
"as long as needed"	14	15	13
not stated	12	10	16

Source: Youth Cohort Study, Cohort 4, sweep 3 (Employment Department 1993).

Table 6.7   *Economically active people of working age in Great Britain receiving job-related training during the previous four weeks, by sex and highest qualification (%)*

| | % receiving training | | |
Highest qualification	All	Men	Women
All people	13.5	12.9	14.2
Degree or equivalent	24.2	22.8	27.9
HE, less than degree	24.6	20.9	27.8
GCE A level/equivalent	14.3	12.9	18.0
GCE O level/equivalent	15.1	16.4	14.2
Other qualifications	9.6	9.0	10.2
No qualifications	4.5	4.6	4.3

Source: Spring 1992 Labour Force Survey figures (Employment Department 1993).

training than women, but they are much more likely to be receiving training lasting for more than one month, whereas women are more likely to receive training of up to four weeks. This again suggests that women's apparent advantage in access to employer-provided training in the UK is misleading.[16]

Table 6.7 shows recipients of training classified in terms of their highest qualification attained. Studies have generally found that the chances of receiving job-related training increase with educational qualifications, although there are some odd anomalies. For example, for men – though not for women – those with O Level or equivalent were more likely to receive employer-provided training than those with A Levels. Those most likely to receive training are young people with previous qualifications (those holding some higher education qualification being the most likely to have access to job-related training): "Unto every one that hath shall be given". At the other extreme, *Training in Britain* showed that just over half of economically active adults with no prior qualifications claimed in 1986–7 to have received no training since leaving school. Similarly Labour Force Survey findings suggest that less than 5 per cent of people with no qualification will have received any training in the previous four weeks. Individuals with existing qualifications are likely to be more "trainable" than those without, and are therefore likely to receive more training (whether the employer or the employee ultimately finances the training).

Table 6.8 shows the occupational pattern of training provision. While the provision of training to all occupational groups rose throughout the 1980s, the broad pattern remained the same: those in managerial,

Table 6.8 Employees[a] in Great Britain receiving job-related training, by occupation (%)

Occupation	Men	Women	All
All occupations	13.4	14.1	13.7
Managers & administrators	13.8	16.5	14.7
Professional	23.3	31.3	26.6
Assoc. professional & technical	20.0	26.8	23.5
Clerical & secretarial	14.0	12.3	12.7
Craft & related	11.3	5.3	10.5
Personal & protective	16.6	11.7	13.4
Sales	14.4	10.0	11.4
Plant & machine operatives	5.6	4.7	5.4
Other	6.5	4.9	5.7

Note: [a]Employees of working age: men 16–64; women 16–59
Source: Labour Market Quarterly Review, August 1993.

professional, technical and service occupations were more likely to receive training from employers than other groups. *Training in Britain* found the highest proportion of employees trained to be in managerial or professional posts and the lowest in the skilled/semi-skilled manual categories. However, the latter categories have relatively high levels of days training per trainee, possibly because of the existence of apprenticeship schemes.

Not only does the incidence of training vary, but also the type of training differs by occupation (see Table 6.9). For example three-quarters of the managers and administrators receiving training said at least part of this had been off-the-job training; the figure is higher for craft and related occupations. Not surprisingly, this latter group also had the highest proportion of training leading to a qualification or credit, again probably as a result of the existence of apprenticeships.

This review of training provided by British employers has described a pattern broadly consistent with the implications of the human capital model outlined in Chapter 2. For example, the longer the stream of post-investment returns expected, the more likely an individual is to be receiving training: the UK data confirm that younger people receive more training. Similarly, individuals who have invested in a substantial amount of formal education have demonstrated "trainability", an ability to absorb knowledge and skills quickly: this indicates to employers that the cost of training is lower for them than for the less educated. The data again support the hypothesis that training is positively correlated with prior educational

Table 6.9   Type of training received by employees in Great Britain, by occupation (%)[a]

Occupation	Some on-the-job training	Some off-the-job training	Leading to qualification or credit
All occupations	41.6	71.4	45.0
Managers & administrators	36.7	73.0	32.7
Professional	40.5	73.0	32.7
Assoc. prof. & technical	43.7	73.6	51.4
Clerical & secretarial	40.1	68.6	41.4
Craft & related	42.9	77.3	66.4
Personal & protective	46.5	67.1	56.6
Sales	43.3	66.0	52.5
Plant & machine operatives	47.9	59.0	45.5
Other	37.7	70.6	55.5

Note: [a]Percentage of all employees receiving training
Source: As Table 6.8.

achievement. These and other patterns in the data indicate that firms and individuals act rationally in the training field.

Nevertheless, this still leaves open the possibility of the sort of market failures which we discussed in earlier chapters. And UK governments have certainly not been content to leave training entirely to the market.

THE GOVERNMENT AND TRAINING

There were some initiatives to encourage technical education in Britain in the nineteenth century, but large-scale central government involvement began with the First World War (Sheldrake and Vickerstaff 1987). The imperatives of wartime shortages of labour impelled the Ministry of Munitions in 1915 to pioneer training schemes for men and women to turn them rapidly into semi-skilled workers. Later in the war the Ministry of Labour began preparations for training disabled ex-servicemen, and for some of those able-bodied men who had missed out on training as a result of entering war service. With the advent of peace these schemes were oversubscribed and the Ministry of Labour was obliged to offer cash grants instead of training to many of those on the waiting list.

By the mid-1920s, economic recession had created a whole new set of problems leading to a considerable expansion of government-financed training schemes, usually based in specially equipped training centres. Nearly two million people passed through these schemes in the interwar years. The schemes were seen as responses to particular problems, rather than as replacements for traditional apprenticeships or other means by which the private sector trained employees. Nor did the experiences of the Second World War fundamentally alter matters. Although training needs obviously increased as labour was diverted to the war effort, the system of "reserved occupations" prevented the chaotic stripping from the factories of skilled labour which had characterized the early stages of the First World War. The main initial need was for engineering workers, and later for shipbuilders and mineworkers. Government Training Centres were expanded rapidly, courses were shortened to increase the throughput, and in 1941 women and girls were admitted to these formerly male preserves.

But it was always clear that such training was to be a temporary expedient. Ernest Bevin, as Minister of Labour and National Service in the wartime coalition government, was keen to prevent "dilution" of skills and the undercutting of skilled labour when peace returned. Penetration of government trainees into long-term employment was resisted by unions. Management, which for much of the postwar period was to tolerate and sometimes even encourage trade unions in the belief that this brought "order" into industrial relations, acquiesced in this return to the *status quo*.

After the war concern about training slipped down the agenda. Government Training Centres were run down, and any political interest concentrated on the problems of young workers. In 1948 the Juvenile Employment Service was set up, but there were few further developments.

The 1950s was a buoyant period for the British economy, but by the early 1960s there was a widespread awareness of Britain's relative decline as other countries recovered from the war. This was the period of "stop–go" in macroeconomic policy, and it was argued that skill shortages were among the factors constraining the economy in periods of boom. The Conservative government, at the height of its enthusiasm for corporatist economic planning, published a White Paper in 1962 calling for improvements in the quality and extent of provision of training, and arguing for the expense of training to be spread by a levy system on employers. The Industrial Training Act was passed in March 1964, setting up a Central Training Council (including six employer and six trade union representatives) and making provision for tripartite Industrial Training Boards (ITBs) to manage the new system of training grants and levies.

Industrial Training Boards grew rapidly; by May 1966 there were 7½ million workers in the industries covered by them. But from the beginning there were criticisms; by the end of the decade there was a consensus that the Act had failed in its objectives. One line of criticism came from small firms, which paid the levy and had to deal with an increasing amount of paper-work but were often unable to claim back grants because they could not spare workers for the off-the-job training which the ITBs emphasized. The unions, by contrast, thought the powers of the Central Training Council were too limited and called for a greater element of central direction plus an extension of the Training Board system throughout industry. Other criti-cisms included the view that there was too much duplication, each ITB funding training in skills that were common across industry. The Donovan Commission in 1968 took the view that many of the skills problems in British industry arose from restrictive practices and the traditional narrow systems of apprenticeship which gave rise to them; these had not been tackled by the ITBs. By 1971 the Confederation of British Industry was calling for exemption of small firms from the levy and an emphasis on retraining to promote greater labour market flexibility.

It was against this background that the Heath administration set up the Manpower Services Commission (MSC) to play an active role at the national level in promoting labour market efficiency in general and improv-ing training in particular (Ainley and Corney, 1990). Direct government training, through the Training Opportunities Scheme (TOPS), was to be expanded, with a focus on general, transferable skills.

Over the next few years the MSC proved unable to develop a significant reorientation of training at the national level, tending rather to react to events. It was during this period that rising unemployment forced the government to respond by developing a series of *ad hoc* initiatives, the precursor of the jungle of job creation and training schemes which were to be a feature of the 1980s.

The election of a Conservative administration in 1979 might have been expected to lead to a cutback in spending on programmes such as those funded by the MSC, but this was not to be the case. On the contrary, total spending rose considerably. This was partly an almost inevitable conse-quence of the recession of the early 1980s, when unemployment rose to unprecedented postwar levels and youth unemployment in particular was seen as a major socioeconomic problem. But it was also in part the result of a genuine conviction that here was one field where, by contrast with other areas of economic policy from which the government sought to disengage, increased government action was called for.

However, training policy had an ideological edge. Since 1979 successive Conservative administrations have emphasized that training should be employer-led. The training levy system was effectively abolished: it sur-vives in attenuated form only in construction and (on a voluntary basis) in engineering. The Manpower Services Commission was seen as an over-centralized body, associated with a corporatist philosophy that had failed. It was reformed, renamed and eventually abolished.

RECENT DEVELOPMENTS

In place of the Manpower Services Commission were eventually established over one hundred business-led Training and Enterprise Councils (TECs) in England and Wales, and Local Enterprise Companies (LECs) in Scotland. Locally based organizations headed by employers, TECs and LECs are responsible for promoting training throughout industry and the community to eliminate Britain's "skills deficiency".

Amongst other things, they are responsible for encouraging more effective employer investment in training and encouraging more individuals to take responsibility for their own training needs. They were never established as training providers, but a major part of their responsibilities involves administering government programmes and acting as intermediaries between government and training providers. They form contracts with external providers in industry, voluntary organizations, professional trainers, and so on. They aim to ensure the provision of a minimum standard of training for those on government training schemes (most notably Youth Training and Training for Work) and for specific groups in the community.

The system is modelled on the Private Industry Councils developed in the United States (discussed in Chapter 5). Like the PICs, TECs were intended to attract more and more private investment to reduce the level of central government funding of training (which had reached over £3 billion by the end of the 1980s) over a number of years. However, in both countries little external funding has been forthcoming.

Of the 47 per cent of 16-year-olds who do not stay in education, some will enter employment immediately but more will enter Youth Training (YT), although the numbers doing both have decreased as more young people have stayed on in education (FEU 1993). YT is a two-year state-funded programme (the successor to the Youth Training Scheme) consisting of work experience, training and, in some cases, part-time study. It is in principle aimed at giving young people basic, transferable, vocational skills. It is available to all 16–18-year-olds who are not in full-time study or employment. Individuals are placed as trainees with firms and are given training to enable them to achieve an appropriate NVQ Level Two.

Similar programmes have been developed for the long-term unemployed following recent criticisms levelled at the government over the treatment of this group. A new initiative, "Training for Work", was introduced in April 1993 to replace the former Employment Training Scheme. It targets the long-term unemployed, offering them an opportunity to improve or update their skills, learn new ones, or do work of value to the local community.

TEC responsibility for government training programmes has attracted criticism from various sources, including from within the TEC movement. Part of government funding for the provision of YT and Training for Work is performance-related, dependent on positive outcomes.[17] This creates an incentive to aim for immediate successes and short-term policies, possibly at the expense of the particular needs of disadvantaged groups. A recent survey of TECs by the Equal Opportunities Commission found that the funding system of payment-by-results has discouraged the recruitment of women returners; TECs feel it may take too long to update their skills and prefer not to take the risk (Unemployment Unit 1993). Another survey found that 43 per cent of TECs expect that payment-by-results will force TECs to neglect the most disadvantaged (*Financial Times* 1993).

To increase their short-term funding TECs are therefore tempted to pursue a policy of "creaming off" the trainees with the greatest potential, a policy which has been the subject of major criticism of the PICs in the US. The most disadvantaged people, who require more investment to get a positive outcome, are likely to be neglected.

Alternatively, TECs may use the minimum investment required to obtain a positive outcome. This may mean providing training for the lowest levels of qualifications or providing subsidized training for employers who promise a job at the end of the training period. The former strategy may restrict trainees' future employment to low-level jobs. The latter could encourage the substitution of public for private funding or the displacement of existing workers, as suggested in Chapter 4. Neither policy necessarily helps the long-term needs of trainees.

There appears to be some evidence that TECs aim for the bare minimum: as Table 6.10 shows, the majority of performance payments in 1991–2 were made for the attainment of NVQ Levels One or Two.

With previous government training schemes, there was a minimum requirement of 12 hours per week off-the-job training. This obligation has been removed from YT and Training for Work, indicating that the focus is shifting away from increasing the general level of education and skills of the workforce towards providing very specific job-related skills. As pointed out in Chapter 2, in the context of human capital theory there is unlikely to be market failure in the provision of specific skills. Therefore there may be some element of displacement of funds by providing specific training. Rather than expanding young people's opportunities, critics have said that this form of preparation will merely limit their future prospects.

*Table 6.10   Number of payments to TECs for trainees achieving NVQs,
England and Wales, April 1991–Jan. 1992*

	Number	*% of payments*
YT		
NVQ level 1	3,015	6.35
NVQ level 2	34,221	72.05
NVQ level 3 or more	10,262	21.60
ET		
NVQ level 1 or 2	19,060	90.68
NVQ level 3 or 4	1,293	6.15
NVQ level 2 (special groups)[a]	555	2.64
NVQ level 3/4 (special groups)[a]	111	0.53

Note: [a]Special groups: skills shortage trainees and labour market returners who also gain
employment
Source: Unemployment Unit (1993).

TECs claim to be hampered by continued dependence on Treasury
funding, which restricts the scope of their operations and imposes irksome
bureaucratic rules. This has led some TEC members to argue for a return to
the system of "industrial levies", abandoned by Mrs Thatcher. A recent
survey found that 68 per cent of the TEC respondents believed that
government spending is too low. Nearly half wanted the return of a levy
system to pay for training people at work.

The government is unlikely to introduce compulsion into training
provision, however, through either a revived training levy or a requirement
to provide young people with training. Although ministers continue their
efforts to engender a "training culture", the emphasis remains on the carrot
rather than the stick, and on the whole the carrots have been modest in
proportion.

One recent innovation has been the development of Training Credits
(renamed Youth Credits), aimed at giving young people (and more recently
adults) the power to purchase training from the provider of their choice and
encouraging employers to provide training since they will have to foot only
part of the bill.[18] This scheme is one of the first real attempts to put into
practice a "voucher" scheme of the kind that free market economists have
been advocating for many years, and it is an interesting experiment. One
problem which has emerged is that, since employers are not obliged to give
individuals time off for training, few employees receive training leave and
many have to spend their credits on evening courses (NATFHE/Youthaid

1993). This report found that in the first full year of operation 42,000 credits were issued but only 21,400 people used them, a 51 per cent take-up rate.[19]

Financial incentives are also in place to induce individuals to invest in their own training. Tax relief on individual investment in skills has been available since April 1992 to people pursuing NVQs and SVQs (their Scottish equivalent). Career Development Loans have been in existence for some time and have expanded recently to help people pay for their own training,[20] and the government is also looking at the idea of individual training accounts, where the individual and the employer jointly contribute to an account which builds up over time to fund the individual's training. National Training Awards, both for individual and company achievement offer financial rewards and the opportunity of good publicity to the firm for investments in worker training.

CONCLUSION

There is a great deal going on in education and training policy in the United Kingdom. In education, there has been a move towards tighter control of the school curriculum, a growing emphasis on vocationally relevant education, and an expansion of further and higher education as government policy seeks to promote participation rates in post-compulsory education closer to those of the UK's major competitors.

The key elements of the reformed training system are: an emphasis on the market; local analysis of needs and provision of training; direct employer involvement; and an increase in the acquisition of vocational qualifications and skills.

How successful these policies will be in producing a higher level of commitment to education and training, and a more highly qualified workforce, remains to be seen. Even if proximate goals (such as the National Education and Training Targets) are met, however, it does not follow that the economic performance of the UK will improve dramatically. For that to be the case, the original diagnosis – that the United Kingdom's apparently weak record in training and education is a prime cause of its relative economic decline – would need to be correct. We will be in a better position to evaluate this claim later in the book.

NOTES

1. See, for example, Stevens and McKay 1991; Layard *et al.* (1992); Mayhew (1991); and various articles from the *National Institute Economic Review*, 1988–93.

2. There are some minor variations in the ages when children are first expected to attend school between England and Wales, Scotland, and Northern Ireland. Below the age of compulsory education, nursery provision is very patchy compared with most European countries. Some commentators have seen this as one of the major failings of the UK educational system and have argued for a transfer of public funding from higher education to nursery schools (National Commission on Education 1993).

3. Further education colleges operate not just for young school-leavers but also for a much wider age range. Full- and part-time courses cover certified academic and vocational courses, personal development/recreational courses and short courses for firms and government training schemes. Young school-leavers do not even form the bulk of students in further education colleges. In 1989 there were 2.2 million students enrolled in further education establishments, 80% of whom were part-timers (FEU 1993).

4. GCE A Levels are broadly equivalent in level to the high school diploma in the US, the *baccalauréat* in France and the *Abitur* in Germany, although more narrowly focused.

5. See *The Times Educational Supplement*, 2 October 1992.

6. The targets also include commitments to "lifetime learning"; to ensuring that all employees undertake some training or development; and to half of all medium-to-large firms becoming accredited "Investors in People".

7. The foundation level is being piloted from September 1993, to be fully operational from September 1994.

8. The issue of gender inequality in the labour market is explored further in Chapter 12.

9. In addition to the old and new (polytechnic) universities, there remain significant numbers of higher education students in smaller colleges of higher education and further education.

10. Accreditation of Prior Learning (APL) now enables students to receive credit for previous formal learning in areas relevant to their degrees, while Accreditation of Prior Experiential Learning (APEL) similarly enables skills learnt at work or in the community to be recognized.

11. In 1991, 92,000 young people, 500 schools and colleges and about 9,000 employers were involved in this initiative, soon to be extended nationwide (FEU 1993).

12. It was intended that CTCs should attract private sponsorship so that they would gradually become self-financing. Few appear to have attracted significant sums from businesses (Beckett 1993), perhaps unsurprisingly given the economic analysis of general training and education outlined in Chapter 2.

13. The Labour Force Survey in the UK is part of a wider European Labour Force Survey (see Chapter 9).

14. Although there may be some under-reporting of on-the-job training. As we saw in Chapter 2, in a human capital perspective there is no clear demarcation between on-the-job training and learning-by-doing through work experience. If a firm has a formal system of structuring work experience this may be reported as training, while similar experience elsewhere is not thought of in this way.

15. The logic is that firms facing fierce competition need to innovate faster and thus have increased training requirements. This is to assume, however, that training is solely undertaken as a means of enhancing productivity. It is possible to argue, as we saw in Chapter 3, that employer-provided training performs some other functions, for example as part of a remuneration package, and here the association with competition is more doubtful. Indeed, it is possible that firms in a more protected market may have more discretion to provide training. This could also explain why firms may cut training expenditure in recessions.

16. Women's access to training is considered in more detail in Chapter 12.

17. Positive outcomes are defined as trainees attaining qualifications (minimum NVQ Level Two) and/or employment (for more than 15 hours per week) or entering full-time further education or training.

18. Youth Credits can be worth between £500 and £5,000, but are more typically worth about £1,000. They are allocated to trainees to exchange for training in a firm, private

training establishment or educational institution, provided the training leads to at least an NVQ Level Two qualification and the provider is approved by the TEC. The scheme was expanded in 1992 to include credits for careers and training advice for unemployed adults.

19. Although some young people will have re-entered full-time education this still indicates that a large proportion are not making use of their credits.

20. To date almost 40,000 people have borrowed over £100 million (since the scheme's launch in 1988), with an average loan of nearly £2,800, and the programme is being expanded to make 120,000 Career Development Loans available. A loan can range from £200 to £5,000 to contribute up to 80% of fees (with a contribution to living expenses for full-time courses) and can be used to fund a variety of ventures, from the cost of "accreditation of prior learning" to a full-time post-graduate course. The government pays the interest on the loan during the training period and up to three months afterwards.

7. Training in Germany: the Best in Europe?

INTRODUCTION

Because it is widely believed that there is a connection between Germany's postwar economic success and the generally high qualification standard of its workforce[1] compared with those of other industrial nations, the system of training and further education in the Federal Republic of Germany has figured prominently in a wide range of economic and social research studies. Alfred Marshall argued over 70 years ago that "all the world has much to learn from German methods of education" (Marshall 1919). This popularity was compounded by the achievements of the West German *Wirtschaftswunder* of the 1960s and later. As European unemployment remains stubbornly high, training has gained in perceived importance; the German model of training provision has frequently been held up for emulation, especially in Britain. Particularattention has been devoted to initial vocational training, as Germany compares particularly favourably in this respect with its European partners.

In this chapter we outline the legal, institutional and organizational structure of German training provision. We focus in particular on the dual apprenticeship system, its origins, development and current problems (including recent events in the East German labour market). We also examine the training opportunities open to the German unemployed.

THE HISTORICAL BACKGROUND TO THE DUAL SYSTEM

The first elements of dual vocational training – the provision of training in the workplace coupled with vocational college-based education – had

already been introduced by the turn of the century, although initially with
no systematic character. Between 1878 and 1897, and then again in 1908,
the enforcement of training in manual trades and the improvement of
further education were at the top of the agenda of the German Reichstag.
This took place in the context of the "middle-class policy" of protecting
craftsmen, merchants and small farmers. Greinert (1992) notes that

> the major amendment, the so-called Law for the Protection of Manual
> Tradesmen (*Handwerkerschutzgesetz*) of 1897, permitted the establishment of
> manual trade chambers as corporations under public law, allowing
> independent tradesmen to protect their common interests and created . . .
> compulsory guilds with the aim of limiting competition.

The amendment, of particular importance for apprenticeship training,
incorporated general and specific regulations targeted at manual trades.
For example, "a 'minor eligibility certificate' was then passed . . . from
then on only a certified master was entitled to train apprentices" (ibid.).
Between 1885 and 1914 vocationally orientated compulsory schools were
introduced to supplement these training reforms, and the foundation for
a dual system was laid.

Around the same time, industry as a whole became increasingly com-
mitted to improving industrial vocational training. In 1919 the German
Committee for Technical Schooling (*Deutscher Ausschuß für technisches
Schulwesen*) called for theoretical instruction to be carried out in schools
and to be separated from firm-based apprenticeships (Pätzold 1980).
However,

> the basis for standardizing the very fragmented public vocational schooling
> system was not created until the school administrations of the individual states
> was centralized in a "Reichs Ministry for Science, Education and Public
> Education" (*Reichsministerium für Wissenschaft, Erziehung und Volksbildung*)
> in 1934 – although this also created the basis for ideological control by the
> National Socialists. (Greinert 1992).

After the end of the Nazi era, the division of the West German territory
into eleven *Länder* (states) went hand in hand with the establishment of a
"federal order of educational policy" through which regional policies of
education and training became almost solely the responsibility of state
ministries of education (the *Kulturhoheit der Länder*). This reflected the
development of a postwar political consensus supporting the idea of
pluralism and displacing the totalitarian principles of the Hitler years. The
role of the state in education and training, however, was relatively limited,

concerned with setting broad legal boundaries and a regulatory framework.

Although they have been described as a period of "stagnation in education" (Herrlitz *et al.* 1981), the 1950s in reality saw significant changes in educational policies. Entry requirements for further education were eased considerably, leading to substantial growth rates in the number of students, reflecting the increased demand for higher educational certification. Between 1952 and 1960, the number of students in intermediate (*Realschule*) and higher secondary colleges (leading to the final school certificate, the *Allgemeine Hochschulreife*) grew by 43 per cent and 25 per cent respectively (Führ 1988). Publicly financed schools and financial support schemes for university students were introduced along with the first tentative movements towards primary and secondary school education for adults (*Zweiter Bildungsweg*). It was also in the 1950s that several educational committees were formed (the Federal Committee For Education and Training – *Deutscher Ausschuß für das Erziehungs- und Bildungswesen* – for example) which were targeted at the public awareness of the importance of education and training. At the time they did not lead to significant changes in policies but they opened up the debate on education and training issues, setting off lively exchanges among expert groups and politicians, and providing some common ground for reform in the 1960s.

The economic successes of the 1960s *Wirtschaftswunder* led to big changes in education and training policies. The call for increased government intervention in the field of education and training was associated with the claim that higher-quality training would improve West German competitiveness. Public budgets for education and training accordingly expanded rapidly. Between 1965 and 1973, public expenditure for education and training rose from DM15.7 billion to DM44.6 billion. This was not, however, sufficient to assuage West Germany's hunger for human capital; for although additional opportunities for education and training were provided, increasing numbers of students took advantage of them, leading to further demands for additional funding. In particular, the number of higher secondary and university students increased dramatically. Between 1965 and 1975, the number of students in intermediate and higher secondary colleges rose from about 1,529,000 to 2,210,000. During the same period, the number of university students more than doubled (from 308,000 to 696,000). The 1969 Vocational Training Act, which will be discussed in subsequent sections, confirmed the increasingly important role public bodies now had to play, especially in the field of adult education and vocational training.

With the recessions of the 1970s and 1980s, however, the period of ever-growing public expenditure on education and training came to an end (Hüfner *et al.* 1986), and it was not until the late 1980s that education and training expenditures rose significantly again. As a result of the costly reunification in 1990 the financial future for education and training now looks rather bleak once more. With the 1992 amendments to the Labour Promotion Act (*Arbeitsförderungsgesetz*), sharp cuts in training provision have already been made. They have been targeted, in particular, at further education and retraining for the unemployed. This action provoked an outcry amongst private pressure groups, which described these cutbacks as "socially unjustified" and expressed their fear that the short-term benefits of public savings will be offset by the long-term consequences of a less skilled workforce (Arbeitskreis Alternative Arbeitsmarktpolitik 1993).

INSTITUTIONAL AND ORGANIZATIONAL STRUCTURE OF THE DUAL SYSTEM

Within the German education system there are many different routes which can be taken following primary school. German youngsters may stay on in general education, aiming for intermediate school qualifications (*Realschulabschluß*) or final certificates (*Fachhochschulreife*; *Allgemeine Hochschulreife*). They may also leave compulsory education, usually at the age of 15 or 16. In the latter case, the majority (over 70 per cent) enters the labour market as apprentices. However, the German apprenticeship system doesn't consist solely of those who have left general education at an early age. An increasing number of German apprentices possess final school certificates (*Abitur* or *Fachhochschulreife*) which would enable them to enter higher education, should they wish to do so.

The system of training and further education aims to provide general education and vocational preparation rather than firm-specific knowledge. This is certainly the case for initial vocational training in the dual system: every apprentice is not only required to spend his or her time in firm-based training programmes either as on-the-job work experience or in company or group workshops, but also in compulsory college-based education for up to two days per week (or even full-time for the first year). Whilst college-based training is intended to provide both general education and the theoretical basis for occupational practice, in-firm training also does not simply involve practical experience but, increasingly, the acquisition of more general work skills and knowledge (Casey 1991). Such training is provided for 378 separate formally defined occupations and takes, as a rule, three years to complete. The most popular apprenticeships are those shown in Table 7.1.[2]

Table 7.1   The ten most popular apprenticeships in West Germany, 1988

	Rank	Numbers	% of total apprenticeships
Males			
Motor vehicle mechanic	1	74,296	7.8
Electrical fitter	2	46,379	4.9
Machine fitter	3	39,941	4.2
Joiner	4	29,010	3.0
Painter & varnisher	5	28,898	3.0
Clerk/wholesale & export	6	28,269	2.9
Plant fitter	7	27,610	2.9
Bank clerk	8	26,255	2.7
Gas, and water fitter	9	25,578	2.7
Electronics technician	10	24,764	2.4
Females			
Hairdresser	1	57,989	8.1
Clerical assistant	2	47,851	6.7
Salesgirl, food	3	45,072	6.3
Doctor's receptionist	4	43,947	6.2
Retail saleswomen	5	43,166	6.0
Industrial clerk	6	41,169	5.8
Salesgirl	7	35,193	4.9
Dentist's receptionist	8	30,488	4.3
Bank clerk	9	28,966	4.1
Clerk/wholesale & export	10	21,924	3.1

Source: Bundesministerium für Bildung und Wissenschaft

On-the-job training costs (operational costs, lower productivity, oppor-tunity costs of resources, etc.) fall on employers initially but also, indirectly, on trainees, who receive "allowances" which are only a small proportion of adult earnings. Casey (1986) claims that in the mid-1980s trainees in Germany were paid between 20 and 25 per cent of adult rates. According to Oulton and Steedman (1992), this pay differential is sufficient to ensure that employers can provide training at close to zero cost, as they obtain a significant amount of "unpaid" productivity which compensates for em-ployers' training expenditure. This conforms to the predictions of human capital theory.

This training follows a company training plan based in turn on a state-wide general training plan. Enterprises which provide training in the dual system must employ at least one person qualified as a trainer, that is, possessing a master (*meister*) or trainer certificate.

Off-the-job training, by contrast, is financed by the public sector. Although the syllabus in vocational colleges is largely technical, the curriculum also includes languages, social studies, economics and accountancy. It is not surprising, therefore, that many sympathetic commentators consider the German training system as better prepared to meet the demands of rapid technological change than any other advanced economy (Sheldrake and Vickerstaff 1987) and as delivering a "high-quality/high-supply equilibrium in both vocational training and vocational education areas" (Oulton and Steedman 1992).

The dual system certainly provides training which is much broader than the immediate job in hand, for example in terms of mathematical knowledge. It has been argued that this gives the worker the flexibility of skills necessary for the modern production process (Steedman 1992). The training itself is also a function of the occupational skills required, so that, though the duration of training is generally three years, the length can be adjusted according to the occupation. Finally, the system has the advantage of minimum standards laid down nationally to which everyone must adhere. Employers thus have some guarantee of the capability of each worker recruited. And employees themselves gain skills recognized throughout the country, irrespective of firm, giving them potential mobility and automatic access to a particular skill status and wage or salary grade. An impression of the coverage of initial vocational training in West Germany over recent decades is given in Table 7.2.

It should be recognized, however, that the system also has its problems. In spite of minimum standards, there is a significant variation in the quality of training provided by firms, especially by small firms. Many have difficulty in guaranteeing quality training which will prepare adequately for the externally set exams, based on what is learnt both at school and in the firm. Dropout rates vary significantly between firms and sectors.

It also needs to be stressed that the dual system ties trainees to employers for a considerable period of time. A large number of German trainees achieve adult worker status – and pay – well into their twenties, and it has been argued that this delay is costly both to individuals and the economy and can reduce the effectiveness with which workers are deployed at their potentially most-productive age (Clarke *et al.* 1994). Moreover, many employees do not use the skills for which they have been expensively trained. In some trades the haemorrhaging of qualified workers is dramatic. In the 1980s nearly half of all qualified pastrycooks, hairdressers,

Table 7.2   Apprentices in West Germany in year and qualification area (in 1000s)

Year	Total	Industry and Commerce	Crafts	Agriculture	Public Services	Free Occupations[a]	Rest	% of the 16–19 years old population
1960	1278.9	743.1	446.6	36.3	19.4	20.4	13.0	54.8
1965	1338.4	752.4	468.0	37.3	23.7	45.5	11.5	57.7
1970	1268.7	724.9	419.5	38.1	20.2	56.4	9.6	53.4
1975	1328.9	634.0	504.7	33.0	46.0	103.2	8.1	48.5
1976	1316.6	611.2	510.4	37.4	43.9	106.6	7.7	46.6
1977	1397.4	643.8	556.1	41.0	44.8	103.4	8.2	47.7
1978	1517.3	692.0	614.9	45.2	51.7	104.7	8.8	50.6
1979	1644.6	748.4	676.2	46.6	53.8	110.4	9.1	53.1
1980	1715.5	786.9	702.3	46.8	53.8	114.3	8.6	53.8
1981	1676.9	771.3	673.6	46.5	54.3	123.6	7.5	52.2
1982	1675.9	764.7	665.5	49.6	58.3	128.5	9.2	52.2
1983	1722.4	791.9	674.9	52.0	63.7	129.7	9.7	54.9
1984	1800.1	841.1	693.2	53.2	69.2	132.4	10.9	59.0
1985	1831.3	874.6	687.5	53.4	72.6	131.5	11.7	62.9
1986	1805.2	882.2	657.8	50.2	73.1	129.9	12.1	66.5
1987	1738.7	866.0	617.8	44.6	71.7	125.1	13.6	68.9
1988	1658.0	827.2	577.9	38.5	67.3	133.6	13.5	71.5
1989	1552.5	783.3	532.5	33.8	62.2	129.3	11.5	72.1
1990	1476.9	756.4	486.9	29.7	63.4	130.3	10.1	74.8

Note: [a] i.e. lawyers, medical surgeons, dentists etc.
Source: Clarke et al. (1994).

123

butchers and medical assistants were working in less-skilled jobs than those for which they trained.

Furthermore, the large number of separately defined training occupations makes for a certain lack of occupational mobility and thus introduces an element of rigidity or inflexibility. Moreover, as firms within a region agree to pay the same rates, trainees are effectively faced by a collective monopsony on the employers' part. Though they are compensated by being on the first rung of a ladder leading to structured career progression (possibly up to the *meister* qualification and beyond), they are kept in an essentially dependent status. After completing training, rigid pay structures continue to limit competition not only in the labour market but also, indirectly, in the market for goods and services. This can also be costly for employers. It is one element of a wider framework of regulated labour relations which incorporates worker representation in firms, generous welfare benefits, job security and emphasis on internal labour markets.[3] Such arrangements do not come cheap. In 1991 total hourly labour costs (including non-wage costs such as pensions) in West Germany were getting on for twice those in Britain (Clarke *et al.* 1994). As a result a growing number of German employers have attempted to get round the problem by hiring immigrant labour, especially from Eastern European countries. This element of labour market segmentation is putting the system under considerable strain.

WHO GETS WHAT TRAINING?

During the 1960s, 1970s and early 1980s participation in initial vocational training was dominated by young men, who constituted well over 60 per cent of 16–19-year-old apprentices. However, since the mid-1980s this picture has changed, and by 1990 almost 43 per cent of all apprentices were female, mainly participating in training courses which lead to qualifications required by industry and commerce.

In addition, it should be mentioned that despite the gender segmentation of training apparent in Table 7.1 (and examined further in Chapter 12), more young women are moving into previously exclusive male strongholds. Whereas in the mid-1970s just under 3 per cent of female apprentices received training in "male work areas" (defined as jobs with an average proportion of male trainees of more than 80 per cent), by 1990 this figure had risen to 9 per cent. Public service professions have experienced very rapid growth in female participation. While in the early 1970s, 78.9 per cent of all training places in these occupations went to men, this proportion had fallen to 53.4 per cent by 1990. In the reverse direction we can also observe

Table 7.3 Incidence of training in the previous four weeks amongst employees, by age, Spring 1989

Age	West Germany	Great Britain
15–19	76	23
20–24	20	19
25–34	8	17
35–44	4	15
45–49	2	12

Source: Organization for Economic Cooperation and Development (1991).

that some previously female-orientated jobs attract a growing minority of
male applicants.

Initial training has rightly received a great deal of attention in discussions of German training provision. It is important to note that Germany
places rather less emphasis on further and continuing training. Further
training tends to be concentrated on the acquisition of additional qualifications (such as the *meister* certificate) by those already well-qualified.
Routine provision of further training for the majority of the workforce
seems unusual. Table 7.3 cannot claim to compare like with like, as
definitions of training and the quality of the training experience vary from
country to country. Nevertheless, the pattern of provision differs quite
sharply between Britain and Germany. The figures are based on Labour
Force Surveys in the two countries; respondents were asked if they had
received training in the previous four weeks. Whereas Germany had far
more of its young employees apparently receiving training than had
Britain, the position was different amongst the older age groups, Britain
having larger proportions of the over-25s receiving some training.[4]

REGULATION

As we have indicated, German training is tightly regulated at federal and
state (*Land*) level. Table 7.4 sets out some of the most important legal and
organizational components of the dual system. Training policies and
standards are the formal responsibility of the federal government, advised
by the *Bundesinstitut für Berufsbildung* (BIBB). At local level, advisory
services and the supervision of training programmes, as well as formal
assessments, are assigned not to the government, but to quasi-public
bodies: the Chambers of Industry and Commerce (*Industrie- und*

Handelskammer) and the Chambers of Crafts (*Handwerkskammer*). The chambers offer nationwide advice and ensure equal standards of vocational qualifications throughout the country as all industrial and commercial companies are members of their local chambers (by German law, chambers are public law corporations and firms' membership is compulsory). In practice, however, the content of training programmes and reform proposals has to be assessed and confirmed by employers' associations, trade unions and the *Länder* (state) governments, all with the same voting power. Unanimous agreement by these parties is difficult to achieve and as a result, as has recently been argued, "procedures for changing training regulations are lengthy and cumbersome" (Shackleton and Lange 1993). Furthermore, firm-based worker councils have an effective veto on those training regulations which are not considered as being beneficial for their trainees.

Nevertheless, because the dual system is part and parcel of the collective bargaining process and is based on employers offering places to trainees, it does have the advantage of being closely bound to labour market requirements. It is essentially the outcome of negotiation and consultation between government and the social partners: the unions play a crucial role. They are

Table 7.4   The dual vocational system of training in Germany

Component of training	Duality	
Place of schooling	Firm	Vocational college
Educator	Vocational trainer (*Meister*)	College teacher
Trainee	Apprentice	Student
Primary didactic principle	Job-orientated approach	Theoretical approach
Supervision	Chambers	State
Finance (explicit cost)	Firm	Public sector
Constitutional order	Federal Government	*Länder*
Aim	Production of capabilities in professional, private and public areas	

Source: Gathered from Benner (1982).

the main defenders of the dual system. "Add-ons" to the system can be made through industry-wide collective agreements (as in the construction industry) and unions also play a key role in monitoring training provision via workers' representatives on the works councils and through participation, together with the employers, in local training and examining bodies.

An important aspect of the system is that it was confirmed through the Vocational Training Act (*Berufsbildungsgesetz*) as part and parcel of a strategy for active intervention in the labour market as embodied in the Labour Promotion Act (*Arbeitsförderungsgesetz*) of 1969. Training and retraining measures were thereby seen as integral to preserving stability of employment and preventing unemployment. They formed a significant aspect of a model of development which Sengenberger (1984) has termed "socially controlled welfare capitalism", aimed at securing and enhancing the social standard of workers, through income security, unemployment insurance and other social benefits, the deployment and training of workers, and improvements in working conditions. In effect, the unions traded off wage restraint against non-wage gains, which included a redistribution of power itself. Crucial to the realization of this model were increased rights given to workers to participate in companies' modernization policies and personnel planning (through the works councils) on the basis of the 1972 revisions to the Companies' Constitution Act (*Betriebsverfassungsgesetz*).

The training system as developed in the 1960s and 1970s was intended to increase flexibility in the use of labour through expanded job content. The reliance on building on the internal labour market noted earlier was confirmed in the 1973 ban (admittedly unsuccessful) on the recruitment of foreign workers. In spite of changes since this time, this original vision of training as being inseparable from an active interventionist employment policy has continued to be reaffirmed. In a Ruhr conference of 1989, for instance, training was explicitly discussed as a means of creating a new skill structure and a measure against unemployment, with the federal government pledging financial support for apprentice training in areas affected by firm closure. It therefore comes as no surprise that it has similarly been an issue of central importance to labour market policies in the former German Democratic Republic in order to prevent a process of mass dismissals (Bispinck 1991). However, German reunification has caused a "cash crisis" in the German training system which has led to significant financial cutbacks in the provision of training and further education – especially for the East German workforce – and corresponding amendments to the Labour Promotion Act.

The dual system of training has the effect of producing a highly segmented labour market, sharply divided between skilled and unskilled. This is because wages, established through centralized collective bargaining, refer – directly or indirectly – to the level of qualifications and are differentiated on this basis (Mahnkopf 1992). Even the level of unemployment benefit is according to qualifications, and those unemployed are not compelled to accept employment below their qualifications. Regional and firm wage differentials remain relatively unimportant in Germany, especially in sectors such as building where rates are at the same level throughout the state. Unlike Britain, therefore, where "poaching" of trained labour for higher rates by firms which do not themselves train remains an issue, wages in Germany cannot be used as a means to poach skilled labour. What is at issue, rather, is the use of labour which falls outside this highly regulated situation. Today this means, above all, labour from East European states. As conditions and wage rates for this labour contrast so sharply with those for regulated labour, immigrant labour has not been "incorporated" but stands as an ever-larger and separate segment of the labour market posing a growing threat to the political economy of "socially controlled welfare capitalism" and thus to the dual system itself.

TRAINING IN EASTERN GERMANY

The picture of recent developments in the German labour market would be incomplete without mentioning the problems of the former German Democratic Republic. The East German labour market faces an unprecedented challenge. Labour market statistics of the Federal employment office (*Bundesanstalt für Arbeit*) show that by July 1993 about 1.17 million people in Eastern Germany were out of work, but the trend depicted in Figure 7.1 underestimates the seriousness of the problem as actual unemployment figures are thought to be much higher (Lange 1993a; Pugh 1993).

Consequently, training and other active labour market policies play an important part in reducing the extent of measured unemployment and, by September 1992, relieved the East German labour market of approximately 1.75 million actual unemployed (Presse- und Informationsamt der Bundesregierung 1992). In the short period from January to August 1992, 640,000 participants in further education and (re-)training programmes were counted and 380,000 people entered work creation schemes (*Arbeitsbeschaffungsmaßnahmen*). In addition, since October 1990 early retirement payments have been offered to East Germans aged over 55 years and, by the second half of 1992, the number of those accepting this offer rose to 835,000 (Commission of the European Communities 1993). However, a greater conformity between training programmes and the skills required by industry and commerce seems to be needed to improve the employment

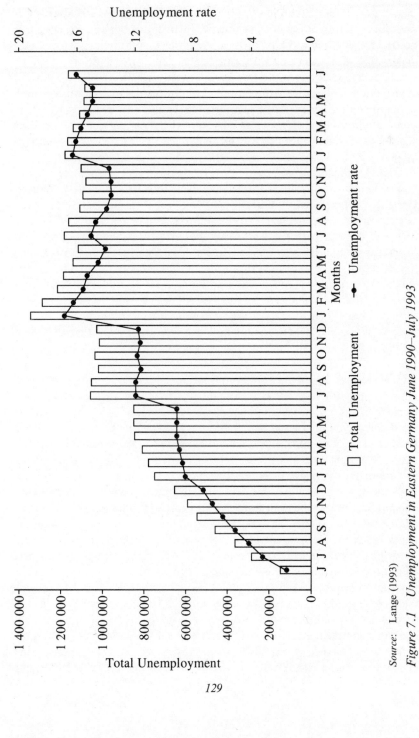

Source: Lange (1993)

Figure 7.1   Unemployment in Eastern Germany June 1990–July 1993

prospects of the East German workforce. Formal qualification programmes suffer from insufficient practical learning opportunities as appropriate equipment in old East German factories is still rare and as specially
designed "employment and training firms" (*Beschäftigungs- und Qualifi-
zierungsgesellschaften*) are often poor substitutes for real-world work
environments. The development of apprenticeship opportunities illustrates the current poor shape of vocational training in Eastern Germany.
Some training experts forecast that over the next few years only 50 per cent
of all East German applicants will manage to enter the apprenticeship
system, the rest either becoming unemployed or moving westwards.

Facing these obstacles, in July 1992 the Federal Government decided to
make changes in its labour market policy. From 1993 onwards, Eastern
Germany experienced significant reductions in the number of training
opportunities. Funding for further training and retraining measures is
now subject to more rigorous selection. Motivation and information
programmes for the unemployed to improve their placement prospects
(under paragraph 41a of the Labour Promotion Act) are no longer funded
and the amount of the adjustment grants aimed at vocational integration of
the unemployed is generally limited to 30 per cent of the wage (it was
formerly 50 per cent) for a period of six months instead of twelve, as was
previously the case (Commission of the European Communities 1993).

TRAINING FOR THE UNEMPLOYED

Further training and other labour market policies for the unemployed in
Germany are based, like initial training policies, on regulations under the
Labour Promotion Act (*Arbeitsförderungsgesetz*). The primary aim of the
LPA, reflecting the period in which it was passed, is to preserve
employment stability and to prevent unemployment, *not* to increase the
re-employment probabilities of the already unemployed. The latter distinction has recently been stressed as many measure the success of German
labour market policies by reduced unemployment figures (e.g. Schäfer
1988). Such evaluations have been described as inaccurate and unfair,
and it has been claimed that attention ought to be centred on LPA's primary targets such as improved occupational mobility and the avoidance
of structural disturbances (Lampert 1989). However, it cannot be denied
that training and retraining have become major public policy issues, in
particular as means of countering unemployment. In what follows, we
therefore comment mainly on their impacts on unemployment.

When assessing training for the unemployed, we effectively mean training for the adult unemployed. This is because, as Table 7.5 illustrates, the

Table 7.5   Youth unemployment rates, 1990

Country	Age group	% unemployed
France	15–24	19.3
Germany	15–24	5.6
Italy	14–24	31.5
Japan	15–24	4.3
Netherlands	15–24	11.1
Norway	16–24	11.8
Spain	16–24	32.3
Sweden	16–24	3.8
UK	16–24	10.0
USA	16–24	10.7

Source: Organization for Economic Cooperation and Development (1993b).

comprehensive coverage of initial training has caused youth unemployment in Germany to be very much lower than in comparable countries.[5] Consequently, active labour market policies have not been primarily targeted at young people, but at the adult unemployed.

There is a wide range of labour market policies in Germany, largely organized by the *Bundesanstalt für Arbeit* (BA) which is responsible for the implementation of these measures under the LPA. Although unemployment benefits, unemployment assistance, programmes for the mentally and physically disabled and miscellaneous measures are the responsibility of the BA, we shall concentrate on those policies which "actively" tackle the problem of unemployment: further training and re-training; work creation schemes; and settling-in allowances.

Further Training and Re-training

As mentioned earlier, public training schemes for the adult unemployed were initially intended to improve existing skills, thus supporting and encouraging occupational mobility in the economy and avoiding structural mismatch. Entry into these schemes was normally direct from employment, and exit was normally back into employment after only a short delay. West German training statistics, however, point to a changing emphasis. Whereas in 1970, on average only 11 per cent of programme participants were previously unemployed, by August 1992 this proportion had risen to over 60 per cent. Not surprisingly, bringing people back to work has become the main objective of these measures.

The operation of further training and re-training schemes now involves a voucher system which gives participants the freedom of choice between entering certified courses and programmes chosen by placement officers of the BA (Disney *et al.* 1992). Training costs usually fall on the BA and employers' organizations, not on individual trainees. This financial support is topped up by subsistence allowances (usually related to previous earnings) for which trainees may be eligible depending upon individual circumstances. As a result of higher unemployment, participation in these schemes has risen significantly. Between January and August 1992, about 340,000 entered further training or re-training programmes – roughly twice as many as in 1970.

Work Creation Schemes

Work creation schemes (WCS) are targeted at the hard-to-place unemployed. The long-term unemployed thus form the largest number of the participants (Spitznagel 1989). The aim of WCS is to place the unemployed in temporary employment, usually for one year. In the short run, placing the long-term unemployed in these schemes seems to be beneficial for the labour market. On average, 380,000 unemployed participated in 1992: they therefore did not appear on the German unemployment register. Work creation is intended only to assist community projects (jobs in health care and environmental improvements, for example). But because of a shortage of suitable opportunities, the creation of sufficient employment in this way proved impossible – a warning for other countries such as Britain where some commentators have lobbied for similar schemes (Layard 1993). In the event, more and more private-sector firms have had to be used to place the unemployed. However, this development has displeased defenders of free market principles; they argue that new jobs for the long-term unemployed can only be created at the expense of potential jobs for young workers entering the labour market and the short-term unemployed (Scharpf 1987). The idea of displacement effects of this sort was introduced in Chapter 4, and will be explored further in Chapter 11. The precise size of such effects in the German context is difficult to measure. Nevertheless, as employment is the first destination for only 22 per cent of WCS participants after leaving WCS (Disney *et al.* 1992), one can assume that significant knock-on effects are created, keeping the short-term unemployed out of work and recreating the same basic problem. Furthermore, WCS do not usually contain any sort of off-the-job training or retraining leading to formal qualifications, and there is little likelihood that they increase unemployed people's chances of entering regular employment after completing schemes (*Wirtschaftswoche* 1993).

Settling-in Allowances

As with work creation schemes, settling-in allowances (SIA) focus on those unemployed who have been classified as "hard-to-place". The initial target population for SIA were older people without formal qualifications and the long-term unemployed – by definition, those who are jobless for more than 12 months. In practice, however, the majority of the participants have been out of work for considerably less than this, with a median duration of about three months (Disney *et al.* 1991), presumably because they are easier to place. In contrast to work creation schemes, SIAs are intended to place the unemployed in private-sector employment. Employers receive wage subsidies of up to 70 per cent, which are usually reduced after six months (Schäfer 1988). Wage subsidies are normally provided for up to two years although workers aged over 50 can be supported for up to eight years (with a wage subsidy of up to 75 per cent). As SIAs are mainly given to private-sector employers for existing jobs, it comes as no surprise that permanent employment rates are significantly higher than those of work creation schemes. One and a half years after being subsidized by SIAs, 69 per cent of the target group are still in employment, 47 per cent with the same employer (Brinkmann 1985). Between January and August 1992, about 21,000 previously unemployed people were subsidized in this way.

As the long-term unemployed were not being reached successfully by Settling-in Allowances, in June 1989 the German government introduced a special scheme – Employment Support for the Long-term Unemployed – aimed entirely at those unemployed who have been out of work for at least one year. Participants are placed in private-sector employment for at least 12 months and must work for at least 18 hours a week. Wage subsidies can reach 80 per cent for the first six months (and 60 per cent thereafter) for an unemployed person who has been out of work for at least three years, 70 per cent (and 50 per cent thereafter) for a person unemployed for between two and three years, and 60 per cent (40 per cent thereafter) for a person jobless for between one and two years. Replacement rates of wage costs are thus considerably higher than for SIA participants and this could be the reason why even the long-term unemployed have relatively good chances of being placed in temporary private-sector employment. Between mid-1989 and early 1993 over 100,000 long-term unemployed found employment under the programme; 90,800 of the placements in permanent jobs supported by the programme thus far were in the old *Länder* compared with 9,300 in the former GDR. The programme is due to run until 1994 and has a current budget of DM2.15 billion (Commission of the European Communities 1993). However, with the recent increases in long-term unemployment, both in eastern and western regions, it seems very likely that the initial plan period will be extended beyond 1994.

CONCLUDING REMARKS

In this chapter we have shown the considerable importance attached to training and vocational education in Germany. Commentators have usually concentrated on the initial training provided in the dual system. We have shown how this provides a relatively smooth transition from school to work, though the process can be lengthy. Apprentices receive a broad general education as well as a grounding in occupational skills, and obtain qualifications which are widely understood and appreciated. However, the degree of labour market regulation implied by such a system limits the transferability of the model to other settings such as the UK or the USA, where the political consensus is unlikely to support it. It is also arguable that the problems of Eastern Germany and the influx of labour from Eastern Europe are likely to undermine the German model of socially controlled welfare capitalism in its heartland over the next few years.

Whatever the merits of the dual system, it certainly has not prevented the emergence of high levels of unemployment in Germany. The plethora of active labour market measures taken to combat unemployment in recent years suggest that despite its high level of labour productivity and its well-educated workforce, Germany faces problems in the 1990s that are not so different from those faced by countries with less commitment to training and education.

NOTES

1. In the late 1980s, about 40% of the workforce in the Netherlands, 50% in France and over 60% in Britain had no formal qualifications. In West Germany only 26% were similarly unqualified: in East Germany the proportion was even smaller (Clarke *et al.* 1994; Lange 1994).
2. Note that the occupations chosen by girls are very different from those chosen by boys, with predictable consquences for future employment and earnings opportunities. See Chapter 12 for a discussion.
3. With the exception of Japan, Germany has the highest average job tenure in the developed world (Organization for Economic Cooperation and Development 1993b).

4. Indeed, the differential was so marked in the older age groups that it more than offset the clear German advantage in the younger groups: overall, 14.4% of the British employees were receiving training as against only 12.7% of Germans.
5. See Schmid (1988) for a discussion.

8.   Education and Training in France: A Heavily Regulated System

INTRODUCTION

Of the four countries we are examining in detail, France has the system of vocational education and training which is the most highly regulated and centralized. For example, the central government, in the form of the Ministry of Education, has far more control over education than anywhere else in Europe or North America, despite recent attempts to devolve some responsibilities to local and regional levels. It has consequently attracted both praise and criticism from different quarters.

Another key element of the French system is the emphasis on general academic education at all levels, including vocational qualifications, and the heavy reliance on school-based vocational education and training. However, a highly structured vocational pathway into the labour force exists for all qualification levels and there is generally a well-defined framework for assessing the level of qualifications and equivalent occupations. Although increasing emphasis is placed on continuing training, this too is dominated by an "academic" model, with formal off-the-job training the rule.

In this chapter the structure and role of French education and training are examined in more detail. Their distinctive features are discussed and the main benefits and drawbacks of the system are highlighted.

COMPULSORY EDUCATION

Children must attend school between the ages of 6 and 16[1] in France. However, the vast majority will already have attended nursery school, which local authorities are obliged to provide, and it has become the norm for young people to remain in full-time education after the age of 16.

The first stage of compulsory secondary education consists of a common national curriculum for the first two years, generally taught in *collèges*.

Following this students may decide to pursue a general education scheme, studying virtually the same subjects with some additional compulsory and voluntary classes, or they may opt for a vocational programme by transferring to a different institution. The Haby Reforms of 1975 were introduced to ensure that all 12–16-year-olds get some introduction to technical or practical education whilst at school. So even if students subsequently opt for an academic route they will have received some vocational education (Noah and Eckstein 1988). Students opting to stay in *collèges* are normally awarded a general education certificate, the *brevet d'études du premier cycle*, at the age of 16. This enables them to continue to general post-secondary education.

Vocational education, however, is mainly acquired at a *lycée d'enseignement professionnel*, where pupils from the age of about 14 study a three-year full-time course culminating in a *Certificat d'Aptitude Professionnelle* (CAP). Some 10–15 per cent of the age group take this route. Students often enter the labour market directly after finishing, although they are increasingly encouraged to remain in education. Alternatively students can do part-time supervised work and part-time schooling in preparation for registering as a full-time apprentice later on, whilst working towards the CAP from a largely work-based apprenticeship (Dundas-Grant 1989).

The CAP is a recognized trade qualification, completed either in full-time education or via an apprenticeship, and is intended to give students general basic training in conjunction with occupation-specific training, including a work placement. However, there has been a high dropout and failure rate from the full-time course (Dundas-Grant 1989).

POST-COMPULSORY SECONDARY EDUCATION

Following compulsory education young people can either enter the labour market or remain in education. In France 80 per cent now take the latter option, a marked increase in the last decade (Wolf 1992). Those remaining in full-time education again have the option of pursuing either a general or a vocational programme of education. Some students progress after the *brevet d'études du premier cycle*, rather than earlier, to study for either the CAP or the more general *brevet d'études professionnelles* (BEP). Both qualifications were intended to be of the same standard (approximately the equivalent of five GCSEs in the UK), although BEP is generally recognized as being the more demanding of the two. Both take just two years when compulsory secondary education has previously been completed.

The BEP is intended to "promote adaptability, mobility, responsibility and independence" (Department for Education 1993a: 3). It is a more general qualification than the CAP, covering 31 broad industrial and occupational areas – reduced from 76 in 1989 – whilst the more specialized CAP can be taken in 250 occupational groupings, down from 315 in 1989 (FEU 1992). As such, it is hoped that it will provide more employment opportunities than the very job-specific CAP.

The BEP corresponds to a group of CAP occupations, so students can enter for both qualifications simultaneously (Wolf 1992). In recent years BEP has become more popular, with young people starting it after completing their secondary education at the expense of CAP registrations, numbers of which are declining.

After completion students may enter the labour market (possession of a BEP would normally mean starting on a higher grade than with a CAP) or remain in education. The BEP allows individuals to pursue higher vocational qualifications whilst at work through, for example, registration with the Chambers of Trade to complete the *Brevet de Maîtrise* (Master's Certificate), which allows them to establish their own business and train apprentices. Or they could study for the *brevet professionnel*, taken at college on a day release basis, equivalent to the same level as the *baccalauréat professionnel*. Alternatively individuals may pursue higher vocational qualifications on a full-time basis, completing a *baccalauréat* or the more specifically vocational *Brevet de Technicien*. The latter is a three-year course, of a slightly lower level than the *baccalauréat*, but more practical, covering twelve broad industrial sectors such as building or textiles.

We turn to the more traditional academic qualifications. The internationally respected *baccalauréat*, taught in *lycées*, is roughly the equivalent of A Levels in the UK, the *Abitur* in Germany or the associate degree in the USA. It is awarded after a three-year course, in which several subjects are examined.

In the past only a general course or a technical *baccalauréat*, both academic in nature, were available to students. They both involve the completion of a general course in the first year followed by greater specialization in the second and third years, depending on which *baccalauréat* is being pursued. Currently there are five general and three technical *baccalauréats*, made up of various options, although it is intended to reduce the number of programmes (Department for Education 1993a). Several subjects (including French, a foreign language, maths and human sciences) are compulsory, so even the technical courses contain an element of general education. The '*bac*' is the basic entry requirement for academic higher education and the majority of *baccalauréat* students continue with full-time studies, those with the technological version opting for technical higher education.

An addition to the system was introduced in 1985, the vocational *baccalauréat* qualification, *baccalauréat professionnel*. This programme, taught in *lycées professionnels*, is less academic than the other *baccalauréats*, generally lasting only two years. It is intended to increase the overall quality of vocational education and provide students who have already acquired an intermediate vocational qualification, such as the BEP, with a good mixture of general and vocational education to take into the labour market. It is not particularly intended as being a pathway into higher education; approximately 80 per cent of students are expected to enter the workforce (the reverse of the situation for other *baccalauréat* students), to obtain managerial and supervisory roles (ibid.).

Since its inception the *baccalauréat professionnel* has proved exceedingly popular, attracting many students at the expense of other vocational qualifications, in particular the *Brevet de Technicien*. Whereas a mere 1,157 students sat the pilot exams in 1987, by 1991 this figure had increased to 70,000. Of these 55 per cent were female (ibid.).

The *baccalauréat professionnel* curriculum is made up of several elements: vocational subjects, including mathematics; communication and general knowledge; art and design; and physical education. There are 26 broad fields of study, covering all the main industrial sectors such as building, motor vehicle engineering, clothing, administration, business, and hotel and catering. It is similar to the BTEC qualification in the UK except that students in France will have already completed a previous vocational course before starting this. Assessment involves a combination of written examinations, continuous assessment and an oral exam. In addition the student is obliged to undertake a work placement of at least sixteen weeks, eight each year. As in other countries, we find that most subject areas tend to be dominated by one or other of the sexes. Thus women make up less than 10 per cent of those enrolling in engineering and construction, for example, while men account for less than 10 per cent of students on business administration courses.

The *baccalauréat* is generally taken at the age of 18 or 19, and has effectively become a school-leaving certificate as fewer and fewer students leave school at 16. In 1990–1 of approximately 700,000 16–18-year-olds in total, nearly 500,000 were enrolled in some form of *baccalauréat*, 57 per cent on the general course, 28 per cent on the *baccalauréat technologique* and the remaining 15 per cent on a professional programme (ibid.).

HIGHER EDUCATION

Higher education is provided in state universities, *grandes écoles* and several private establishments. The state controls the length of courses, their entrance requirements and broad features of the content. However, the universities may allocate their budget and specify their courses as they wish.

State universities tend to offer arts and humanities courses, the first two years of which lead to a general diploma, *Diplôme d'Études Universitaires Générales* (DEUG), combining compulsory and optional subjects. The following two years give the student a *licence* after the first and a *maîtrise*, the equivalent of a masters degree, after the second. A further three years (usually) culminates in a doctorate or alternatively, after the *maîtrise*, a student may decide to complete a one-year training course for a profession, graduating with a *Diplôme d'Études Supérieures Spécialisées* (DESS).

Grandes écoles have a great deal more prestige than state universities, offering three-year business, science and engineering courses, and as a result entrance is highly competitive. In order to sit the compulsory entrance examination students generally complete a 2–3-year course at their *lycées* following their *baccalauréat* so that graduates will have had at least seven years' post-compulsory education before qualifying to degree standard. Again, students study for a diploma, although some *grandes écoles* are postgraduate institutions.

Dropout rates from universities are high in France: up to 50 per cent in some institutions. The figures are much lower for *grandes écoles*, not surprisingly given the ability and preparation needed to obtain entrance in the first place (Incomes Data Services 1992).

A student not wishing to attend university to study for an academic degree can work for a vocational diploma in a scientific, technical or commercial field, or alternatively attend vocational higher education institutions. A *Brevet de Technicien Supérieur* takes two years of study following either a technical or vocational *baccalauréat* or a *Brevet de Technicien*. *Instituts Universitaires de Technologie* offer students two-year specialized courses in vocational areas such as social work and commerce, providing graduates with a *Diplôme Universitaire de Technologie* (DUT). These were developed at the request of industry, and business representatives sit on the Boards of Trustees and participate in teaching (Blachère 1992). The DUT either prepares students directly for the labour market or enables them to transfer to a university, exempting them from part of the course.

In 1991, 28 Institutes of Applied Sciences, *Instituts Universitaires Professionalisés* (IUPs), were established to deliver three-year vocational diploma courses. At least half the staff in these institutions are professionals recruited from industry. *Instituts Universitaires de Formation des Maîtres* (IUFMs) were also opened in 1991 to provide university-level preparation for those involved in training in industry (Blachère 1992).

REGULATION

Commissions Professionnelles Consultatives (CPCs) are statutory bodies established to advise on the content and standard of secondary-level vocational education, each corresponding to the various industrial sectors of economic activity. The members of each of the 18 CPCs[2] are representatives from employers and trade unions (in equal numbers), government departments (appointed by the minister concerned), the Centre for Studies and Research on Qualifications (CEREQ), the Association for Adult Vocational Training (AFPA) and other interested parties, such as teachers, parents, and Chambers of Commerce (Department for Education 1993a).

CPCs advise and formulate policy proposals. They examine new reforms, curricula and certification to assess suitability, to prescribe any necessary regulations such as entry requirements or length of course. They try to ensure that each syllabus contains a minimum level of both general and specific education, and is not too narrow in its focus. They are, however, only advisory bodies and the state retains overall policy control over the education system. National criteria apply to curricula, qualifications, and administration and finance, so that courses are largely uniform across the country. In addition the state takes responsibility for the recruitment and training of all teachers. Even in privately run establishments, the state maintains a large element of control by providing some funding in return for management of standards and staffing. As a result, education is nationally validated, culminating in national qualifications with common national standards.

Advisory boards are also being developed for vocational higher education. Twenty CPNs exist for *Diplômes Universitaire de Technologie*, and national advisory committees are being established for DUTs and IUPs to involve industry professionals. To date, however, employers have a more limited role than they do on CPCs (Blachère 1992).

OVERVIEW OF THE EDUCATION SYSTEM

So much for the bones of the system: Figure 8.1 provides a summary. We now turn to take an overview of French education. One of the main

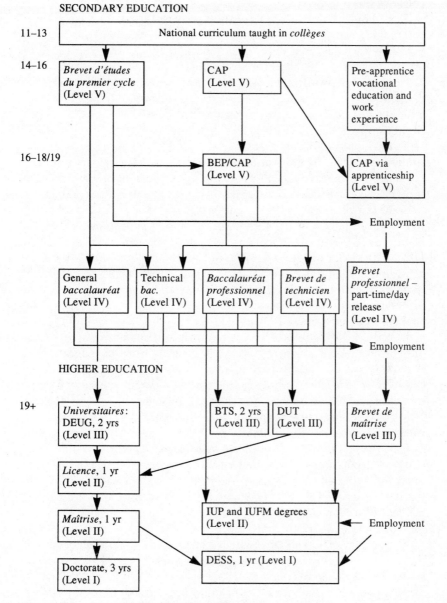

Figure 8.1   Vocational education in France

successes of the French system is thought to be the broad element of general education[3] in most courses at all levels, including vocational courses. However, as we shall indicate, there are some critics who consider this a drawback.

The administration of initial vocational education and training is largely centralized, run by the Ministry of Education, although powers have gradually been devolved since 1983 to local and regional authorities in an attempt to make the system more responsive to local needs. The state provides about two-thirds of the total, reflecting the extent to which it directs the system, determines policy directions and objectives, pays staffing costs and so forth. Central government will also provide money for special projects or national policy objectives (Blachère 1992).

The regional authorities are responsible for day-to-day operations, running and building costs of institutions. In addition they are now also responsible for assessing their local economy and defining its education and training needs in order to draw up a provisional investment programme.

Some critics take the view that, despite the appearance of consultation, the degree of state control is such that the industry–education link exists in name only (FEU 1992). As in many other developed countries, such as the UK and the US, there is criticism from French employers about the basic educational standards of school leavers, particularly about the quality of *lycée professionnel* graduates and the fact that initial training caters inadequately for a still-sizeable minority of young people who fail to complete qualifications (CEDEFOP 1987).[4]

It is also possible to hear in France, as in other countries, pleas from business to eliminate the perceived gap between industry and education, so that schools teach students to prepare for the economic environment they will face. Industrialists emphasize the need for general work skills to be taught in schools, to improve for example the communication skills and attitudes of young workers and for students to be taught about the "real world" (Noah and Eckstein 1988).

Having said this, there has been an increase in French firm–school links covering negotiations concerning work placements, donations, training provision by *lycées*, employers visiting and talking to students and so on. During the academic year 1989–90, 99.1 per cent of vocational *lycées*, 91.7 per cent of technical/general *lycées* and 87 per cent of *collèges* had some form of contact with companies (Blachère 1992).

There has been tremendous emphasis on upgrading the qualifications of the workforce. This is reflected in the expansion of the *baccalauréat professionnel*, to enable individuals pursuing vocational education to attain higher-level qualifications. As in the UK and the USA, the French government has set targets for further increases in the qualifications of the workforce. The 1989 Education Act set the goal of increasing the numbers of people qualified so that 80 per cent of each cohort will take a *baccalauréat* by the year 2000, in comparison to 66 per cent now (Department for Education 1993a). In addition the government intends that every school-leaver be qualified to at least CAP or BEP level, whereas at present about 15 per cent of school-leavers have no qualification and 45 per cent of young people leave the education system with a CAP or BEP their highest qualification (FEU 1992).

The government is trying to introduce flexibility into vocational education by introducing credits and work placements and reducing the number of occupational categories, in order to make courses more general. For example, the vocational *baccalauréat* and a number of courses within CAP, BEP and *Brevet de Technicien Supérieur* have, on a trial basis, used independent modules, or "credit units", to make up the whole course (Organization for Economic Cooperation and Development 1990). It is intended that this will facilitate adult part-time continuing training courses by enabling individuals to complete the course in their own time, and also so that account can be taken of their previous experience.

From the outside, all this activity looks most impressive. In recent years the always formidable French educational system has expanded and innovated, especially in the vocational field, on a scale which has been greatly admired abroad. As in the United States, but unlike Germany or the UK, the emphasis in initial vocational training is on the achievement of qualifications before entry to the job market. There is only a small amount of official interest in apprenticeships or employer-provided initial training. However, unlike the USA, qualifications are tightly regulated by the state, which has a virtual monopoly on awards. Possession of appropriate qualifications is necessary in order to practise a very wide range of trades.

As a result a system of nationally recognized and defined levels of qualification and equivalent occupations has easily been constructed, something which is taking a long time to achieve in Britain following the establishment of the NVQ framework (see Chapter 6).

Vocational and academic qualifications are categorized into six levels corresponding to different occupations. The highest is level I, covering professional occupations which require a PhD or equivalent. Level VI, the lowest, represents unskilled occupations requiring no formal qualification or training beyond compulsory schooling.[5]

This easy categorization reminds us that the French educational system, in both its academic and vocational manifestations, is a hierarchical one, concerned with status. French training experts talk of "formation professionelle", a notion which conveys preparation for a niche in a clearly defined occupational structure rather than simply the creation of a set of skills. Some writers see an emphasis on formal qualifications, associated with a rather inflexible pay hierarchy and reliance on seniority in determining promotions, as an element in internal labour markets which have characterized an important part of French industry (Méhaut 1993). In view of the changing competitive environment, internal labour markets may not always be as important or appropriate.

Indeed, it is worth mentioning that, despite the efforts and resources which have gone into developing vocational education in France in recent years, French young people do not appear to be markedly more successful than their counterparts elsewhere at achieving jobs on entering the labour market. Since the middle of the 1980s, for instance, youth unemployment in France has been significantly higher than in the USA, the UK or Germany (Organization for Economic Cooperation and Development 1993b).[6]

TRAINING FOR THE WORKFORCE

Moving on from preparation for entry into the workforce, we now examine the provision of training for those in employment. Such further or continuing training has grown rapidly since the early 1980s. One indicator is the percentage of wage costs spent on training activities. Amongst companies with 500–2,000 employees this rose from 1.81 to 3.12 per cent between 1982 and 1991; for those with more than 2,000 employees the corresponding proportions were 3.06 and 4.67 per cent (Méhaut 1993).

One reason for the growth in firms' expenditure is the legal requirement to spend a minimum proportion of wage costs on training or pay a tax: a levy system operates in France. The Act of 16 July 1971 set up a requirement to pay a *taxe de formation professionelle continue* to help fund vocational training. There is also a *taxe d'apprentissage* dating back to the 1920s to pay for training for young workers.

The levy system introduced in 1971 obliged firms with more than ten employees to produce a training plan and allocate a percentage of their wage bill to further vocational training, either by spending it themselves on formally recognized training activities (which means off-the-job training in France) or paying it into state funds or intermediary bodies.[7] In 1984 total expenditure on training from company taxation (from both the apprenticeship tax and the continuing training tax) amounted to the equivalent of £2.9 billion, or £320 per employee, including wage costs during training (Méhaut 1992). Employers are also obliged to grant employees individual leave to do a course of their own choice, using training funds. The *taxe de formation professionelle continue* has been increased several times since

1971; it is now 1.5 per cent of the gross salary bill (Incomes Data Services 1991). The apprenticeship tax is set at the same rate and is paid, like the further training tax, in the form of cash or equipment, either direct to the state, education institutions or Chambers of Trade or Commerce to be used for vocational education and training. One problem that has emerged from this system is the uneven distribution of resources for schools and colleges; obviously certain institutions may benefit more than others (Department for Education 1993a).

Firms with fewer than ten employees have only recently been subject to levy legislation (since January 1992), and are now obliged to spend 0.15 per cent of the wage bill on training (Incomes Data Services 1991).

Recent increases in the level and scope of taxes reflect not only the higher priority being given to continuing training in general, but also the government's commitment to devolving responsibility to firms. As an added incentive to increase spending by firms the government has introduced a system of credits to reward firms allocating more than the statutory requirement to training. These credits enable firms to reduce the amount of tax they pay on their annual profits.

Apprenticeship colleges (CFAs) receive about 30 per cent of their funding from the apprenticeship tax and 20 per cent from members of the Chambers of Trade or Commerce by way of member contributions. The remainder is generally obtained directly from either that portion of the apprenticeship tax given direct to the Chambers of Trade or Commerce or direct funding from employers for the provision of specific training.

The national government and regional governments also contribute money towards continuing training by allocating money to such projects as the National Centre for Distance Learning (CNED). The state-run National Employment Fund provides short-term assistance for firms facing reorganization and training for the long-term unemployed. The Adult Vocational Training Association (AFPA) provides training schemes to enable the unemployed and job seekers the chance to gain a qualification.

In addition to *lycées*, institutions such as *groupements d'établissements* (GRETAs) and *centres de formation des apprentis* (CFAs) also provide post-secondary level education, generally full- and part-time vocational education and training to those in employment and the unemployed.

There are 350 GRETAs in France, voluntary institutions set up by *lycées* and *collèges* for the purposes of adult vocational education, and funded partly by *lycées*, partly by employer taxes: they also receive some funds from the state government for training programmes for groups such as women returners and the unemployed. The *lycées* and *collèges* are legally obliged to make some provision for adults, which explains their role in the funding of GRETAs, although employers will pay the commercial cost of training. Eighty per cent of enrollees are employed; about half attend full-time, one-quarter attend for 2-2½ days per week over two years and the remaining 25 per cent complete short courses (Department for Education 1993a).

A large proportion of work-related training is provided by external training bodies, though paid for by the firm, although according to Méhaut (1992) the level of internal training increases with the size of the firm. However, he estimates that even in large firms with comprehensive training plans only 60 per cent of the training courses are provided within the firm.

Approximately 15 per cent of 16-year-olds leave school to become apprentices. They are bound by contract to their firm, studying part-time at an apprentice training centre, a CFA, run and generally funded by a Chamber of Commerce or professional association jointly with labour unions. The two- to three-year course involves both general and occupation-specific education, and apprentices are obliged to attend the training centre for at least 400 hours per year. Firms are not obliged to employ apprentices when they qualify, and according to Michiels (1991) only a few remain with their training company.

Apprenticeships are controlled by the Ministry of Education and managed by a national co-ordinating committee and regional organizations. A firm must be approved by national vocational education inspectors to be able to employ apprentices. They are assessed in terms of training provision, adequate resources and so forth. Firms must have one approved *maître* for each apprentice (Department for Education 1993a).

Apprenticeships are considered as part of the education system in France, rather than viewed as work-based training as they are in the UK: they therefore tend to be included in the education statistics rather than in formal training data. Traditionally limited to the CAP, apprentices are now encouraged to also prepare for the BEP, the *baccalauréat professionnel* and the *brevet de technicien*.

WORK-BASED TRAINING

On-the-job training is not formally recognized[8] as training by the state, firms or employees and so is included in neither the legal framework of training nor many of the statistics. Furthermore the official figures for employer-provided training are likely to be distorted because data refer to training on a particular date rather than over, say, a period of a year.

Table 8.1   *Proportion of French enterprises reporting some training activity*
and/or training expenditure, and training incidence among em-
ployees, by size of enterprise (%)

	Enterprises reporting training	Training incidence
All firms	55.8	29.2
< 10 employees	n/a	n/a
10–19 employees	35.3	7.9
20–49 employees	55.4	10.7
50–499 employees	81.3	20.9
500–1,999 employees	97.5	33.9
⩾ 2,000 employees	97.5	49.3

Source: Organization for Economic Cooperation and Development (1991).

The implication is that the reported levels of training will often underestimate the actual provision of training.

As we have seen, French firms tend not to spend a significant amount of money on initial vocational preparation, leaving this responsibility to the state; instead they focus their attention on further work-related training (Méhaut 1992). This is the cause of some criticism since virtually all initial training is school-based, and as such may be limited in its relevance to work situations.

In the mid-1980s, nearly 25 per cent of the working population, almost 5 million workers, took part in training, and total expenditure amounted to approximately FF70,000 million in 1986. This includes costs of trainee pay, administration, trainee accommodation and transport. A narrower measure, concentrating on resources directly expended in training, would put the figure for the same date in the region of FF30,000 million (CEDEFOP 1990a).

In 1986 firms spent on average 2.34 per cent of their wage bill on training even though at that time they were only obliged to contribute 1.2 per cent. However, training provision varies with the size of the firm such that this average increased from about 1.1 per cent for firms with 10–19 employees to nearly 4 per cent for firms with 2,000 employees or more; and it has been suggested that most firms spend the statutory requirement or less on training, with the average figure boosted by the training provision of a few large firms (ibid.).

Expenditure on training and incidence increased between 1975 and the late 1980s in firms of all sizes. For example, in 1975 firms with 10–19

Table 8.2 Classification of French industries in terms of expenditure on training

High spenders	Middle-range spenders	Low spenders
Financial institutions	Chemicals	Construction
Electricity	Iron and Steel	Textiles
Gas and Water	Pharmaceuticals	Leather products
Combustible	Electronic goods	Several service sector
minerals	Insurance	industries
Petroleum	Automobiles	
Transportation		

Source: Organization for Economic Cooperation and Development (1991).

employees spent 0.7 per cent of the wage bill on training, increasing to 1.33 per cent in 1989, with incidence increasing from 3.6 per cent to 7.8 per cent of employees receiving training. Similarly, expenditure rose in firms employing 500–1,999 employees from 1.49 per cent to 2.92 per cent of the wage bill, with increased coverage of 19.5 per cent to 36.1 per cent of employees (Organization for Economic Cooperation and Development 1991).

Table 8.1 provides proportions of companies training staff, by size of enterprise, the figures reflecting the observation that larger firms are more likely to train any staff than are smaller firms, and that larger firms also tend to train a greater proportion of their workforce. Firms employing at least 2,000 people offer training to nearly half their workforce.

The Organization for Economic Cooperation and Development (1991) suggests that there is a lot of variation in the amount of training by size of firm in France because data are dominated by formal training. By contrast the differences are much less in, say, the UK because of the wider definition of training. The implication of this observation is that small firms tend to provide relatively more on-the-job training, a logical conclusion since many small firms probably do not have enough staff to cope if one member of staff attends a formal training course; the opportunity cost of a trainee's time is likely to be greater in a small firm than a large firm.

As with all other countries, training in France varies significantly between industries. Different data sources give different results, with 1987 state administration data finding that office machinery, electricity and finance were above-average trainers, whilst textiles, clothing and construction provided below-average proportions of their workforce with training.

Similarly the 1989 French Labour Force Survey found office machinery as a high-incidence trainer, but in this case also gave education a high rating. Textiles and clothing were again classified as low-incidence trainers (Organization for Economic Cooperation and Development 1991).

In contrast to other countries, retail trade in France was found to train an above-average proportion of its workforce, probably due to the relatively high proportion of contract apprentices in the industry; about 35 per cent of all apprentices are in retail trade (ibid.). Furthermore it is likely that industries with high turnover rates, such as retailing, will frequently have to provide induction training, thereby boosting the overall training figures. According to CEDEFOP (1990a), industrial sectors with above-average incidence of training in the late 1980s were energy, office machinery and information science, transport, financial agencies, and posts and telecommunications, each sending more than 40 per cent of staff on a training course each year. At the other extreme, in the manufacturing of consumer goods, agri-foodstuffs and building and civil engineering, firms typically provide training for a much smaller proportion of their staff.

Table 8.2 shows industries classified in terms of whether they spend above-average proportions of their wage bill on training (high spenders), an average or middle-range amount, or if their expenditure is just above or below the minimum legal requirement (low spenders). The low spenders may be driven largely by the law and rely more on apprenticeships and on-the-job training, neither of which are covered in the formal reporting of training for the purposes of the levy, and there are also relatively high proportions of small firms within these industrial categories (Organization for Economic Cooperation and Development 1991). This highlights an important point about the analysis of training in France (and other countries): dividing industries and firms into high and low trainers implies high is "good" and low is "bad", but this is not a complete picture since many of these "low spenders" will supplement formal training with informal training, and on-the-job training may be more appropriate for some jobs.

In common with other countries there is a relationship between occupation and level of training received; supervisors, technicians and technical staff are most likely to receive training (47.5 per cent received some training in 1986), whilst only 14 per cent of labourers were given formal training in 1986 (CEDEFOP 1990). This could, however, partly reflect the nature of the work; labourers may be more likely to receive on-the-job training, in which case the training would not be considered formal training and so would not be included in official statistics.

An odd result from the French Labour Force Survey is that unskilled workers are apparently more likely to receive training from their employers

Table 8.3   Incidence[a] of training among employees in France as measured
in Labour Force Survey, by age and sex, March 1989

	All persons	15–19 years old	20–24 years old	25–34 years old	35–44 years old	45–49 years old	50+ years old
All	4.6	43.2	9.2	4.6	2.3	1.5	1.5
All[b]	3.5	10.2	8.2	4.5	2.3	1.5	0.6
Men	4.7	49.7	7.8	4.8	2.3	1.5	0.7
Men[b]	3.3	9.5	6.6	4.7	2.3	1.5	0.7
Women	4.5	34.4	10.7	4.3	2.2	1.7	0.5
Women[b]	3.7	11.5	9.9	4.2	2.2	1.7	0.5

Notes:
[a] Incidence refers to number of employed people who said they were receiving training at the time of the survey divided by the total number of permanent salaried employees.
[b] All people excluding apprentices.
Source: 1989 LFS data, reproduced in Organization for Economic Cooperation and Development (1991).

Table 8.4   Incidence[a] of employer-provided training among employees in
France, 1988[b] (%)

All persons	26.6
Men	28.8
Women	22.8

Notes:
[a] Incidence refers to employees who took at least one formal training period within the company's training plan, divided by number of permanent employees at the end of the calendar year.
[b] Based on returns under 1971 law on training finance: covers only companies with at least ten employees.
Source: Organization for Economic Cooperation and Development (1991).

than skilled non-manual workers. However, we can probably explain this in terms of the way data are classified: contracted apprentices are counted as unskilled workers (Organization for Economic Cooperation and Development 1991). Otherwise the incidence of training amongst employees is related to their previous qualification levels, with individuals generally more likely to receive training the higher their level of previous education.

Table 8.3 shows how training incidence varies with age and sex. The basic pattern shows that the young are most likely to receive training with incidence declining with age, as in the UK and Germany. According to CEDEFOP (1990), men are more likely to attend continuing training courses than women and, as Table 8.4 shows, are more likely to receive employer-provided training than women, although the figures for women are increasing at a faster rate.

GOVERNMENT TRAINING SCHEMES FOR THE YOUNG AND THE UNEMPLOYED

Various government-funded schemes exist which are applicable to specific groups of the population, for example the long-term unemployed, the disabled and women returners. A system of subsidizing job and training initiatives caters for 16–18-year-olds. Young school-leavers may enter a contract of *emploi-formation* for a minimum of six months: here they receive training either from their employer or at a training centre.

Under the *contrat de qualification*, available to 18–25-year-olds, the government gives employers tax credits and a minimum wage to the employee in return for the guarantee that the young people receive some work-related training. The employer is not obliged to provide a permanent position at the end of the contract. In a similar vein *contrats d'orientation* give three- to six-month courses to introduce people under the age of 22, with no professional qualifications, to work. Similarities can obviously be drawn with the system of training credits and Youth Training in Britain (see Chapter 6) and the JTPA in the US (see Chapter 5).

The unemployed are dependent on the state for training, whilst employees rely on firms or themselves for work-related training, as is the situation in the other countries which we look at in this book. In the late 1980s it was estimated that 30 per cent of the unemployed attend training schemes funded by public authorities (CEDEFOP 1990). Though some schemes are funded regionally or locally, they are still regulated nationally and aim to provide trainees with nationally recognized qualifications.

SOCIAL PARTNERS

As indicated earlier, the "social partners" (organized business and labour interests) are involved in education via bodies such as the *Commissions Professionelles Consultatives*. In this way their influence is felt in discussions with government over the nature and content of initial vocational education. At the level of continuing vocational training, consultations between the social partners lead to interprofessional agreements which the state will adopt as much as possible, modifying the proposals where necessary (Blachère 1992).

Social partners have a greater role to play in continuing vocational training because firms finance a great deal of their own training. The levy system obliges firms to draw up a training plan, which is done in consultation with trade unions and works councils. The unions are also involved because qualification levels are commonly used as reference points for occupation and remuneration and are included in collective agreements so that employees know in principle precisely what occupation grade and income they can expect when they achieve each level of qualification. The advantage of this, and the increasing number of collective agreements which include sections on training, is that further training and career advancement ladders are increasingly well-defined.

CONCLUSIONS

France has maintained a rigid division between education and training, with initial vocational education the responsibility of the state and conducted in schools whilst training is specifically related to the firm and the prime responsibility of employers. Essentially the state treats compulsory education and initial vocational education and training as pure public goods; the state provides the system, charging society via levies and taxes.

There are many positive aspects to this system: students leave school or college with a sound foundation in both general education and occupation-specific studies. The system provides a much broader range of academic and vocational options than was the case in the past, and this has resulted in a larger and larger proportion of young people entering the labour market with formal qualifications. Students are rigorously tested and their qualifications are widely respected, to the extent that pay scales reflect their educational achievements to a greater extent than in, say, the USA or the UK.

The system has its downside, however. Employers are given only a limited role in initial training, and critics charge that this may be inhibiting the process of reacting and adapting vocational education and training to the overall economy's requirements. This problem is associated with the fact that initial training is concentrated in schools and may not be appropriate to the rhythm of the workplace. The majority of school-leavers will have had only a few weeks work experience as part of their vocational courses. Consequently there is likely to be some duplication of funds as firms will still have to pay for some initial training just to acclimatize young people to working and to their role within that specific company. Moreover, problems are compounded, it is alleged, by the "inflexibility of the training apparatus": state control and bureaucracy mean that the introduction of a new course or amendments is a time-consuming process (CEDEFOP 1987).

For all its logical structure, the French qualification system has some problematic areas. One is at the lower levels, with basic vocational qualifications such as the CAP and BEP not always being recognized by collective agreements when workers initially join companies. As a result workers may have to start at a lower grade than they are actually qualified for, to gain experience before they are recognized as skilled workers (Lefresne 1992). Further up the scale, the contraction of traditional industries and restructuring of markets and firms has reduced opportunities for promotion, so that the link between achieving higher qualifications and a higher position in an internal labour market has been broken.

Furthermore, the strictly defined and regulated system tends to prevent both re-entry into the system and the accreditation of informal learning, since officially training does not include informal on-the-job learning.[9] Because of the bias which the levy system gives towards formal, off-the-job training, the tendency to concentrate continuing training on the already well-qualified is accentuated. Since one of the original purposes of the 1971 Act was to offset the disadvantages suffered by the less well qualified, this is unfortunate.

NOTES

1. This does not take into account some students who may leave earlier or later, depending on whether they are more or less advanced than the average pupil (Department for Education 1993a).
2. There are 17 CPCs covering each industrial sector and one relating to training in the agriculture sector.
3. By contrast, British vocational education is often held to be too narrow (Prais 1989).
4. Noah and Eckstein (1988) claim that in France, Germany and the UK "the most frequent criticism voiced is that schools provide an inadequate and inappropriate preparation into work".
5. The other levels can be briefly outlined as:
   Level II: An occupation normally requiring training to at least masters level or equivalent such that the post requires four years of education following the *baccalauréat.*
   Level III: Training to *brevet de technicien supérieur* level or a diploma from the first cycle of higher education, i.e. *baccalauréat* level plus two further years of education.
   Level IV: Refers to education up to, and including, a technical *baccalauréat* or a *brevet de technicien.* Occupations covered would normally be technician and supervisory posts.
   Level V: CAP or BEP qualifications and qualified blue- or white-collar workers requiring these as a minimum.

    Level Va: Occupations that only require a short education/training course of up to a
year and lead to the *certificat d'education professionnelle* qualification or an equivalent
(Blachère 1992; FEU 1991).

6.   Some sources (*The Economist* 1993c) see the high rate of youth unemployment in France
as being in part a consequence of the national minimum wage, set at just under half of
average earnings.

7.   The legal requirement stimulated a growing market for continuing training, and this led
to bodies being developed which allowed firms to retain some control over the use of
their levies. For example, small to medium enterprises pay about a third of their levy
into mutual funds (*Fonds d'Assurance Formation*), administered jointly by employers
and unions: these enable firms to rearrange the timing of their training investments to
meet their needs, rather than paying out so much every year (Verdier 1994).

8.   The 1971 Act established the model of off-the-job training, involving a predetermined
sequence of studies. These were to be conducted outside the workplace with specially
prepared learning materials. This "academic" model of further training was relaxed
somewhat in the 1980s. Practical training in the workplace was permitted as a use of the
training levy provided employee representatives were informed (Verdier 1994).

9.   The Labour Force Survey-recognized training includes full- and part-time education,
day release from work, training courses and apprenticeships.

9.   A Broader Perspective

INTRODUCTION

In the four previous chapters we have examined the experience of four separate countries. We have seen that there are substantial contrasts between
these countries in terms of training provision and government policy. In
Germany a traditional reliance on apprenticeships going back into the
nineteenth century has developed into the modern dual system with a high
degree of government regulation supported by co-operation between the
"social partners" representing capital and labour. In France, the emphasis
on vocational preparation in the state-run education sector has been accompanied by a levy system to support employer-provided training. Although the UK has had a limited levy system in the past, and although
manufacturing traditionally employed a substantial number of "time-serving" apprentices, in the last decade or so the structural changes in the UK
economy have been associated with considerable expansion of publicly
funded training for young workers and the unemployed. Nevertheless, much
of this training has been employer led, as has been the development of new
forms of competence-based skill certification. In the United States, state
funding has played a much smaller role. Furthermore, employers have traditionally provided little formal training; apprenticeships have not been
important in this century. On the other hand, individuals have typically
financed higher levels of post-compulsory schooling than has been the case in
Europe: much of this education has had a vocational slant.

Despite these differences, in each country training has assumed a higher
profile in recent years than in the past – symbolized in the case of the UK,
France and the United States by the setting of skill targets for the beginning
of the next century. One reason for this is a perceived problem of competitiveness in relation to the economies of the Far East, most notably that of
Japan. The astonishing success of the Japanese economy in the postwar
period has excited widespread admiration. Numerous commentators have
associated this prowess with the use to which labour has been put within
firms; training is an important aspect of this, and the first thing we do in this

chapter is outline the most important features of the Japanese system of education and training.

We then broaden our comparisons by looking at available comparative data on training in a wider range of advanced economies. Much of the data relate to members of the European Union, and we briefly outline some EU initiatives in training and relate them to common economic and demographic problems facing European countries.

JAPAN

One non-quantifiable generalization that appears to hold for both the United States and much of Europe is fear of the prowess of the Pacific Rim economies – especially Japan. Such fear is often exaggerated; in its naive forms it often amounts to a belief that trading relations are a zero-sum game, and that Japanese gains are matched by European or American losses (Krugman 1994). Nevertheless, the Japanese economic growth rate since the war has been so rapid, and its ability to maintain low levels of unemployment even in the changed world environment since the 1970s so impressive, that it is natural to look at Japanese education and training for lessons to emulate. Yet such lessons are not easy to discern, for features of the Japanese system seem to contradict a number of conventional wisdoms.

The Japanese have long seen education and training as key elements in achieving economic success. This is reflected in the tight control exercised by the government over the educational curriculum, and by the Ministry of Labour's development of national Basic Vocational Training Plans (NEDC/MSC 1984). The Japanese system is usefully examined under three headings: general education, vocational education, and vocational training.

There is a great deal of concentration in Japan on formal general education. The country has a highly developed system of internal labour markets, with markedly less interfirm mobility than is the case in other advanced economies (Organisation for Economic Cooperation and Development 1993b: ch. 4). The emphasis is therefore on recruiting the best candidates leaving the educational system, and so there is a premium on educational attainment. At all levels from primary school (where there is sometimes fierce competition to get into good lower secondary schools[1]) to university the emphasis is on hard work; pupils typically spend far longer hours in study than their European or American counterparts,[2] in preparation for the all-important examinations. The curriculum, highly detailed and involving the use of compulsory, officially approved textbooks, is controlled by the Ministry of Education, Science and Culture and incorporates core subjects such as Japanese, mathematics and English. Examinations, however, are set largely by the prefectures (for admission to upper secondary school) and universities to meet their own entrance requirements. Despite having to pay significant fees for upper secondary school attendance, around 95 per cent of all young people stay on at school beyond the age of 15 (when compulsory education ends). Over 35 per cent of the relevant age group enter higher education (though this is a somewhat broader category in Japan than in some European countries).

The general educational achievements of Japanese school students are considerable. In mathematics, for instance, 13-year-old Japanese students outscore their European and American counterparts, in the case of the USA by a factor of two (*The Economist* 1990; Commission on Workforce Quality and Labor Market Efficiency 1989). In standard intelligence tests the average westerner scores 100, while the average Japanese pupil scores 117. Functional illiteracy amongst Japanese adults is virtually unknown, whereas in the USA it is suspected to be over 10 per cent.

Japanese education is not without its critics: it relies heavily on rote learning in schools; its students are not encouraged to be critical or creative;[3] its curriculum is politically controlled; and (despite their high entry standards) its universities do not work their students particularly hard (Hendry 1987). However, it provides an impressive base on which vocational training can subsequently be erected.

The bulk of such training is provided by employers. None is provided during the period of compulsory education, where the curriculum is heavily academic. Although students may opt to enter vocational schools on completing lower secondary school at 15, only about 25 per cent choose to do so (a proportion which has declined considerably since the 1960s). They mainly attend technical and commercial schools. As in many other countries, vocational education of this kind carries less prestige than academic education in Japan, but the average standard of student entrant seems reasonably high, and the syllabus indicates that the work expected (which includes continuing with a significant range of academic subjects) is of a standard approaching that of some craft-level vocational qualifications in Europe (Prais 1987). However, the levels actually achieved are less clear. To graduate from vocational school it is sufficient simply for a student's achievements to be satisfactory. Some students choose to take industrially recognized trade tests, but they are a minority of the vocationally educated. There does not appear to be the same emphasis on vocational certification in Japan as there is in Europe.

Japanese firms seem to prefer to conduct the bulk of vocational training themselves. It is well known that a characteristic of much of the Japanese economy is the lifetime employment system. The importance of this system

Table 9.1   Tenure of job with current employer, 1991

| | Average current tenure[a] | | | % of employees with |
	Men	Women	All	tenure under 1 year
Finland	9.4	8.5	9.0	11.9
France	10.6	9.6	10.1	15.7
Germany (1990)	12.1	8.0	10.4	12.8
Japan (1990)	12.5	7.3	10.9	9.8
Netherlands (1990)	8.6	4.3	7.0	24.0
Spain	10.6	8.2	9.8	23.9
UK	9.2	6.3	7.9	18.6
USA (1992)	7.5	5.9	6.7	28.8

Note: [a]Average number of years employees have been with their existing enterprise.
Source: Organisation for Economic Cooperation and Development (1993b).

can be exaggerated; it applies primarily to large firms and to male Japanese workers, women and immigrant workers being largely excluded. Nevertheless the greater importance of continuing attachment to the firm than is the case in many other countries can be inferred from Table 9.1.

Two indicators, average[4] current tenure and the percentage of employees who have been employed for less than one year, both tell the same story. Japan has (for men at least) the highest average tenure and the lowest proportion of recently joined employees. At the other extreme, the USA has a much higher degree of interfirm mobility and a correspondingly lower continuity of employment. European countries tend to fall somewhere in between.

The significance of the differences in average tenure shown here lies in the relationship which is thought to exist between stability of employment and employer-provided training. As we have seen in earlier chapters, greater continuity of employment is associated with higher levels of training in both a human capital and a labour market segmentation framework. Although comparable data between countries are hard to obtain, within one country (the United States) there is evidence of quite a strong negative relationship between another indicator of tenure, labour turnover, and the incidence of formal training, simple correlation coefficients varying between -0.193 and -0.504 (Organisation for Economic Cooperation and Development 1993b: ch. 4).

Even allowing for differences in tenure, moreover, Japanese firms seem to provide far more training for their employees than most American and many European firms. In particular, Japanese firms emphasize on-the-job training, which is part of a wider emphasis on human resource development. It features such elements as job rotation, transfers between plants, group working and participation in quality circles, together with planned career progression, rather than focusing on particular occupational skills as in most other countries (NEDC/MSC 1984). This has been one reason, it is argued, why Japan is able to adjust to product market downturn and technical change without major job losses.

In addition to a culture which encourages and expects Japanese workers to study further in their own time and commit themselves to a goal of continual self-improvement and lifetime education, the government also plays a role. Although Japan devotes a much smaller proportion of its GDP to direct public spending on training than is the case in Western Europe or the USA, the government is active in forecasting skills trends and setting training targets in the Basic Vocational Training Plan. Tax incentives are provided to firms and individuals to expand training and continuing education. And although the Vocational Training Law makes it clear that training is primarily the responsibility of employers, there is a limited amount of direct provision by the state and the prefectures in such areas as upgrading training, occupational capacity redevelopment training and instructor training.[5]

There are no easy lessons from the Japanese example for Europe and the USA. The system of lifetime employment and heavy reliance on internal labour markets which is associated with high levels of firm-provided on-the-job training seems unlikely to be replicable in Britain and the US, where the free market liberalism and structural change of the 1980s has undermined whatever tendencies existed in that direction. Given the labour market problems currently faced by France, Germany and the other countries of continental Europe, further movements towards security of employment seem unlikely to be feasible in the near future. The only clear lessons are negative ones: substantial state funding of training does not seem a necessary condition for success – and neither does a large scale system of skill certification of the kind found in Germany.

COMPARATIVE DATA

We now move on from looking at the experience of particular countries to see what we can infer from the broad statistical indicators covering education and training which have been used and abused in international comparisons.

Statistical data on training and education present considerable problems. Definitions of terms often differ (for example, much informal training provided in the UK and the US would not be classified as training in

France); information is collected in different ways and from different parties (this matters because employer-provided data may give higher figures for training than employee-provided data: it is sometimes collected in order to claim tax credits or reclaim levies, and there are thus built-in incentives to exaggerate); employer-provided data may often be confined to firms over a certain size (and the size distribution of firms differs from country to country); quantitative data tell us little about quality; and above all, figures need to be put into the context of particular economic and social systems.

But for all these caveats, there is some merit in at least seeing what information is available. In recent years increasing energy has been put into developing cross-national indicators of training effort. International bodies such as the Organization for Economic Cooperation and Development (OECD) and the European Commission, as well as national governments, have taken an interest in the area. So have broadly based bodies such as the US's Commission on Workforce Quality and Labour Market Efficiency, interest groups such as the Confederation of British Industry, and a host of researchers based in universities and research institutes.

The UK's Department for Education, for instance, has for some years published relatively "hard" data on participation in education and training by young people in advanced economies. Recent figures are given in Tables 9.2 and 9.3. Perusal of the footnotes to these tables immediately suggests some of the problems of comparing like with like. However, some general impressions come over. One is that all the countries shown now have a majority of 16–18-year-olds participating in post-compulsory education or training – although Italy and the UK have relatively low proportions of full-time students.[6] Over the 1980s most countries (except those with already high participation rates) experienced an increase in the proportion with some involvement in education or training. In the case of some countries – notably France, Belgium and Spain – this increase was quite dramatic. This probably reflects the abnormally high youth unemployment rates in these countries during the 1980s, rates which encouraged many more young people to delay entry into the labour market.

In most countries male and female young people show approximately the same participation rates. However, Spain, Italy and (more surprisingly) the Netherlands display significantly higher male participation rates. In the case of Spain the big jump in participation between 1986 and 1990 seems to have been an exclusively male phenomenon.

It has been suggested that the differences between countries demonstrated in Table 9.2 partly reflect differences in the employment status of young workers between countries. For instance, many young workers in the UK have employee status. If they attend college on a day-release or evening basis, they will be classed as participating in education or training

Table 9.2 *Participation of 16–18-year-olds in education and training[a] (%)*

	Persons			Males			Females		
	1982	1986	1990	1982	1986	1990	1982	1986	1990
Australia	59	66	69[b]	65	69	71[b]	53	63	66[b]
Belgium	73[c]	81	87[d]	72[c]	77	85d	74c	85	88[d]
Canada	67	75[e]	78[e]	na	75[e]	78[e]	na	74[e]	79[e]
Denmark	72[6]	77	79	na	76	78	na	77	80
France	66	74	82	65	71	81	68	76	84
Germany	84	90[g]	89	87	92[g]	90	82	88[g]	87
Italy	65	na	na	77	na	na	53	na	na
Japan[h]	69	80	79	na	na	76	na	na	82
Netherlands	79[c]	86	87	83[c]	89	90	75[c]	83	84
Spain[i]	47[f]	52	61	46[f]	52	65	48[f]	53	58
Sweden	73	78[d]	73	72	77[j]	73	74	78[j]	74
United Kingdom[k]	65	64	71	67	64	72	64	63	71
USA[l]	79	80	82	80	81	83	78	80	81

Notes: na = not available
[a] Includes apprenticeships, Youth Training and similar schemes.
 Includes higher education for some 18-year-olds
[b] 1989
[c] 1983
[d] 1988
[e] Excludes certain part-time students: 10% at 16–18 in 1986, 16% in 1989
[f] 1981
[g] 1987
[h] Includes estimates for special training schools and Miscellaneous schools
[i] Higher education estimates for all HE 1981: universities only 1986
[j] 1985
[k] Includes estimates for public-sector evening study and for private-sector further and higher education, including training courses with employers
[l] Includes private sector higher education
Source: Department for Education (1993d).

Table 9.3 *Participation in education and training by mode of study, 1990: percentage rates for 16–18-year-olds*

	Full-time	*Part-time*	*All*
Australia (1990)	52	17	69
Belgium (1988)	82	4	87
Canada[a]	78	–	78
Denmark[b]	79	–	79
France[c]	82	–	82
Germany[d]	89	–	89
Italy (1983)	47	18	65
Japan	76	3	79
Netherlands	77	10	87
Spain	61	–	61
Sweden[b]	73	–	73
United Kingdom	40	31	71
USA	81	1	82

Notes:
[a] Excludes certain part-time students: 16% at 16–18 in 1989
[b] All regular formal education now classed as full-time
[c] Apprenticeships are classified as full-time
[d] Dual system participants classed as full-time
Source: Department for Education (1993d).

part-time. German young workers, as we have seen in Chapter 7, will normally be apprentices in the dual system: they may sometimes be classified as trainees rather than employees. Hence, even if they only spend the same amount of time in formal training as their UK counterparts, they could be counted as full-time participants in education and training (Department for Education 1993d). That having been said, it is nevertheless interesting that the UK retains a strong tradition of part-time vocational education, which is also carried forward into rather older age groups.[7]

Within the European Union, comparative data are available from a number of sources: for example the EU Labour Force Survey, which covers a large sample (60,000 in the UK) of the workforce in member countries (Thomas 1992). It has some limitations: for example, it is a household-based survey, and its sampling frame excludes collective households (such as student halls of residence) in some countries. Although sample sizes are set by EUROSTAT[8] in order to ensure that estimates of key variables such as unemployment rates are reliable, calculation of sampling errors and data cleaning are the responsibility of national statistical offices, where practices

Table 9.4   Percentage of 25–49-year-olds in employment receiving training
in the previous four weeks, Spring 1989

Netherlands	19
Denmark	16
UK	11
Germany	6
Ireland	4
France	3
Spain	3
Luxembourg	3
Belgium	2
Italy	2
Portugal	1
Greece	1

Source: Commission of the European Communities (1991).

differ. Moreover, in the training field the LFS suffers from the problem that there are no common questions asked. Instead, each member state is free to set its own questions, reflecting national practices. Although this is understandable, it does mean that "because of the uncertainties arising from the interpretation of guidelines in collecting, categorising and analysing results in each country, further investigation is needed before training statistics from the EC [now EU] Labour Force Survey can be quoted with confidence" (Employment Department 1990: 125).

Some attempts are made. For example, EUROSTAT has published the data shown in Table 9.4. This shows that, across the EU, 6 per cent of all prime age adults in the labour force reported that they had received employment-related training in the previous four weeks.[9] But there were considerable national variations around this figure. Although definitions vary, and nothing can be inferred about the nature and quality of the training provided, the Commission does draw the tentative conclusion that "there was more training activity in the North of the Community than in the South" (Commission of the European Communities 1991: 134).

Instead of asking individuals about their receipt of training, another approach is to ask firms to provide data. One source of information on training across the European Union is the Labour Costs Survey which each country conducts under agreed common definitions. The main problem with this is that only a small part of employers' total "real" expenditure on training is identifiable from the LCS data: on-the-job training, for example, may often not give rise to explicit costs (Employment Department 1991:

*Table 9.5   Vocational training costs as a percentage of total employers'
              costs, 1988*

	% of total costs	Total monthly costs per employee (ECU)[a]
Belgium	0.2	2391
Denmark	2.3	2171
Germany (West)	1.6	2504
France	1.8	2138
Italy	1.3	2063
Netherlands	0.7	2194
United Kingdom	1.5	1732

Note: [a]Converted from national currencies at 1988 annual average
Source: Adnett (1993).

108–9). However, the figures may give some indication of the relative significance of training costs in different countries. The most recent available data are summarized in Table 9.5.

The previous sources pick up both public and private activity. Data for a wider range of countries are available covering government expenditure on training activities. Table 9.6 sets out information on two indicators: training narrowly defined, and a wider measure which covers all active labour market policies. The latter include employment subsidies, counselling services, placement services, and so on; these may often have some element of training involved.

The table groups countries into "high", "medium" and "low" spenders on publicly funded training. There is no clear pattern linking public and private spending. Germany, with its high youth training commitment through the dual system and its relatively high proportion of labour costs devoted to training, is up amongst the leaders in public spending too. On the other hand, Italy, which seems to provide relatively little private-sector training, is also a big public spender – while Japan, which, as we saw earlier, devotes considerable resources to on-the-job training (NEDC/MSC 1984), spends very little public money directly on training. The United States likewise spends relatively little public money on training; on the other hand, its firms are also thought to provide rather little, as Table 9.7 seems to indicate.[10]

It is however difficult, given the limitations of the data and the way in which the various indicators may point in different directions, to draw significant conclusions about the incidence of enterprise-based training

Table 9.6   Public expenditure on training and active labour market policies, 1992

	Public expenditure on training[a] *as % of GDP*	*Public expenditure on all active labour market policies*[b] *as % of GDP*
High Spenders		
Denmark	0.66	1.56
Finland	0.49	1.76
France (1991)	0.57	0.88
Germany	0.65	1.64
Ireland (1991)	0.83	1.51
Norway	0.50	1.14
Portugal	0.68	0.86
Sweden (1992–3)	1.61	3.21
Medium Spenders		
Canada (1992–3)	0.44	0.68
Greece	0.21	0.39
Netherlands	0.26	1.12
New Zealand (1991–2)	0.41	0.74
UK exc. NI (1992–3)	0.36	0.59
Low Spenders		
Australia (1991–2)	0.14	0.34
Austria	0.10	0.30
Belgium (1991)	0.14	1.04
Japan (1990–1)	0.03	0.13
Luxembourg (1991)	0.13	0.28
Spain	0.14	0.57
Switzerland (1991)	0.02	0.27
United States (1991–2)	0.12	0.25

Notes
[a] Publicly funded training for unemployed and those at risk, and for unemployed adults; support of apprenticeship and related general youth training; remedial education, training or work experience for disadvantaged youth.
[a] Includes training, employment subsidies, job creation, support of enterprise schemes, placement and counselling services, geographical mobility allowances, work for the disabled, etc.
Source: Organization for Economic Cooperation and Development (1993b).

Table 9.7   Share of new young recruits who received any formal training from their employers (%)

France	
20–29-year-olds in 1980 with training between 1980 and 1985	23.6
Germany	
dual system apprentices, 1989	71.5
Japan	
new hires from high school, 1984	67.1
first year at firm, worker recall responses, 1989	32.3
United States, 1980s	
first job after leaving school	4.8
training at any job within 7 years after leaving school	10.2

Source: Organization for Economic Cooperation and Development (1993b).

between different countries. As the OECD points out "there is simply no generally recognized or standardized definition of types of enterprise training" (1991: 142). Thus many popular generalizations about the relative significance attached to training in different countries lack adequate quantitative support (Organization for Economic Cooperation and Development 1992).[11]

Rather than attempt to compare incidence between countries, a more promising approach may be to seek common patterns of provision in different countries. A number of observations are possible. One is that "better educated workers are nearly always more likely to receive additional training compared with less educated workers" (Organization for Economic Cooperation and Development 1991: 135). Although the definitions of training and sources of data for Table 9.8 vary considerably from country to country, the same broad pattern is discernible. Training may thus act as a complement to education rather than a substitute. In a human capital perspective, prior education may increase the "productivity" of investment in training, thus raising the rate of return and encouraging a higher level of investment by individuals and firms. In a labour market segmentation approach, of course, the correlation between training and education suggests again how markets may work to amplify initial disadvantage. Rationing of "good" jobs with access to training (see Chapter 3) by education is a likely outcome.

Another generalization is that while women in many countries (e.g. the UK, Germany and the United States) are as likely as men to be undergoing some kind of training, they are less likely than men to receive formal com-

Table 9.8   Incidence of training among employees, by level of educational attainment[a]

Educational attainment	France	Japan	Spain	Sweden	USA
Less than upper secondary	1.3	67.7	0.2	17.6	17.1
Completed upper secondary	3.8	70.1	4.0	30.3	31.0
Completed some post-secondary	4.1	68.9	8.7	38.1	41.9
Completed at least one university degree	4.9	85.0	4.2	42.4	55.6

Note: [a]As percentage of all employees in attainment group. Each country defines training, and the period over which it is received, rather differently.
Source: Organization for Economic Cooperation and Development (1991).

pany training or employer-sponsored outside training.[12] This point is taken further in Chapter 12 and will not be pursued here.

We could add to this the observation that people from ethnic minority backgrounds may be less likely to receive good-quality training than their counterparts from the majority population, even though they appear to possess similar qualifications. For example, virtually all ethnic minority groups in the UK currently have participation rates in post-compulsory education which are higher than those of whites, and amongst young people many ethnic groups such as Indians, Chinese and Africans are on average better qualified than whites. Yet the occupational distribution of these minorities remains unfavourable. Thus only 30 per cent of Pakistani and 23 per cent of Afro-Caribbean men with A Levels or higher qualifications are in higher occupations, as opposed to 37 per cent of white men with the same qualifications. And although LFS data show that they are slightly more likely to be receiving some training than whites, it is probable that the number of training days ethnic minority trainees receive is lower (Walsh 1994). In the United States, whites are distinctly more likely to receive company training than are blacks or Hispanics (Amirault 1992).

Another generalization is that in all countries there is marked variation between industries in the incidence of training. Because this presumably reflects such factors as technology, differential turnover patterns, the size of enterprises and the age and gender composition of the workforce – factors which can vary from country to country – there is not an immutable ranking of industry training incidence. However, it is very common to find high levels of training in finance, health care and public administration and markedly lower levels in such industries as textiles and agriculture.[13]

There are very clear occupational differences in training incidence in all countries. However, occupations are very hazily defined, and although there has been some useful work within the European Union on standardizing definitions, wider comparisons are less feasible. It is apparent that in all countries people in non-manual jobs typically receive both more formal and on-the-job company training than those in manual jobs. Within the non-manual category, those in the higher-level occupations (professionals, managers, etc.) receive more training than those in the lower level (clerical, office workers). However, the picture within the manual classification is more obscure. There is some evidence that skilled manual workers receive more training than the unskilled, although there are countries in which the reverse appears to be true.[14]

Finally, the OECD has examined the relationship between age and receipt of training. There are two patterns: "in some countries, especially those with strong systems of apprenticeship ... the incidence of training declines consistently from the youngest to the oldest", while in other countries "training incidence tends to increase with age, reaching a peak within the 30–44 age band" (Organization for Economic Cooperation and Development 1991: 135). Thus although Germany has a higher proportion of its 16–19-year-olds in training than the UK, a greater proportion of British 25–34-year-olds appear to receive training than their German counterparts (as noted in Chapter 7).

THE EUROPEAN DIMENSION

Comparative work on training is much more advanced within Europe, and especially within the European Union, than elsewhere. A number of recent studies have suggested that there are trends which are common to the labour markets of European countries, and which are likely to have implications for training provision. First, demography (Johnson and Zimmermann 1993; Commission of the European Communities 1992): over the period 1990–2000, the number of young people across Europe will fall rapidly. In the UK 15–19-year-olds will fall by around 8 per cent, 20–24-year-olds by around 25 per cent, and 25–29-year-olds by just under 20 per cent. Significant falls of similar dimensions are going to occur across most of the EU. At the same time, the total population will continue to rise, albeit slowly. The result is that the average age of the workforce will increase.

Until recently, the bulk of resources devoted to training have gone to support initial vocational training for young people. The implication is that both public and private resources will need to be redistributed towards continuing training and retraining of older workers. This would be economically rational if a shortage of skilled labour drove up wage rates and therefore raised the rate of return on training for older workers. It should be noted, however, that theoretical analysis of the implications of demographic change (Blanchet 1993) suggests that the optimal pattern of training will also depend on the (changing) structure of the particular economy in question. Furthermore, in some countries the position may be affected by inflows of immigrants from Eastern Europe. So we should be wary of inferring that there is any simple relation between current demographic trends and training needs.

Another change which is likely to be common across Europe is the greater attention paid to the role of women in the workforce. Activity rates for women have risen significantly in the EC over the last twenty years. In some of the less-developed regions where female economic activity rates were previously quite low, the proportionate increases have been dramatic. Over the 1980s, for example, the increase was of the order of 25 percentage points in Spain and Greece. Women's share of total employment in the EU is projected to rise from 40 to 45 per cent between 1990 and 2000. More startlingly, as much as 73 per cent of all new entrants to the workforce over this period will be female. As we indicate in Chapter 12, at the moment women typically train for "women's" occupations such as hairdressing, medical or dental receptionists, retail sales, and so on; this may have to change.

Women are the overwhelming majority of part-time workers. Across Europe, part-time work is increasing (Commission of the European Communities 1992: 142–4). It rose during the 1980s to constitute over 20 per cent of the workforce in countries such as Denmark, the UK, and the Netherlands (where it rose spectacularly from 16.6 per cent to 33.2 per cent between 1979 and 1990).

The growing importance of part-time work is only one aspect of the trend towards "atypical employment" which analysts have seen developing across Europe. A growing number of workers are on fixed-term contracts, for example. By 1990 around 12 per cent of all male employees in the then European Community, and 8 per cent of females, were working under such arrangements (ibid.: 145). And there has been a growth in self-employment, homework, telework and employment in the black economy. In all such areas, training provision is currently limited or non-existent.

Changes in employment status of this kind are part of a wider pattern of change in the labour and product markets which has ramifications for training provision. Economic restructuring across Europe is the result of the Single Market, technological change, increasing competition from Asia, privatization, deregulation, outsourcing, and so on. It is leading to a decline in the relative importance of large firms in employment – a tendency perhaps exacerbated by the switch from manufacturing to services (services were 44 per cent of EUR12 employment in 1970, 61 per cent in 1989) – and in public-sector employment relative to private-sector. As large firms and the public sector have historically been disproportionate providers of training in most countries, these trends again have implications for future training provision.

A final challenge which European countries face in common is rising unemployment – and particularly long-term unemployment. While the implications of this for training are explored in Chapter 12, we can note here that the long-term unemployed constitute over half the large total of unemployed in Belgium, Italy and Spain – and things are little better in France, Britain and Germany.

EUROPEAN UNION POLICY

Given this background, it is not surprising that the European Union has been active in promoting training, and providing resources for publicly funded training over and above those provided by individual member states. Interest by the Community in training goes back to article 123 of the Treaty of Rome, which set up the European Social Fund "to render the employment of workers easier and increase their occupational and geographic mobility within the Community", and to article 128 which calls for the development of "general principles for implementing a common vocational training policy". In addition, article 118 states that the EC should "promote close co-operation between member states in the social field, including basic and advanced vocational training" (Milner 1992; Addison and Siebert 1992).

The means to achieve these objectives are somewhat circumscribed. Education policy, for example, is supposed to be excluded from the EC's direct influence.[15] The Social Fund (which has worked together with the other structural funds, the European Regional Development Fund and the European Agricultural Guidance Fund) has to be matched by equivalent funding from national governments. This has restricted the selection of projects to those which member states are themselves willing to support. In practice (though this is not supposed to happen) this has frequently meant that the structural funds have paid for training which national governments would otherwise have provided themselves,[16] although some women-only training would probably not have been provided without the ESF.

The Council of Ministers decided in April 1963 on two principles for vocational training; first, that every Community citizen should have the opportunity to attain the highest standard of education and training required to carry out his or her occupation; and second, that the mutual

Table 9.9 *European Community/European Union vocational training action programmes*

Programme	Description	Budget (million ECUs)
Initial vocational training and young workers		
PETRA	Promotes vocational training of young people through exchanges and international partnerships	1992–4: 177
Youth for Europe	Support for networks, study visits, training of youth workers, etc.	1989–90: 17.5 (new budget for 1992–4)
Continuing training		
FORCE	Dissemination of good practice, to promote training schemes with a European dimension, to collect information on continuing training	1991–4: 24
Higher education		
ERASMUS	Exchanges of students and staff	1990–4: 192
COMETT	University–industry partnerships to promote training in advanced technology. Emphasis on small to medium firms	1990–6: 700
Human Capital and Mobility	Creating research networks	1992–4: 500
LINGUA	To improve teaching of Community languages	1992–4: 500
TEMPUS	To encourage training links with Eastern Europe	1990–5: 20
Miscellaneous		
EUROFORM	To set up Community-wide transnational consortia to plan and implement training and employment measures at sectorial and regional levels	1990–3: 300

Table 9.9   European   Community/European   Union   vocational   training
action programmes – continued

Programme	Description	Budget (million ECUs)
Miscellaneous—*continued*		
NOW	To encourage employment and training measures targeted at women	1990–3: 120
HORIZON	To assist training/employment of handicapped	1990–3: 200

Sources: Addison and Siebert (1992); Milner (1992).

recognition of qualifications should be encouraged in order to promote
the free movement of labour between countries. The first of these principles
is somewhat vacuous, but the second has led to a great deal of activity,
particularly since the foundation of the Centre for the Development of
Vocational Training (CEDEFOP) in 1976. This body has done much to
document the variations in training systems in Europe. From the mid-1970s
EC law accepted a range of directives instituting mutual recognition for
professional qualifications in such fields as medicine, dentistry, architecture
and pharmacy. In 1989 a directive was passed, as part of the Single Market
initiative, to require mutual recognition of all higher education diplomas
requiring at least three years' study; compliance with its provisions has,
however, been patchy. Co-ordination and recognition of intermediate and
lower skill levels have proved more difficult because of variations in qualification levels and training methods: most of CEDEFOP's work has been
confined to classification of work content and competencies in broad
groups of occupations (Milner 1992).

The EU has developed a wide range of training initiatives in recent years.
One new impetus to this has been the reform of the structural funds in 1989,
when the reduction of long-term unemployment became a "priority objective for policy action" (Commission of the European Communities 1992:
180).[17] Training is a key element in the EU's policy towards unemployment
and structural change, together with various forms of job creation and
wage subsidy.

Table 9.9 lists some of the EU's more important vocational training action programmes and initiatives, together with an indication of the scale of
funds available. Although the total EC funds deployed to promote training
are substantial, they remain marginal to the training policies of most large

member countries. Although the general drift of the policies favoured suggests a willingness on the part of the Commission to see convergence towards something like the German model (there is frequent emphasis on the role of "social partners", for example), with an emphasis on a high skill equilibrium as a means of increasing European competitiveness against the Far East, there remain important differences of emphasis within national economies which are likely to preclude very much more substantial harmonization of EU training systems for the foreseeable future.[18]

CONCLUSION

Part II of the book has looked in detail at training provision and policies in four advanced economies, and has taken a broad overview of many more. The relative importance of initial versus continuing training, on-the-job versus off-the-job, formally certificated versus uncertificated, varies from country to country. So does the role of the state: although governments intervene in all countries, the degree of involvement is much more marked in France, say, where initial vocational preparation is seen very much as a government responsibility and where firms are taxed to support training, than in the United States. In continental Europe the "social partners" – organized labour and employer associations – are encouraged to play an active role. Such thinking is anathema in the United States and the UK, while in Japan the focus of labour-management cooperation is the firm itself.

At the same time we observe that in most countries there has been a growing importance attached to training in the last decade or so, as a result of rapid changes in the world economy which seem to suggest that the skill levels of the workforce in advanced economies need to be raised. Despite the very different institutional approaches we see that countries do face similar challenges and opportunities.

In Part III we therefore look in detail at three topics which have emerged as common issues from our cross-country comparisons. First, we examine some general principles concerning the role of education as preparation for entry to the workforce. Second, the most urgent economic problem facing many of the countries which we have surveyed is that of the very high levels of unemployment, and especially long-term unemployment, which we have become used to in recent years. We therefore devote a chapter to this specific topic. Finally, we have seen that women are a large and growing section of the labour force, and that their training experiences have typically been rather different from those of men. The implications of this are therefore explored in Chapter 12.

NOTES

1. Competition can start even earlier. In Tokyo there are tutorial institutions which charge large fees for preparing very small children for entry into particularly good kindergartens, where the demand for places exceeds the supply (Hendry 1987: ch. 6).
2. Japan has a longer school working year than most countries – 243 school-days a year, compared with 193 in England (Prais 1987). Perhaps more importantly, a large proportion of Japanese schoolchildren spend several evenings a week in supplementary private classes in order to improve their chances in examinations. In Tokyo up to 75% of 10–12-year-olds are enrolled in such classes. One survey in 1989 indicated that junior high school children only had two hours a day free from work and travelling (*The Economist* 1990).
3. We should be wary of stereotypes. Some attempts are currently being made to broaden the Japanese school curriculum and to foster greater individualism by the introduction of pupil projects. However, examinations are still heavily based on multiple-choice and short-answer papers (*The Economist* 1992b).
4. Data for median current tenure show roughly the same ranking.
5. See NEDC/MSC (1984). Spending on public training facilities is around 0.03% of GDP. (Organization for Economic Cooperation and Development 1993b).
6. In the case of the UK, however, it should be remembered that children start school at an earlier age than children in most other countries and have a longer period of compulsory education than any other country except the Netherlands. Moreover the post-compulsory education participation rate has risen sharply since 1990, the last date shown here.
7. There are, for example, about 2.5 million "mature" (aged 25 plus) part-time students in the UK.
8. EUROSTAT is the Statistical Office of the European Union.
9. This period is chosen as "a compromise between asking about training on a particular day, which would give a very small sample, and asking about training over the whole of the last year, in which the respondent may well have forgotten about training received earlier in the year" (Employment Department 1991; 109). A problem with choosing this indicator is that there is no reliable way of estimating from it the total amount of training received in a year.
10. The differences between the US and other countries in the overall incidence of training may be exaggerated by Table 9.7 because this concentrates on young people. There is, as we have seen, evidence that in the US older workers tend to receive relatively more training than they do in some other countries.
11. In British debate it is well-nigh universally accepted that the UK trains less (and less well) than its competitors (Shackleton 1992). This is held to justify an active training policy. The European Commission also bases much of its argument on the belief that training in some parts of the Union is less adequate than in others (Addison and Siebert 1992: 15). While both these views may be correct, examination of available statistical data will not conclusively demonstrate their correctness.
12. For example, "in the United States, women appear to participate less in formal company programmes, and if they receive schooling as a source of skill improvement, it is less likely to have been employer-supported compared with men" (Organization for Economic Cooperation and Development 1991: 148).
13. Organization for Economic Cooperation and Development (1991: Table 5.6). However, it is important to remember, as we have seen, that incidence is only one indicator of commitment to training.
14. A possible explanation is that some apprentices and other trainees may be classified as unskilled.
15. Although a number of judgments in the European Court have permitted some encroachments in the area of higher education.

16. Although this is supposed to be prevented by the "additionality" principle, it is almost impossible to prevent. The result is a further example, at the European level, of the kind of displacement effect outlined in Chapter 4.

17. The priority objectives now recognized are: first, the promotion of growth and adjustment of "Objective 1" regions, those which are lagging behind the rest of the Community; second, to support "Objective 2" regions which are badly hit by industrial decline; third, to combat long-term unemployment (Objective 3); fourth, to integrate young people into the workforce (Objective 4); and fifth, to adapt agricultural structures and promote rural development (Objectives 5a and 5b).

18. Greece and Holland, for example, have reservations about the appropriateness of a common pattern of training across the Community (Milner 1992: 19). And Robert Lindley has also argued, in a study funded by the European Commission, that the skill needs of the European economies are more complicated than EC policy suggests (Lindley 1991). In some countries and occupational fields, workers may be over-qualified and there exists a danger of "educational crowding out" (see also Chapter 10).

PART III

Issues

10. Education for Work?

INTRODUCTION

It seems likely that employees are going to be more receptive to training if they have received an appropriate education, so in looking at particular national training systems in previous chapters we have also given some indication of the educational set-up. In this chapter we discuss in more general terms the ways in which formal schooling prepares young people for the job market.

Increasingly, young people stay on at school or college beyond the age at which they are legally required to do so. It is pointed out that both the private and social rate of return indicate that post-compulsory education is normally a profitable investment, although analysts differ on the reasons for this.

It is frequently argued that traditional "academic" education, emphasizing learning for its own sake, is ill-suited to the needs of a substantial proportion of young people. As a consequence, educational systems often "fail" individuals who have in principle much to offer. Educational "planning" and a more thoroughgoing vocational education, with an emphasis on work-related knowledge and skills, is often called for. We discuss the case for such policies.

We note that evidence from many countries suggests that, where separate provision is made for a technical or vocational stream or track in educational institutions, such streams typically carry less prestige than their academic counterparts. The reasons for this are explored and some conclusions drawn.

THE ROLE OF EDUCATION

Employer-provided training has to build upon the educational base provided by the school and, for some students, the university and college system. Formal education of this kind is largely the product of the last

Table 10.1   Public expenditure on education, 1988

Country	Total public expenditure[a] on education as % of GNP
Australia (1987)	5.0
Belgium	4.9
Canada	7.1
Denmark	7.8
France	5.3
Germany (West)	4.2
Italy (1987)	4.8
Japan	4.3
Netherlands	6.8
Spain	4.3
Sweden	6.7
United Kingdom	4.6
USA	5.3

Note: [a]Includes subsidies to private sector.
Source: Employment Department (1993).

two centuries. In today's advanced economies, the bulk of such education is provided by the state (although a substantial part of the indirect costs of education, especially past the age of compulsory schooling, are borne by individuals and their families).[1] Such economies typically spend around 5 per cent of their GNP on publicly funded education. Table 10.1 shows that there are some variations from country to country, but these may partly result from differences of definition and too much should not be read into them. Certainly, educational outcome in terms of qualifications, still less economic performance (often held to be the motive for devoting further resources to education), bears little obvious relation to the ratio of government educational spending to GNP.

Education has many functions. Some people continue to see it primarily as an end in itself; in economists' language, as a consumption good. There is undoubtedly some element of truth in this, as many people do value the intrinsic rewards of study and even the status of being a student. Nevertheless, there has always been a strong disposition to see education as a means to an end. In early modern times, education was often advocated as a means of social control. As Adam Smith saw it, an educated population would be less subject to wild enthusiasms and revolution: it was something to be encouraged by the propertied classes (Shackleton 1976). Others saw education as a strictly utilitarian task, teaching reading, writing, arithmetic and some simple technical skills appropriate to the station of life to which most people were called. As it was felt that the poor either couldn't or wouldn't educate their children, charitable and (later) state subsidy was often advocated.

Religion was, of course, an important factor in the equation. For Victorian evangelicals, education was a high-minded proposition, particularly in the reconstructed "public" (i.e. private) schools of mid-nineteenth-century England. Here the emphasis was on a rather muscular Christianity and the classics, with little attention to science and still less on vocational preparation (unless a knowledge of the ancient Romans and Greeks be considered essential preparation for the activities of the rising Imperial Civil Service).

Already, however, there was a different tradition of organized state education growing up in continental Europe, soon to be copied in some respects by the United States. In Germany and France in particular the education system was seen as a means of promoting nationhood, state power and domestic industry. Such objectives tended to be treated with disdain in England (Barnett 1986). The British education system grew up in a haphazard manner, with significant variations between the countries of the United Kingdom and from region to region, and with a large and continuing role for voluntary and religious provision. Unsurprisingly, no national curriculum developed until the late 1980s.

In the twentieth century state education also came to be seen as a means of social engineering. In the liberal rhetoric of Britain and the United States it was seen as an important avenue for individual social mobility. In the totalitarian regimes, however, it became a means of indoctrination and a mechanism for creating the new men and women envisaged by fascist and communist ideologists.

EDUCATIONAL ECONOMICS

Nowadays, as we saw in Chapter 2, it is common to think of education in a human capital framework. Here the emphasis is on individuals choosing to undergo periods of education during which they incur costs (including the opportunity cost of their time) in return for benefits in the form of higher earnings in the future. It is often objected that individuals (or their parents, in the case of younger students) lack the information necessary to enable them to predict likely returns on investment, and that in any case they may take a short-sighted view which discounts future earnings very heavily.[2]

Surprisingly little evidence has been collected to support the view that decisions to stay on in education beyond the end of the period of compulsory schooling are made on economically rational grounds. However, a study by Pissarides (1981), using 1973–8 data for England and Wales, models the staying-on decision as a function of a number of explanatory variables; his work broadly supports the hypothesis of rationality. From first principles, we would probably expect economically-rational young people to be more likely to stay on in education (a) the lower are the real earnings of young people; (b) the higher the real earnings of university graduates; (c) the higher is youth unemployment; and (d) the lower is graduate unemployment. For young males, coefficients on all these variables have the predicted sign and are significantly different from zero. For young females, the evidence is less clear-cut. The unemployment variables are insignificant: there is still, however, a significant relationship between the two earnings variables and the staying-on rate.

Another way to approach this question is to look at the evidence on the rates of return to investments in education. While not conclusive, evidence of positive rates of return is at least compatible with the view that such investments make financial sense for individuals.

Rates of return can be calculated in two ways (Johnes 1993; ch. 3). If we have full information about the costs of education, the likelihood of individuals completing courses successfully, future earnings profiles, probabilities of unemployment, and so on, we can in principle calculate the discount rate at which the presented discounted value of the costs is just equal to that of the benefits associated with spending, say, an extra year in education.[3] This can be done for both private (costs and benefits to individuals) and social calculations. The difference between the two arises principally from the existence in most countries of subsidies to education, and the fact that individuals pay income tax and thus lose some of the benefits of enhanced pay to the tax authorities.

This method requires a great deal of data in order to capture all the relevant costs and benefits of an extra year's education. A cruder method was pioneered by Mincer (1974, 1979). At its simplest it involves estimating an equation of the following type:

$$\ln Y = a + bE + cX + dX^2 + u \qquad (10.1)$$

(where $\ln Y$ is the natural logarithm of earnings, E is years spent in full-time education, X is years of employment experience and u is an error term).

If we hold all other factors constant, staying on an extra year in education raises $\ln Y$ by b. If the extra cost of a year's schooling is taken to be its opportunity cost in earnings forgone, the coefficient b can be

Table 10.2   Rates of return to education in some advanced economies

| | PRIVATE | | SOCIAL | |
	Secondary	Higher	Secondary	Higher
Canada	16	20	12	14
France	12	10	10	11
Japan	10	9	9	7
Netherlands	9	10	5	6
UK	11	23	9	7
USA	19	15	11	11

Note: All figures are percentage rates of return. They are derived from a number of different studies, conducted using different methodologies, at different times; they should be treated very cautiously.
Source: Psacharopoulos (1985).

interpreted as an approximation to the rate of return on investment in an extra year's education.[4] This approach needs less data, but it makes some strong assumptions[5] and it is obviously only able to generate private as opposed to social rates of return.

Table 10.2 provides some figures from a number of countries, based on a variety of sources and methods. Little importance should be attached to the precise estimates, but they do provide some support for the view that it is reasonable to analyse education as a form of investment; on average it seems to provide private rates of return which make it worthwhile.

What can be inferred from the figures for the social rate of return is less clear. In order to read anything into them we must assume that educated people's enhanced earnings reflect the value of their augmented marginal productivity, and that this increase in productivity is the consequence of the educational process undergone. We saw in Chapter 3 that both these assumptions can be queried. For example, some critics of human capital theory argue that formal education adds little to productivity. Qualifications achieved simply perform a "screening" role for employers or a "signalling" function for workers. There are presumably substitutes for education in both these roles.[6] Some credence is given to these critics by studies which have suggested that significant numbers of workers are "over-educated" for the work which they actually perform.

OVER-EDUCATION?

For example, for the United States Rumberger (1981) claimed that the match between skill requirements and years of schooling had worsened

*Table 10.3   Distribution of job skill requirements and educational attain-
ment of employed population, USA, 1976*

Years of schooling	% of employees with this education	% of jobs requiring this education
0–4	1.8	1.6
5–7	4.1	13.2
8–10	16.8	29.8
11–12	44.7	35.4
13–16	25.8	16.1
17–18	6.8	3.6

Source: Rumberger (1981), quoted in Johnes (1993).

between 1960 and 1976. As Table 10.3 indicates, there appeared to be a substantial part of the workforce which was educated above the level strictly required for adequate performance of their jobs. In another US study Sicherman (1991) revealed that 40 per cent of a representative sample of male workers reported themselves as over-educated for the jobs they carried out. Lindley (1991) has pointed out that in the Netherlands those "working below their level of qualification" rose from 7 to 26 per cent between 1960 and 1977. He warns of the more general possibility of "educational crowding-out" in European labour markets, as the more highly qualified replace the less highly qualified even in fairly low-skilled jobs.

One group which is particularly likely to be working below its level of educational attainment is made up of women returners to employment, who often take pay cuts and a decline in occupational status on re-entry into the labour market. Of UK women with degrees, for example, only one-third work in professional or managerial jobs, and one in ten of those with A Levels work in semi- or unskilled jobs (Payne 1991). This question is further explored in Chapter 12. In a similar way, some academically well-qualified individuals from ethnic minorities seem to be disadvantaged compared with apparently similar individuals who are white. White men with given qualifications (A Levels, for example) in the UK are more likely to be in higher occupational categories than men from ethnic minorities with similar qualifications. They are also less likely to end up unemployed (*The Independent* 1993).

Does this mean that qualifications don't really matter? Caution should be exercised before coming to such a conclusion. Qualification levels are imprecise (data typically do not distinguish the class or grade point average of degree-holders, for example), as are job requirements. And it should not be assumed that the "over-educated" gain no long-run advantage from their qualifications: their apparent status may be transient. For example, it is well known that young entrants to the labour market typically switch jobs a number of times in the early stages of their careers as they search for appropriate employment. Similarly, older workers may switch from more-demanding to less-demanding jobs as they move towards retirement. Although "snapshots" of the workforce may show considerable job-qualification mismatch at any moment, over a working lifetime things may look different.

Critics of the human capital model argue that observed over-education fits rather well with Thurow's job competition model, discussed earlier. In this view, remember, potential employees queue for "good" jobs, which carry higher pay and other desirable attributes including training. Employ-ers rank applicants in order of their educational qualifications, which are taken as proxies for characteristics such as inherent ability, motivation, flexibility, trainability, and so on. It has been argued that each individual finds it profitable to secure higher educational qualifications to improve their position in the queue. Unless the supply of "good" jobs – assumed to be determined exogenously – increases, however, there can be an educa-tional "arms race", with first degrees replacing A Levels, high school completions or *baccalauréats*, followed by masters' degrees replacing first degrees as the requirement for success. Individual rationality thus creates collective irrationality.

It is difficult to believe, however, that such a scenario can be common. It implies that the wages in "good" jobs are invariant to the supply of appropriately qualified labour, and thus that employers will continue to pay high wages for ever-higher qualifications, rather than develop alter-native mechanisms for selecting employees.

Whatever the interpretation of the evidence on apparent over-educa-tion, it does serve as a useful corrective to "exaggerated claims, based upon extrapolation from special cases, about the burgeoning job content of the economy as a whole and the need for educational levels to rise to keep pace with the increasing sophistication of the modern world of work" (Lindley 1991: 194). We shall return to this point shortly.

HUMAN RESOURCE PLANNING

One government response to mismatch between job requirements and qualifications is to attempt to forecast skill needs and then try to manipulate student preferences and/or availability of educational provision in order to improve matters. This process of "manpower planning", now renamed "human resource planning", has been practised in many countries since the early 1960s.

Human resource planning involves the production of a forecast, conditional upon projected growth rates of the economy, of the likely number of workers required in broad occupation categories five, ten or whatever years from today. Such forecasts rely on a variety of information sources and techniques. Some are based on employers' estimates of future demand for labour,[7] some are in effect based on input–output relationships held to be characteristic of the economy in question. Others assume that patterns of labour demand characteristic of countries at more advanced stages of economic development will be replicated in other countries at a later date: what the USA does today, Europe does tomorrow. The forecasts may be economy-wide, or may simply concern some sub-group of the workforce which is of concern: scientists, engineers, doctors, teachers.

The forecasts can then be compared with projections of entries to and retirements from the labour force to determine the requirement for additional recruits. Where there is a clear educational route to occupational status, as in the examples just cited, the forecasts may inform planning of the courses to be provided by universities and colleges, and possibly the pattern of incentives to students to enrol in such courses.

Over twenty years ago, Mark Blaug delivered a powerful attack on the theory and practice of human resource planning (Blaug 1972). He pointed out that the common assumption in these exercises of a fixed relation between educational attainments and job requirements ignored economists' emphasis on substitutability amongst productive inputs, and the role played by prices of all kinds. In effect, human resource planning is subject to the same sorts of criticism raised against economic planning in general. It assumes that planners have access to knowledge not available to the private sector, that individuals will follow the plan's requirements irrespective of the pattern of incentives they face, and that planners pursue some conception of the public good. On this last point, Blaug is particularly scathing: "it is a useful rule to regard all references to 'manpower needs' with the suspicion we usually accord to the emotive argument of special-interest groups" (ibid.: 145).[8]

Some other writers take a more favourable view of human resource planning, however. Geraint Johnes argues that educational planners may indeed have knowledge not freely available to potential students. In the absence of published forecasts, individuals will form their own subjective estimates of likely future demands for skills, and they may be badly wrong. "The planners' forecasts do not need to be perfect; in order to be useful they need only be better than the forecasts implicitly made by the consumers of education" (Johnes 1993: 63).

The same author points out that, although the heyday of human resource planning may have passed, governments in a wide range of countries still publish both general and sector-specific forecasts of labour demand, and use them to inform policy. Even in the UK, where scepticism about this sort of exercise has been very marked, both public and private forecasts abound. And the UK government's recent attempts to cut back social science provision in universities in favour of expansion of science and engineering suggests a continued willingness to try to outguess the market.

VOCATIONAL EDUCATION

Apart from attempts to plan provision of post-compulsory education in relation to specific occupational requirements, another common thread of policy in many countries is the attempt to make secondary education more work-orientated. The charge is that schools tend to be dominated by "academic" concerns: a concentration on knowledge for its own sake, discipline-based rather than interdisciplinary, unrelated to real-world problems and standards, and failing to focus adequately on preparation for the demands of employment. For a minority of students, this may not matter; by family background or personal attitude they are sympathetic to learning, and do well in the educational ratrace.

The charge is, however, that a large proportion of young people are not so inclined. They include the droves of young people who still leave school with no significant qualifications in the UK, high school dropouts in the USA and so on. It is argued[9] that they require a more practical, vocationally orientated curriculum. Such a curriculum would concentrate on skills and competences, rather than abstract knowledge. Because its subject matter would be more obviously relevant to future careers, it would engage the attention of many who would otherwise be turned off school. They would then acquire qualifications which would improve their chances in the labour market and provide a firm basis on which employers could build further and more specific training.

Many countries have pursued the goal of vocational education to some degree – but, in the eyes of critics, hardly ever enough. In the UK it has been a long-standing lament that governments "have persisted in keeping vocational education and training out of the education system" (Steedman 1990: 50). In recent years the French system has been most prominent in UK discussion. As we saw in Chapter 8, the French have in recent years developed a school-based model of vocational preparation which contrasts sharply with the work-based training which is such a strong feature of the German system. However, this is still a comparatively new development the long-term consequences of which have still to be seen. So far it has not led to markedly lower youth unemployment in France than elsewhere.

There are certainly difficulties with getting vocational education right. In the UK, the National Institute of Economic and Social Research has been a consistent advocate of improved vocational education in the UK. It has argued, however, that there are weaknesses in much of the thinking characteristic of vocational educators in the UK – such as their down-playing of workshop practice, their "intellectualization" of practical education (Bierhoff and Prais 1993), and the emphasis on "competence-based assessment" at the expense of pen-and-paper tests which at least reveal something about basic literacy and numeracy (Prais 1989).

One problem is said to be that, almost universally, vocational education is seen as an alternative to academic education, rather than as an integral feature of education for all pupils in schools. Although there are gestures towards preparing all students for the world of work (such as the TVEI and Enterprise in Higher Education Initiatives in the UK), by and large the academically bright are steered into studying traditional academic disciplines while the less obviously able are directed towards more utilitarian interests. From time to time efforts may be made to ration academic places in line with conceptions of national "needs", as we suggested earlier. The attempt is then made to divert young people to more vocational studies.

There are endless examples of the ways in which students try to circumvent such restrictions on their choices. In a famous paper written many years ago, Foster (1965) described the "vocational school fallacy" then prevalent in developing economies. Because agriculture dominated many of these economies, educational efforts were often focused on agricultural matters. However, other skills such as numeracy and literacy were imparted alongside agricultural techniques, and graduates would make use of these skills to move to the city to further their education or take white collar jobs. More generally, "vocational" students frequently see their qualifications as a second chance, a means to leapfrog back into what is perceived to be the educational mainstream.

Take the UK's Business and Technician Council Higher National Diplomas, developed in the 1970s and 1980s and offered by the then polytechnics. They were intended to lead into employment, and the curriculum and methods of assessment were designed with the supposed "needs" of employers very much to the fore. These courses typically required one A Level for entry, while degrees required at least two A Levels. On successfully completing an HND, however, students could often transfer into degree courses with advanced standing. These courses were therefore very attractive to those who had done badly in their A Level examinations, irrespective of their actual content. In some institutions a large proportion of successful HND students transferred back into "academic" degrees.

Is this preference for academic courses irrational snobbery? There may be some element of this. But for young people, taking academic rather than vocational courses can make economic sense. They seem to lead on to a wider range of better-paying careers. For example, Psacharopopoulos, reviewing studies from a range of countries, finds that "contrary to what might be expected (because of the non-specificity or non-technicality of the curriculum) social sciences, economics and law graduates are doing rather well" (Psacharopolous 1987: 200).

Certainly, there is little evidence that having a vocational rather than an academic education is a positive advantage to young people in the labour market. In the United States, Grasso and Shea (1979) found an advantage in hourly rates of pay for vocational graduates only among women; amongst men there was no pay advantage in the short run, and possibly some disadvantage in long-run career outcomes. Gustman and Steiner (1981) found that vocational school graduates have no advantage over general programme high school graduates, while Bishop (1991) reached a broadly similar conclusion: vocationally trained school students only do better when they go into a job directly related to their training. In practice large numbers do not do so.

In similar vein, UK evidence suggests that social science graduates have private[10] rates of return on their education as high as engineers (Department of Education and Science, 1988), while Bennett *et al.* (1992) claim that the rates of return on vocational qualifications generally fall markedly short of those on academic qualifications. They estimated the expected lifetime earnings profiles for individuals with different qualifications, using 1985–8 General Household Survey data. They found that rates of return to vocational qualifications were less than those to academic qualifications for both men and women. GCSEs or O Levels led to higher lifetime earnings than low-level vocational qualifications, and degrees offered higher returns than higher vocational qualifications.[11]

These results would not surprise Mark Blaug, who has been a long-standing opponent of excessive emphasis on vocationalism, which he says is "profoundly wrong and is actually grounded in a total misconception of what it is that makes formal education economically valuable" (Blaug 1993: 2). In his view it is the "unintended consequences" of education (socialization, team working, a critical mode of inquiry) that matter more than any particular skills. Going further than Lindley, whose scepticism about the apparent need for ever-higher qualifications we noted earlier, he has also provocatively claimed that "most jobs in a modern economy require about as much cognitive knowledge and psycho-motor skills as are necessary to drive an automobile" (Blaug 1993: 28).

Blaug argues that heavily vocational secondary education is unpopular with students and is taught by teachers with little industrial experience or by recruits from industry who know little about teaching. Equipment is frequently outdated and in any case the ambience of the classroom fails to catch the "rhythm and pace" of industry. It is, as Psacharopoulos (1987) has shown, typically more expensive than academic schooling. Added to its lack of success in terms of pay or job opportunities, the indictment is complete. Blaug quotes the American Department of Education's document *What Works*, a compendium of research results in education. It concludes that students with basic skills of literacy and numeracy and positive work attitudes are more likely to find and keep jobs than those with "vocational skills" alone. Such a conclusion, incidentally, is consistent with the idea that employers value educational qualifications more for their "screening" function than their content. In the absence of any better information, *abiturs*, *baccalauréats* and A Levels provide some evidence of motivation, commitment and achievement. It also squares very much with the view of those employers who blame schools for failing to concentrate on the "basics", and who continue, not at all perversely, to be more concerned about the quality of graduates' general communication skills and ability to learn than with their degree subject.[12]

CONCLUSIONS

Education is valued more than ever before as a means of promoting economic growth through assisting in the accumulation of human capital, and all advanced economies spend growing sums of public and private money on it. At the level of individuals and their families, evidence suggests that it is not unrealistic to assume that investment in post-compulsory education is made on a fairly rational basis, given available information: education usually tends to boost earnings, and private rates of return are positive and sufficiently high to make investment worthwhile. However, qualifications are not an automatic passport to success. For some groups in the population, qualifications do not lead on to high status occupations. Furthermore, there is a more general possibility of overqualification and educational crowding-out, although the evidence so far is not totally convincing.

The belief that civil servants have access to more information than individuals leads most governments to attempt to plan provision and determine educational curricula. As with other forms of central planning, choices made by individuals nevertheless often frustrate the planners.

Finally, one recurrent theme stressed by governments of right and left is the apparent need for education to be more vocational. The evidence suggests, however, that narrowly vocational education is not attractive to individuals or firms. Educational reformers may be better employed in trying to improve basic skills of literacy and numeracy rather than seeking to impose an excessively utilitarian curriculum.

NOTES

1. However, there remains a private sector of varying size. In Europe typically 5–10% of education is privately provided: in the United States and Japan the figure is significantly higher (Johnes 1993: 83). Quite what determines the appropriate mix of public–private provision is unclear. Some economists (Blaug 1972, for example) would argue that there is no more reason for the state to provide education directly than there is for it to produce, say, bread. If there are arguments (presumably on externality or income distributional grounds) for subsidizing education in some way, this can be done by educational vouchers or cash transfers.
2. This is part of the alleged justification for compulsory schooling, although West (1965) has argued that the spread of compulsory education owes more to "producer power": lobbying by professional educators.
3. See Chapter 2.
4. The change in $\ln Y$ is approximately equal to the proportionate change in Y. Thus $(1 + b)$ will be the approximate ratio of earnings with the extra year's schooling to earnings without it, and b can be read as the private rate of return on the extra education.
5. For a discussion, see Johnes (1993: 28–31).
6. For example, employers could make use of aptitude tests, intensive interviews, trial periods of employment and so forth. However, such methods can be expensive and are not always reliable. Very few employers would use such methods while totally ignoring evidence of educational performance.
7. Always a somewhat dubious approach. As the late Lord Zuckerman once ruefully put it, after his experiences on the UK Committee on Scientific Manpower, "one of the least reliable ways for finding out what industry wants is to go and ask industry" (quoted in Blaug 1972: 147).
8. We spoke of the role of pressure groups in stimulating demand for increased training in Chapter 4. In the area of education such special pleading dressed up as concern for the public good arguably reaches its apogee.
9. As if it were self-evident. Rather little research appears to have been done on what young people themselves would like from their schools and colleges.
10. The *social* rate of return on social scientists appears to be significantly higher, presumably because of the lower costs involved.
11. In a human capital framework, one plausible explanation for the differential for degrees over higher vocational qualifications would appear to be the traditional "rationing" of higher education places by entry standards in the British educational system (much less marked in the USA and continental Europe). In recent years such rationing has eased as more higher education places have become available, and theory would predict some convergence of rates of return on different qualifications in the future.
12. A recent study of employers conducted by Birmingham University concluded that "for many of the employers the subject of a student's degree was of little or no relevance. Even where graduates went on to jobs linked to their degree, specialist factual knowledge was not given a high priority. It is far more important for graduates to be willing to continually update their knowledge" (Sanders 1994).

11. Training for the Unemployed

INTRODUCTION

The high rates of unemployment experienced in developed countries in the last fifteen years or so stand as a reproach to governments and the economists who advise them. Although virtually all countries now display higher unemployment rates than in the earlier postwar period, the problem is particularly marked in Europe. There is, of course, no dearth of theories which attempt to explain the rise in unemployment since the 1970s, and its persistence at levels which many experts would have thought impossible in the 1950s and 1960s.[1] The simple-minded Keynesian view, that unemployment was in large measure the consequence of aggregate demand deficiency, was discredited by the simultaneous increases in unemployment and inflation in the 1970s. At a theoretical level, the development of the expectations-augmented Phillips curve analysis (Friedman 1968), and (later) the popularization of rational expectations by New Classical economists (Lucas 1981; Peel 1990), seemed to suggest that an economy could only temporarily be disturbed from its natural rate of unemployment[2] by shifts in nominal aggregate demand. If the unemployment rate was perceived to be too high, this was because of "rigidities" in the labour market, resulting from such factors as excessive government regulation, over-powerful trade unions, and the incentive pattern generated by the tax and social security systems (see, for example, Minford *et al.* 1983). The cure for excessive unemployment involved appropriate "supply-side" remedies rather than the use of fiscal or monetary policies to stimulate aggregate demand.

In the 1980s, there was something of a retreat from the position that "demand doesn't matter". Experience of recession on a scale unprecedented since the 1930s suggested that sharp cutbacks in aggregate demand could have a lasting effect on unemployment – the *hysteresis* effect.[3] Furthermore, "new Keynesian" theorists (Shaw 1990) demonstrated that the wage (and price) rigidity associated with continuing unemployment could have a variety of alternative explanations to those proposed by the New Classicals.

As these new ideas developed, labour economists focused their attention on wage rates and earnings as the most important characteristics considered by workers and employers when rejecting and offering jobs. In particular, attention was paid to the reservation wage, the wage below which workers are not willing to take up employment.[4] Amongst other variables, training and education are influential forces affecting the level at which reservation wages are set.[5] As we have seen earlier in the book, the idea that education and training serve as determinants of earnings is a key feature of human capital theory, and the decision to invest in skill enhancement is made in the expectation that costs incurred now have a payoff well into the future.

In this chapter we first address some underlying theoretical issues relating education and training to unemployment. Second, we look at empirical studies intended to bridge the gap between theory and the real world.

DURATION DEPENDENCE, SCREENING AND HYSTERESIS

On theoretical grounds, it is suggested that training can affect the level of unemployment in two (not mutually exclusive) ways. First, bear in mind that amongst the jobless the probability of *remaining* unemployed varies considerably. For example, the longer an unemployed person has already been out of work, the more difficult it is to find a job. Economists refer to this as *duration* or *state dependence*. On the employees' side, reasons for this may include falling motivation and lower search intensity as the unemployment spell lengthens. Employers, on the other hand, may see the longer-term unemployed as being insufficiently prepared to meet the challenges of ongoing technological change. Human capital will depreciate, as individuals are no longer receiving the continuing training necessary to maintain their productivity: "the unemployed have no opportunity to maintain and update his/her skills and knowledge. The longer the period of unemployment, the larger these human capital losses and the lower the probability of finding a job will be" (Bourdet and Persson 1992).[6]

But does the depreciation of human capital suffice to explain persistent high rates of unemployment? And can the provision of remedial training improve the situation? It is here that the second potential influence of training comes into play.

Instead of looking at training achievements simply as a means of accumulating and maintaining the human capital stock, we need to remind ourselves that involvement in training also has a *signalling function*. As noted in Chapter 3, training and educational achievements may be taken

Table 11.1   Long-term unemployment as percentage share of total unemployment

Year	Britain	Germany
1981	22.0	16.2
1983	36.5	28.5
1985	41.0	31.0
1986	41.1	31.9
1987	40.8	31.8
1988	39.6	32.9

Source: Organisation for Economic Cooperation and Development (1991).

by employers as proxies for inherent abilities, diligence and other not-easily-observable personal characteristics which help determine the employability of workers. Thus training has a *sorting* (or *screening*) function for employers faced with an excess of job applicants.

It is reasonable to assume that both mechanisms – duration dependence and sorting/screening – play a significant role during economic downturns. "An economic downturn increases the inflow rate of unemployed with less competitive characteristics and reduces their outflow rate . . . we may expect an increase of the ratio of long-term unemployment to total unemployment in times of economic downturn" (Bourdet and Persson, 1992). Another way of putting this is to say that we may expect a decrease in the ratio of completed to uncompleted unemployment spells. Such developments have indeed been witnessed, and Tables 11.1 and 11.2 give some calculations of this kind for the labour markets of Britain and (West) Germany during the 1980s.

As pointed out earlier, economic recovery on its own need not necessarily lead to falling rates of unemployment. For example, the fall in GDP in the UK in the early 1980s ceased after 1981, but total unemployment (and within this, long-term unemployment) continued to rise for a further five years. Similarly, following the German recession of the early 1980s, positive growth rates reappeared in 1983 – but unemployment continued to rise until 1985, while long-term unemployment did not fall until the late 1980s. The persistence of high unemployment after demand shocks is, as we have noted, now described by economists as the hysteresis effect. It is argued that unemployment is not only affected by present macroeconomic conditions but also depends upon the unemployment history of a country. Over time, economic recovery may lower the level of unemployment somewhat, but it will not be enough to bring it back to its level before the downturn. There

Table 11.2   Completed and uncompleted spells of unemployment in Britain and Germany

Year	Completed duration of all spells (Cs) (months)		Uncompleted duration of all spells (Us) (months)		Ratio Cs/Us	
	Britain	Germany	Britain	Germany	Britain	Germany
1983	9.0	7.4	18.0	9.2	0.50	0.80
1984	9.3	7.4	20.8	10.5	0.45	0.70
1985	9.2	7.4	22.2	11.6	0.41	0.64
1986	8.9	7.2	24.5	12.5	0.36	0.57
1987	8.7	7.3	24.5	13.0	0.35	0.56
1988	8.0	7.2	24.0	13.6	0.33	0.53

Sources: Department of Employment (Britain), Bundesanstalt für Arbeit (Germany); authors' own calculations. Results obtained by using Kellerer's traditional spell formula: $d(Bb + A) = 2Bab\,(tb - ta)\ /\ A + Z$, where d = duration of completed spell, Bb = number of unemployed in period b, Z = number of unemployment leavers, A = number of entries in unemployment. Crucial assumption: stationary process over time.

are *transitory* and *permanent* components of the hysteresis effect. Bourdet and Persson argue that

> how quickly the transitory hysteresis effects on unemployment will vanish and how large the permanent hysteresis effect will be can be expected to depend in part upon the extent and composition of labour market policy. ... this is the case because labour market policy measures ... can be expected to affect the duration dependency processes and sorting processes. (Bourdet and Persson 1992).

As this chapter is mainly concerned with the effects of training on unemployment, the following sections examine in particular the extent to which training can improve the re-employment probabilities of the unemployed.

SOME THEORETICAL FOUNDATIONS

The effectiveness of training and further education for the unemployed has become a major public policy issue. Before we look at empirical results of particular training schemes, however, we need to explore in more detail the theoretical arguments concerning the effectiveness or ineffectiveness of training schemes.

It is widely believed that certain occupational and individual characteristics inhibit or worsen the re-employment prospects of the unemployed.

This belief is strongly associated with the understanding of unemployment as a "structural" problem. This form of unemployment arises because displaced workers possess the wrong skills and inadequate occupational and/ or regional mobility to fill available vacancies. In this view, training can improve matters in two ways. First, if unemployment is solely a problem of observable skill deficiencies, job prospects for the unemployed can be enhanced by offering courses and programmes leading to recognised and appropriate vocational qualifications.

Although nearly everybody agrees on this, in practice matching training to jobs presents considerable problems. Stiglitz (1975) made the point that "educators often talk of the importance of matching an educational programme to the needs and abilities of our students". However, the matching process is rather like a marriage: its needs are dynamic. Just as a couple, however initially well-suited, need to adjust over time to inevitable changes in the domestic and external environment, so do firms and individuals. "As the characteristics of the economy, the individual, and the firm change over time, matches that were once good can become bad" (Devine and Kiefer 1991: 3). The matching process thus necessarily goes hand in hand with a degree of uncertainty as the relevance of skill qualifications to work performances of potential employees cannot be perfectly foreseen. Labour economists refer to this situation as a "noisy state", where "uncertainty and incomplete information are prevalent" (ibid.). When we add to this the view that initially unobservable characteristics of adaptability, honesty and diligence are going to play a crucial role, this leads on to the second function which education and training performs.

As already pointed out, unobservable heterogeneity among workers can be partially overcome by employers using prior education and training as "screening devices". It is argued that employers are not simply interested in specific knowledge or general work-related skills (the "cognitive effects of training"). They are also interested in attitudes, motivation and social skills (the "non-cognitive effects" of training). The latter are virtually impossible to test and employers are likely to use superficial characteristics, including training credentials, for their hiring decisions. As the Organization for Economic Cooperation and Development has put it:

> in its strong version, the sorting–screening perspective treats education [and training] as producing information about pre-existing individual aptitudes and behavioural traits ... rather than [as] any cognitive development or psycho-motor skills gained through education [and training]. ... weaker versions of this perspective provide a role for cognitive developments and formation of psycho-motor skills but nevertheless argue that empirical estimates of the rates of returns to schooling inflate the pay-off to this development. (Organization for Economic Cooperation and Development 1989: 3).

So the training process can provide a means of screening or sorting for "good" workers, and by helping these workers signal their desirable characteristics to employers can improve their re-employment prospects. Similarly, prior training and educational qualifications will also assist in the screening process. However, two problems suggest themselves.

First, it is clear that there is not a 100 per cent match between credentials and worker productivity. Nor is there, of course, an exact match between credentials and pay. However, if the fit between pay and credentials is better than that between productivity and credentials, there will inevitably be differences between private and social returns to education and training – a problem addressed in previous chapters.

Second, in a world where there is known not to be a perfect match between certification and productivity, employers are likely to use other personal characteristics as well as, or instead of, formal qualifications. In many developed countries it is in principle illegal to use such characteristics as gender, ethnic status or age as a means of allocating scarce jobs; in practice, legislation is often ineffective. We have pointed out elsewhere in the book that there are differences in access to occupations and associated training for different groups, even when prior education and other economically relevant characteristics seem broadly comparable. To the extent that employers accord importance to such characteristics as gender and ethnic status, training will be less effective as a means of improving the re-employment prospects of the unemployed. This truth, however, may be concealed if training places go disproportionately to favoured groups, as we have indicated before. For example, if white males are favoured by employers who are recruiting staff, and if white males are over-represented amongst trainees on a particular scheme, training may be seen as the cause of their success in the job market. Black females undergoing identical training, however, would not do as well on completion of their courses. This point can be further emphasized by reference to a model developed by Phelps (1972).

PHELPS'S MODEL OF DISCRIMINATION

Suppose that employers are able to measure the performance of potential employees in some kind of test, y_i, which is proxied by a measure of the applicant's degree of qualification, q_i, plus an error term, μ_i:

$$y_i = q_i + \mu_i \qquad (11.1)$$

The qualification term q_i is estimated by introducing a social characteristics variable, x_i, which, in Phelps's model, is believed to be race-related such that

$$q_i = \alpha + x_i + \epsilon_i \tag{11.2}$$

with

$$x_i = (-\beta + \epsilon_i)c_i, \qquad \beta > 0, \tag{11.3}$$

where $c_i = 1$ if the applicant is black and zero otherwise.

Developing Phelps's model a little further, in order to take into account other "socially disadvantageous" factors, x_i can also be interpreted as a vector of several personal and occupational characteristics such as gender, age or prior educational status. If certain characteristics are believed by the employer to be socially disadvantageous, then one might expect to find lower predictions of q_i for those groups with these characteristics than for those groups without them, although both groups may have equal test scores. Note, however, that only in the special case of $\epsilon_i = 0$ is this strictly true. As in Phelps's model, this crucial assumption is made to supply a highly stylized illustration (Figure 11.1) where prediction curves relating q_i to y_i for groups with disadvantageous characteristics lie parallel and below the prediction curves of those groups without these characteristics.

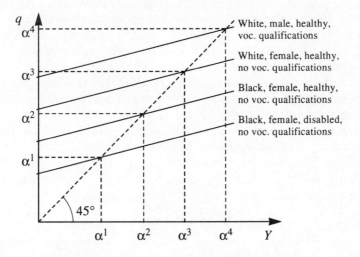

Figure 11.1   Prediction curves and personal characteristics

The more significant the discrimination on grounds unrelated to vocational qualifications, the less retraining and further education schemes have to offer to the unemployed. This has led some commentators (Köditz 1990; Lange 1993a) to argue for moving away from training schemes as such towards counselling and placement services for the unemployed and potential employers. Such services can try to address the specific problems individuals face; such problems, as we have indicated, may only partly, if at all, be caused by skill deficiencies.

PROGRAMMES AND SCHEMES

In previous chapters we have already seen how government training provision can differ from country to country. The aim of this section, therefore, is not to detail particular schemes but to outline some of their common elements.

Training schemes and other active labour market policies for the unemployed can be classified under three main headings. First, the unemployed may participate in training and further education schemes targeted at the inadequacy of their vocational skills and qualifications. Courses of this kind are mainly full-time and can last several years.[7] They may vary considerably as to type, content and location. Some countries give particular emphasis to firm-specific vocational content (in the UK, for example), whereas in others participants are required to attend college-based education combined with firm-based training (in Germany). Training and further education courses are seen to be of particular importance for those unemployed people who previously worked in declining industries or in areas where formal vocational qualifications were of lesser importance. In the past, these programmes were primarily targeted at young people; but with an increasing proportion of the unemployed being classified into "prime-aged" and "older workers" categories this has changed (Lange 1993a).

The second group of schemes consists of work-creation measures. Schemes of this kind are primarily targeted at the "hard-to-place" unemployed. The long-term unemployed thus form the largest group of participants. We can further distinguish between two broad types of job-creation measures. In one, the unemployed may be placed in schemes which are intended only to assist community projects (jobs in auxiliary health care and environmental improvements, for example), and do not directly compete with private sector activity. However, an increasing proportion of the unemployed in some countries, notably Germany, find publicly financed, temporary employment in the private sector, where employers' willingness to take on the unemployed is encouraged by a subsidy which covers a large part of their wage bill.

It is mainly this latter type of work creation with which defenders of free market principles take issue. It is argued that these jobs for the unemployed, especially the long-term unemployed, can only be created at the expense of

Table 11.3 Entries into labour market programmes, as percentage of the workforce[a], unemployment[b] and long-term unemployment[c]

Country:	Germany	France	Ireland	Netherlands	Portugal	United Kingdom
U-Rate	8.7	10.0	16.7	8.3	5.8	8.2
LTU (as % of total unemployment)	32.9	44.8	65.8	51.2	56.6	40.8
Training and Further Education[d]	4.1	4.1	3.6	1.4	1.2	1.1
(i) for the unemployed[e]	3.7	2.5	1.7	1.4	—	1.1
(ii) employed	0.5	1.7	2.0	—	1.1	—
Training for unemployed youth	0.7	2.8	3.3	0.9	0.6	0.8
Subsidy schemes[f]	1.5	1.2	1.6	0.3	0.4	0.2
(i) private placement	0.1	0.4	0.2	0.1	0.1	—
(ii) public placement	1.4	0.7	1.3	0.2	0.3	—
(iii) incentive scheme for self-employment	—	0.2	0.1	—	—	0.2

Notes:
[a] in 1991; for the UK in 1990; Germany includes Eastern Germany.
[b] in 1988.
[c] in 1988; Ireland and Portugal in 1987.
[d] Due to missing information or unclassified measures, some data may not sum up in total.
[e] or those under threat of becoming unemployed.
[f] As [d].
U-rate = Unemployment rate.
LTU = Long-term unemployment.
Sources: informisep 1993; OECD 1992; Bundesanstalt für Arbeit 1992.

potential jobs for young workers entering the labour market and the short-term unemployed (Scharpf 1987). Problems of deadweight loss and substitution effects have already been addressed in Chapter 4; they add additional force to this criticism.

The final type of measure can be described broadly as "counselling services" for the unemployed. Guidance and counselling have gained in importance as other policies have frequently been accused of being insufficiently targeted on the needs of the heterogeneous groups consti-tuting the unemployed. According to Köditz (1990), the most important instruments of counselling activities include provision of job information; assessments of aptitudes and abilities by means of guidance interviews (tests, group sessions); recommendations (on the basis of assessments); and help with placement or job-hunting. It is believed that counselling services are of particular help for the most disadvantaged groups among the un-employed, i.e. the disabled, older and long-term unemployed workers. There are, of course, other programmes which may enable the unemployed to find work, such as financial incentive measures for self-employment. However, these schemes are not as common in all countries as those out-lined above. Table 11.3 illustrates how widely particular programmes are used and how the coverage of these schemes compares to the rates of un-employment and long-term unemployment across a range of European countries.

MACROECONOMIC EFFECTS OF TRAINING AND JOB CREATION

When assessing the overall effects of training and job creation programmes economists usually focus their attention on two variables: the level of em-ployment, and real wages. These variables feature in a diagram employed by the OECD to analyse the effectiveness of active labour market policies and show how such policies produce new equilibria in the labour market (Or-ganisation for Economic Cooperation and Development 1993b: 47). This diagram, of the kind popularized by Layard and Nickell,[8] is reproduced as Figure 11.2.

In the diagram, an upward-sloping wage-setting curve, indicating the positive relationship between higher employment and higher real wages, intersects with a conventional labour demand schedule and determines equilibrium levels of real wages and employment. The various effects of particular schemes can now be analysed, provided that the employment le-vels shown on the horizontal axis are interpreted as "net employment", i.e. excluding participation in labour market programmes.

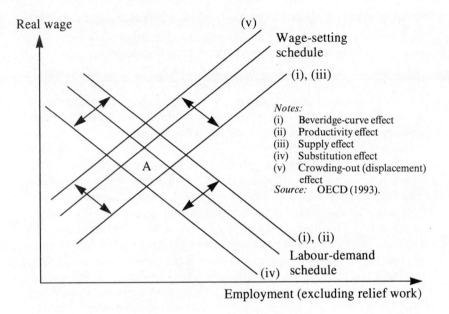

Figure 11.2   Macroeconomic effects of training schemes

First, if the efficiency of the matching process can be increased through training, a "Beveridge-curve effect" (fewer vacancies per given number of jobseekers) occurs, which consequently results in reduced wage pressures (a downward shift of the wage-setting schedule in the Layard–Nickell set-up). In addition, hard-to-fill vacancies (frequently associated with so-called skill shortages[9]) are often seen as extremely expensive to employers because hiring costs increase (repeated advertising, positions temporarily filled by workers with skills below requirements, and so on). If training can reduce the number of these vacant positions and respective costs, the labour demand schedule may tend to shift to the right. Both of these effects lead to higher levels of employment.

A second effect can arise because of positive externalities of on-the-job training, especially in work creation and other subsidized employment schemes. As indicated in Chapter 2, the "new growth economics" stresses this point: human capital embodied in a worker may well lead to increased productivity of colleagues (Lucas 1988). Hence, though such heuristic models are not as yet supported by a great deal of empirical evidence, there is at least the theoretical possibility that labour productivity may generally increase, leading to outward shifts of the labour demand schedule which, in turn, increases employment and wages.

When training and other active labour market policy measures are particularly targeted at the long-term unemployed, another potential effect of programmes comes into play. It is generally believed that those jobless who are out of work for a considerable period of time do not in effect compete any more in the labour market. By reducing the number of long-term unemployed and other disadvantaged people in the labour market, therefore, competition for jobs may increase and wage pressure may be reduced.[10] The corresponding downward shift of the wage-setting schedule leads to higher levels of employment.

Thus far the analysis has suggested only the positive employment effects of active labour market programmes. Unfortunately, there are also distorting effects which must be looked at closely to understand the limitations of training and other active measures. We have seen that subsidized job-creation measures may, in theory, lead to increased labour productivity. However, subsidized employment programmes are, by definition, incentive schemes for employers who are compensated for their willingness to take on the (mainly long-term) unemployed by partial public financing of their wage bills. It therefore becomes profitable for employers to substitute regular and "expensive" employees by "cheap", subsidized workers. Effects of this kind are quite common, as explained in previous chapters: one British analysis reported substitution effects of up to 20 per cent (Deakin and Pratten 1987). The implication is that unemployment is created elsewhere: the labour demand schedule shifts to the left and regular, unsubsidized employment is therefore reduced.

Finally, by reducing the loss of income and the risk of (long-term) unemployment, schemes may have adverse effects on wage-setting as unions and individuals are less inclined to wage moderation. In diagrammatic terms, this produces an upward shift of the wage-setting schedule which, in turn, reduces regular employment.

We have seen, therefore, that the macroeconomic effects of active labour market policies, however well-intentioned, may in principle go either way. We certainly cannot conclude *a priori* that government-sponsored training and other active labour market programmes necessarily reduce unemployment: it all depends. To explore this point further, we shall survey some of the empirical work on this topic.

EMPIRICAL SPECIFICATIONS

We have learnt that under certain circumstances training and other active labour market programmes may provide effective help to bring people back to work. Over recent years the average share of active programme expenditure (as opposed to passive spending, such as that on unemployment benefits) in total government labour market spending has increased steadily (from about 33 per cent in 1985 to almost 37 per cent in 1990). The trends depicted in Figure 11.3 also show that over the same period of time average unemployment rates in OECD countries have decreased (from 7.9 per cent in 1985 to 6.49 per cent in 1990). Nothing can be inferred from this about the direction of causation, however. Serious analysis of the question has been based on microeconomic studies.

In the last decade there has been an explosion of microeconomic studies, aided by the increasing availability of datasets and growing sophistication in modelling techniques. Recent studies of this kind include work by Ridder (1986) for the Netherlands, Björklund (1990) and Korpi (1992) for Sweden; Dolton *et al.* (1992a and b) for the UK; Breen (1991) for Ireland; Raaum (1991) for Norway; and Spitznagel (1989) for West Germany.[11] The general approach used for these evaluations is to compare two similar (in the optimal case, two identical) groups of individuals who either did participate (group 1) or did not participate (group 2) in training programmes, and to calculate the impact of participation upon the probability of becoming re-employed.[12] Dolton *et al.* (1992b), for example, use the following specification:

$$P_{it} = F(aX_i + BD_{it}) \tag{11.4}$$

where P_{it} is the probability of employment for the ith individual in period t. F represents a suitable distribution function and aX is an individual specific component which is a linear function of a vector of individual characteristics, X, with coefficient vector a. X usually includes characteristics such as gender, age, race, former education and qualification standards, marital status, regional unemployment rate and so on.[13] In this specification, D is a variable indicating whether the individual participated in training.

Δ_{it} can then be treated as an employment effect where

$$\Delta_{it} = E(P_{it}|D_{it} = 1) - E(P_{it}|D_{it} = 0) \tag{11.5}$$

$$\Delta_{it} = F(aX_i + b) - F(a_i). \tag{11.6}$$

In other words Δ_{it} indicates employment probabilities for two individuals with identical (observable) characteristics, with the difference being their participation in training programmes. Similar models can be found in the studies mentioned above.[14]

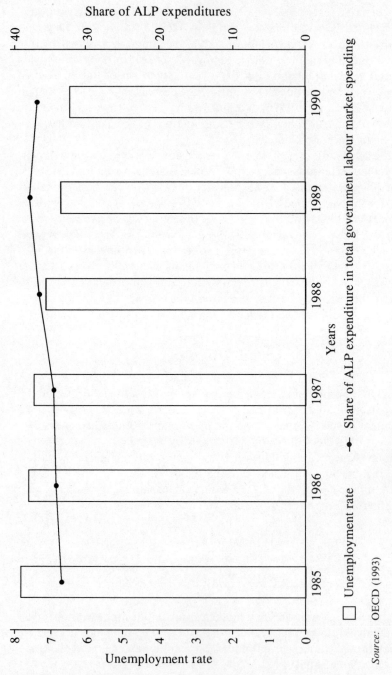

Share of ALP expenditures

Unemployment rate

Years

☐ Unemployment rate

◆ Share of ALP expenditure in total government labour market spending

Source: OECD (1993)

*Figure 11.3 Unemployment and active labour market expenditure
Simple average for OECD countries (excluding Iceland & Turkey)*

At first sight, modelling the impact of training in this way seems highly promising. Provided that data are collected in a coherent manner and that reliable survey results are available, care can be taken about (observable) heterogeneity among the unemployed, and even different types of training provision can be examined and compared.[15] However, of course, all such studies have some drawbacks.

Some Difficulties

The majority of evaluation studies have focused their attention on the length of unemployment spells and respective re-employment probabilities. Although the insights derived from these studies are valuable, questions about the employment stability patterns of "successful" trainees arise almost immediately. Are the new jobs stable, or simply a temporary reprieve from unemployment? This issue "is one that has received relatively little attention in evaluation studies" (Korpi 1992: 2). Dolton, *et al.* (1992b) add that "the conventional approach models the probability of employment at a particular point in time and therefore suffers from the fact that the point chosen is arbitrary and is usually imposed on the researcher by the survey used". Longitudinal analyses are still rare.[16]

Critical attention must be given to the sample chosen to examine the effects of schemes on re-employment. There can be selection biases at work which may affect the outcome of the evaluation. An aspect of this problem has been discussed in earlier chapters in the context of schemes which "cream" potential trainees. Raaum describes the general problem thus:

> Motivation is presumably an individual characteristic important to the quality of job offers received by any unemployed worker. This motivation, however, is impossible to observe in practice. Our estimates of the training effect will be biased if motivation also affects participation, either because the more motivated persons apply for LMT (labour market training) or because the administrator can observe and emphasizes this characteristic when persons are enrolled. Put crudely, a superior employment performance will not reflect an impact of the training but rather the better motivation among participants. (Raaum 1991: 15–16)

Hence, there are not only problems with unobserved heterogeneity but also criticisms of unrepresentative samples which must cast some doubt on the usefulness of evaluation studies.

In sum, though it is interesting to examine whether at a particular point in time certain programmes seem to be better-suited than others to bringing the unemployed back into work, over-confident assertions about the effectiveness of particular schemes need to be looked at with caution.

Some Results

Given these theoretical difficulties with training evaluations, it is un-
surprising that empirical results often appear to contradict each other. While
some of the studies conclude that training programmes have a positive
impact on transition rates out of unemployment, others fail to find any
significant results on respective re-employment probabilities. Gritz (1988)
reports that some public training schemes increase the rate of transition
from employment to non-employment. Private programmes, on the
other hand, produce the opposite effect. Furthermore, he claims that
training is of benefit for women but can lead to decreased transition rates
from employment to non-employment among minorities. Ridder (1986), on
the other hand, found decreased transition rates out of employment for
women, young people and minorities. Korpi (1992) reports that employment durations increase as a result of manpower programmes and that
though previous unemployment had a negative effect on employment
stability patterns, no significant impact of the length of the latest unemployment spell was found. Sehlstedt and Schröder (1989) report no
significant effect of training programmes at all. British evidence by Dolton
et al. (1992b) suggests that ex-trainees obtain jobs at a slower rate than
non-trainees even when the time on the training schemes is excluded.
However, they found evidence suggesting that female trainees obtain
"good" jobs at a faster rate than non-trainees.

Confused? We shouldn't be. Apart from the obvious point that the
content and quality of training schemes for the unemployed differs
from scheme to scheme and even within schemes,[17] there are other reasons
why outcomes may differ: for instance, different data sources. Surveys
are conducted differently asking different questions and are targeted
at different groups of people. Hence, international comparability is
rarely provided. More importantly, however, even if care is taken to
compare identical groups of people (based on observable characteristics),
unobservable characteristics inevitably exist and differ. People grow
up under different economic and social conditions; hence, people are
simply not identical, and neither are their responses to training
programmes.

These results are of undeniable academic interest. However, their policy
implications seem rather limited. Even were there more unanimity in findings, it would need an act of faith to conclude that a training programme
which appears to have worked in country A could be transferred to country
B and produce similar results. Different institutional, economic and social
environments reduce such transferability.[18]

CONCLUDING REMARKS

The high levels of unemployment experienced in many developed countries since the 1970s have led governments to search with increasing desperation for new methods of getting people back into work. New training and re-training schemes for the unemployed have been a common response. Such schemes certainly have an immediate impact by getting people off the un-employment count, but this chapter has suggested that their longer-term effects are more doubtful. Although there are theoretical reasons why training schemes might reduce unemployment, there are also reasons why they might have the opposite effect. Although studies can be cited showing that some schemes appear to increase the probability of individuals being re-employed, in many cases there remain questions about the stability of such re-employment. Moreover, inability fully to control for personal characteristics which affect employability adds further caveats to any conclusions drawn from such studies.

NOTES

1. For a wide-ranging survey of theoretical and empirical material on unemployment, see Layard *et al.* (1991).
2. The natural rate of unemployment is that rate at which the demand for labour and the supply of those willing to accept work is equal; there is no Keynesian, "involuntary" unemployment. At this unemployment rate, which is compatible with any *sustained* expected rate of inflation, there is no tendency for inflation to increase or decrease. Thus it is also known as the non-accelerating inflation rate of unemployment, or NAIRU.
3. In hysteresis models, the natural rate or NAIRU is not independent of the actual rate of unemployment. On the contrary, it is *path dependent:* if a demand "shock" temporarily raises unemployment, workers may not be re-employed when demand returns to normal. There are various reasons for this: one is that workers may be stigmatized by the experience of unemployment. The consequence is that aggregate demand matters for unemployment in the long term as well as the short term. For a discussion of hysteresis in the European context, see Blanchard and Summers (1986, 1988).
4. For a discussion of reservation wage policies and job search models, see Mortenson (1986) and Devine and Kiefer (1991).
5. In the short run, at least, training credentials may increase wage expectations. The longer the unemployed remain out of work, however, the more likely it is that downward pressures are imposed on the wage rate at which employment would be accepted. Over time, therefore, reservation wages exhibit downward dynamics.
6. "However, it should be noted that a necessary condition for this relationship is that the reservation wages of the unemployed are not adjusted downwards sufficiently to offset these losses of skills" (Bourdet and Persson 1992: 2).
7. In Germany, for example, retraining courses can last for up to three years.
8. Such diagrams illustrate the effects of changes in the bargaining strengths of labour and employers in imperfectly competitive markets (Layard and Nickell 1986).

9. However, the causal relationship between hard-to-fill vacancies and skill shortages should be looked at with some caution. The problem of filling a vacant position may sometimes stem from other factors than unskilled labour; for example, low rates of pay or bad working conditions.

10. However, it has also been argued that long-term unemployment is a phenomenon that is not caused by inflationary wage pressures. Whether a reduction in long-term unemployment *per se* will lead to reduced wage pressures is therefore highly questionable.

11. Some results on training participation in Eastern Germany can be found in Bellmann *et al.* (1992).

12. Such studies use statistical methods to separate out the effects of individual characteristics on training outcomes after the event. An alternative approach is to design training "experiments" where scheme participants and control groups are randomly assigned in advance. As we indicated in Chapter 5, a number of such experiments have been conducted in the United States. For various reasons large-scale studies of this kind are virtually non-existent in Europe. They present their own problems. See Organization for Economic Cooperation and Development (1993b: ch. 2) for a discussion and a brief survey of experimental programmes.

13. Note the similarity to Phelps's model (the developed version) discussed earlier in the chapter.

14. For a detailed review on model specifications, see Devine and Kiefer (1991).

15. See, for example, Dolton *et al.* (1992a).

16. An exception is Korpi's (1992) study on employment stability of Swedish youth after training participation. Dolton *et al.* (1992b) provides a similar approach for British Youth Training participants.

17. For example, the quality of work placements in the British Youth Training Scheme is known to have differed considerably from area to area and between ethnic groups.

18. See Clarke *et al.* (1994) for a discussion of the feasibility of transferring features of the German training system to the UK.

12.   Women and Training

INTRODUCTION

The training received by women is of growing importance because their role in the economies of most developed countries has increased significantly in recent decades and seems set to increase still further.

Whilst the contribution women make to the labour force has grown, their economic status remains on average lower than that of men. In all countries earnings are lower and the occupational distribution less favourable. The reasons for this are explored; in particular, the role of education and training is elucidated. Following the analysis of the previous chapters, we see that it is possible to interpret the evidence of inequality in different ways.

A broad outline of the current pattern of education and training for women in developed countries (particularly the UK, Germany and the United States) follows. It is shown that women's experiences of schooling and skill acquisition systematically differ from those of men on all available measures. We conclude with a discussion of some policy options.

WOMEN IN THE LABOUR MARKET

Women's role in the formal economy has changed dramatically in recent years. In Europe in the 1960s, for instance, women formed less than 30 per cent of the working population. But by the 1990s, over 40 per cent of the working population in the States of the European Community (now European Union) was female (Commission of the European Communities 1992), although significant differences continue to exist between member states, as Table 12.1 demonstrates.[1] Women's share of total employment in the European Union has moreover been projected to rise to 45 per cent by 2010 (ibid.).

In terms of female economic activity rates (the female civilian labour force aged 16 and over as a percentage of the female population aged 16 and

Table 12.1 *Women's employment in European Union as a percentage of total employment, 1990*

Country	%
Belgium	37
Denmark	46
Germany	40
Greece	35
Spain	32
France	42
Ireland	33
Italy	34
Luxembourg	34
Netherlands	38
Portugal	42
UK	43

Source: Authors' calculations from Commission of the European Communities (1992).

over), the change in the position of women is even more striking. Labour Force Survey data show a rate by the end of the 1980s as high as 60 per cent for Denmark, 51 per cent for Britain, 46 per cent for France, 42 per cent being the European Union average.

The changes in the demographic characteristics of the workforce in the United States are similar to those experienced in Europe. For example, whereas in 1960 approximately 31 per cent of women with children worked in the labour market, by the late 1980s this figure had risen to almost 65 per cent. Similarly, the economic activity rate of all women over 16 years of age in the US was about 57 per cent in 1991, compared with 34 per cent in 1950 (National Center for Education Statistics 1992b).

It is worth pointing out that the potential for women's participation in the labour market is not exhausted by the levels of involvement experienced or currently projected for coming decades. In the former German Democratic Republic, for instance, the labour market participation rate of women was over 80 per cent. This exceptionally high level of economic activity was associated with several factors which show how women's position in the labour market can in principle be altered: state policies to promote women's employment; only a tiny minority of women (13 per cent) without vocational certificates or college degrees; a dramatic decline (from 51 per cent to 19 per cent) between 1971 and 1985 in the number of semi- and unskilled female workers and an increase in the proportion of skilled female workers; and access to non-traditional sectors and levels in the occupational hierarchy to a higher degree than in the West.

INEQUALITY IN THE LABOUR MARKET

If one reason for paying attention to the issue of women's access to training is their growing importance in the workforce, another is inevitably the question of gender inequality and the way in which training provision may affect, or be affected by, this phenomenon.

It is a commonplace that women in all countries earn less than men on average; Table 12.2 demonstrates this for a range of occupations in the UK and the United States; Table 12.3 for manual and non-manual manufacturing workers in Europe. Over time, these gaps in pay have narrowed a little in most countries, but they remain pronounced. This is despite legislation (such as Title VII of the US Civil Rights Act of 1964, the UK's Equal Pay and Sex Discrimination Acts and a variety of similar laws in Europe) which was intended, and widely expected, to lead to greater workplace equality.

Table 12.2   Female earnings as a percentage of male earnings

UK 1991		*USA 1990*	
Managerial	66	Executive, administrative and managerial	66
Professional	79	Professional	74
Associated professional and technical	74	Technical, sales and administrative support	67
Sales	63		
Clerical and secretarial	83		
Personal and protective service	65	Service occupations	72
Craft and related	58	Precison production craft and repair	65
Plant and machine operatives	65	Operators, fabricators and labourers	69
Labourers and other occupations	68	Farming, forestry and fishing	82

Source: Polachek and Siebert (1993).

*Table 12.3   Earnings differentials in Europe: women's earnings as a per-
              centage of men's in manufacturing, 1988*

Country	Manual	Non-manual
Belgium	74	64
Denmark	84	na
France	80	65
Germany (West)	73	67
Greece	78	67
Ireland	68	na
Netherlands	75	64
Portugal (1989)	68	72
United Kingdom	68	55

Note: na = not available.
Source: IRIS (1992).

Comparisons such as those shown in Table 12.2 are rather simplistic.
For one thing, they are not standardized for hours worked. For example,
female professionals work fewer hours on average than males. Although
their (weekly) earnings are shown in the table as 79 per cent of those of men,
their *hourly* earnings are 90 per cent of the male average. Another qualification to be borne in mind is that "men" and "women" are categories that
are rather too broad. For example, Polachek and Siebert (1993: 139) calculate that in 1985 average earnings of all US women were 63 per cent of
those of all men. However, marital status makes a great deal of difference to
the result. Thus single women earned on average 87 per cent of the earnings
of single men. Somewhat more surprisingly, single men earned only 62 per
cent of the average for married men.

Nevertheless, despite these necessary qualifications, lower levels of pay
are a significant feature of women's labour market experience. One reason
for this is the different sectoral distribution of employment for men and
women. As the European Commission puts it:

> Employment of women and men is concentrated in different sectors. A much
> higher proportion of women in employment work in services compared with
> men ... In 1990, 75% of all women in work were employed in services ...
> whereas 51% of men worked in services. (Commission of the European
> Communities 1992: 135–6)

Moreover, greater disaggregation of sectoral employment in six European
Union countries has revealed that almost one-third of women in employ-

Table 12.4   Concentration of women in "female"[a] *occupations, 1990 (%)*

Country	%
Belgium	68
Denmark	78
Germany	70
Greece	58
Spain	65
France	73
Ireland	69
Luxembourg	70
Netherlands	69
Portugal	67
UK	76

Note:
[a] Occupations are ranked by the proportion of women among all employees in the occupation; those with a high share are described as "female"; those with a low share, "male". The borderline lies where the total number of employees in female occupations is equal to the total number of women in employment.
Source: Adapted from Rubery and Fagan (1993).

ment work in retailing, health services and education alone. By contrast, men's employment is much more evenly spread between sub-sectors of the economy (ibid.: 139).

In a similar way, women and men tend to be concentrated in different occupations. Rubery and Fagan (1993) produce evidence which indicates a high degree of occupational "segregation" by gender in Europe (see Table 12.4[2]). Hacker (1986) gives examples of occupations in the United States which are almost exclusively female (dental hygienists 99.5 per cent; pre-school teachers 98.8 per cent; secretaries 98.4 per cent) or male (loggers 99.0 per cent; auto mechanics 98.3 per cent; tool and die makers 98.0 per cent). And women are significantly under-represented in high-status occupations. In 1989 the proportion of UK managers in top firms who were female was 8 per cent; in the US it was as low as 3 per cent (*Economist* 1991b).

To the extent that rates of pay vary from sector to sector and occupation to occupation, different patterns of male and female employment must imply that average pay levels for men and women will differ to some extent.

This has been taken by labour market segmentation theorists (see Chapter 3) as supporting their hypotheses. Barbara Bergmann claims: "Many jobs are earmarked for one sex or the other. Thus, men and women are selling themselves and their human capital in segregated markets, a

Table 12.5   Gender differences in tenure, 1991[a]

	Mean uncompleted tenure (years)		Median uncompleted tenure (years)	
	M	F	M	F
Australia	7.8	5.4	4.1	2.9
Canada	8.9	6.5	4.8	3.3
Finland	9.4	8.5	5.8	4.9
France	10.6	9.6	7.9	7.0
Germany	12.1	8.0	9.5	5.0
Japan	12.5	7.3	10.1	4.8
Netherlands	8.6	4.3	3.9	2.0
Norway	10.2	8.4	7.4	5.8
Spain	10.6	8.2	7.5	3.3
Switzerland	10.4	6.6	7.1	3.6
United Kingdom	9.2	6.3	5.3	3.7
United States	7.5	5.9	3.5	2.7

Note: [a]Or nearest available date.
Source: Organization for Economic Cooperation and Development (1993b).

separate market for each sex" (Bergmann 1989: 49). According to this approach, women are largely confined to "secondary sector" jobs where wages are low and turnover is high.

High turnover has implications for training in both the LMS scheme of things and the human capital framework. As we pointed out in Chapter 9, it is known that there is a positive correlation between tenure – the length of time an individual spends with an employer – and the probability of receiving training (Organization for Economic Cooperation and Development 1993b: 120). Industries in which average tenure is high are those where training is more common. This is a two-way relationship; high expected average tenure encourages employers and employees to invest in training, while a high level of training encourages lower turnover. Typically, women have lower average tenure than men, as Table 12.5 illustrates.[3] Interestingly, one of the countries where the gap is narrowest is France, where child care provision is widely acknowledged to be much better than most other countries shown in the table. Absence of adequate child care is often suggested as one reason why women leave jobs after children come along.

The "segregation" of women and its economic consequences are in one view largely demand-led: primary-sector employers require, or think they require, characteristics of employment stability and work commitment which women are thought to lack. Employer discrimination is thus the cause of women's economic disadvantage (Kenrick 1981). It should be emphasized that, in the main, employers probably do not discriminate between men and women because they are so crass as to imagine that women are *always* likely to display some undesirable characteristic (such as absenteeism) more than men: clearly the characteristics distributions of men and women overlap. But if the means of these distributions differ, "statistical discrimination" is economically rational[4] – which means that it is difficult to eradicate, even with the assistance of legislation. Women may on occasion break through into "men's jobs", but will have to display exceptional characteristics to overcome employer antipathy.

Other writers in the same tradition stress supply-side factors which restrict women's access to jobs in the primary sector. For example, opportunities in this sector may be limited partly because of efforts by male-dominated labour unions to control the supply of labour. Like employers, unions emphasize the importance of "length of continuous service over other potential criteria in judging fitness to serve" (Rees 1992: 101), and thus women are under-represented in union hierarchies and their concerns are not prioritized.

This view, that women earn less because they do "women's work", has come to be known as the *crowding hypothesis*. Because large numbers of women are effectively confined to a limited range of occupations, wages are depressed in these fields. The hypothesis has testable implications. If it is a significant element in determining female pay relative to that of men, we might expect that if women's occupational pattern were to be the same as men's, their pay disadvantage would largely disappear. However, simulations of such a scenario do not provide a great deal of support for the hypothesis. Polachek and Siebert (1993) cite a number of US and UK studies which demonstrate that giving women the same pay as men within each occupation, but keeping their occupational distribution the same, would be much more effective in reducing pay inequality than would matching women's occupational pattern to that of men but keeping the same gender differentials within occupations. However, Polachek and Siebert recognize that the matter is more complicated than this; for within a given occupation, women tend to be employed in smaller, lower-paying firms. If firm size were corrected for, occupational segregation would be more significant in determining pay – an observation which lends somewhat more support to the labour market segmentation theorists' explanation of pay inequality between men and women.

Polachek and Siebert's own view, it should be said, is squarely within the human capital framework. They see women's pay inequality arising essentially from human capital investment decisions. These include educational

choices. But they also include the choice of occupations – and particular
jobs – which are easy to leave and re-enter without significant loss of pay
(Polachek 1981). Such jobs are likely to have a relatively low training element, and thus less-steep earnings–experience profiles (see Chapter 2) than
those of men. Such choices are, in Polachek and Siebert's view, broadly
rational given that most women expect to participate in the labour force less
than most men over the lifecycle. They take more time out of employment
for family commitments, and retire earlier from paid work. In this view it is
not discrimination by employers or male workers that creates and maintains inequality:

> Rather it is the more subtle forms of social conditioning taking place directly
> within the family, and the power of gender specialisation within the household
> which are important. The specialisation factor is shown by the fact that single-
> never-married women have greater lifetime labour force commitment than
> their married counterparts, as well as a higher level of earnings and better jobs
> ... [it] is also the reason that ... the gender wage gap is smaller for singles than
> for marrieds, smaller at younger ages, and larger for those with
> children.   (Polachek and Siebert 1993: 167)

Their view, essentially, is that the ultimate source of inequality lies outside
the labour market: it lies within the home. The gender division of labour
within the household can be seen (Becker 1981) as the result of rational, freely
chosen specialization on the basis of comparative advantage, exactly ana-
lagous to the international division of labour which leads to hot countries
exporting bananas and cold mountainous countries offering ski holidays.
More critically, of course, gender-based household roles may be seen as
essentially oppressive, with men exploiting female unpaid labour in their
own interests.

Whichever view is taken, however, Polachek and Siebert believe that
things are changing, and that the extent of gender inequality is falling over
time. The traditional family and household division of labour between the
sexes is breaking down, and (cause or consequence?) young women are investing more in education and training.

EDUCATION

There is certainly a good deal of evidence to support the proposition that
women are now entering the labour market with far better qualifications
than their mothers and grandmothers had. The level of educational attainment of women at school-leaving age has been steadily improving over recent
decades, to such an extent that in a number of countries they are now

significantly better qualified than men on leaving school. In Germany this process began with educational reforms in the 1960s which provided broader access to post-elementary education: women were the main beneficiaries. This resulted in what has been called the *Fraulein Wunder*, with female school children achieving more than males in secondary education, with higher participation rates and better grades. This has already fed through into the labour market so that, whilst four-fifths of those economically active have some kind of school-leaving certificate, the majority of these are women. By the 1980s, the equalization of educational opportunities in Germany was such that a higher proportion of women than men were also to be found in full-time post-compulsory education and at the end of the decade women constituted 49 per cent of all university students (Blossfeld 1987: 113).

In the UK a similar picture emerges. In England and Wales girls are higher achievers at each qualification level and fewer girls (5.8 per cent in 1990–1) than boys (8.2 per cent) leave school with no graded results (Department for Education 1992).[5] More young women than young men continue full-time education after the end of compulsory schooling. And in the United States young females are typically better qualified on leaving compulsory education than young males, are less likely to drop out of high school and are more likely to enrol in higher education. In 1991, 67 per cent of female high school graduates enrolled in higher education, compared with 58 per cent of males (see Chapter 5).

Women may therefore start their post-compulsory school life in stronger positions than men. This is important because, for example, in almost all European states it is found that women completing post-compulsory education are more likely to be economically active in later life than women who have not and, in the second place, the degree of education is a key determinant of the ability of workers to acquire new skills and adapt to changes in technology (Commission of the European Communities 1992). Hence we would expect that, as suggested in the human capital model, women would be in a strong position to receive further training, given that previous education and qualifications provide an important indicator to employers of the individual's "trainability", while raising the returns to training for individuals.

However, even when women obtain significant qualifications they are at a disadvantage in the labour market. It seems, for instance, that with the same apparent qualification level they are less likely than men to be employed in high-level occupations; they are in effect expected to be more qualified for the same class of job. In Britain, the Labour Force Survey found in summer 1993 that, of women employees with qualifications above A Level, only 25 per cent were managers, compared with 38 per cent of men, and 13 per cent with A Level or equivalent were managers compared to 21% of men (Employment Department 1994). One-tenth of women so qualified were also to be found in semi- or unskilled jobs (Payne 1991).

Furthermore, any optimism about the improving qualifications of female labour force entrants really needs to be tempered by awareness of the type of qualifications they tend to acquire. At school and college girls and young women move into particular subject areas, as we have pointed out in earlier chapters. In the UK, because of the early stage at which pupils have traditionally had to choose which subjects to pursue, this is perhaps more apparent than elsewhere. At secondary school, girls study modern languages, biology and the arts, whilst boys study physics, chemistry and geography. In further education girls concentrate on the arts, business and secretarial studies, and health-related courses, whilst boys are more likely to choose science, engineering and maths. In higher education women are dramatically under-represented in architecture, maths, physical sciences, engineering and technology. In 1992, for instance, almost a quarter of men at British universities took engineering and technology degrees compared with less than 5 per cent of women. Such a pattern is common in higher education in other countries too. Thus in West Germany, despite some infiltration into traditionally masculine fields, the proportion of female engineers only rose from 2 to 5 per cent during the 1980s (Rubery and Fagan 1993).

These choices are also reflected in the types of qualification which men and women acquire. In England and Wales, for example, young males and young females are approximately as likely to achieve NVQ qualifications at a given level. However, males are far more likely than females to achieve City and Guilds qualifications (associated with manual crafts and skills); females are more likely to get Royal Society of Arts qualifications, which predominantly lead into secretarial and administrative work. The same type of differentiation occurs within higher education: in most countries women are much more likely than men to be taking nursing and teaching qualifications. In the United States, although the proportions of men and women entering college differ little, men are more likely to complete bachelor degrees than women, who are more likely to leave college after completion of associate (two-year) degrees.

INITIAL TRAINING

Initial training is another area in which men and women's experiences are markedly different. In Germany, where a large proportion of young people enter the dual system (see Chapter 7), a larger proportion of young men than of young women secure training places. In 1991 only 76 per cent of young women seeking a training vacancy received an apprenticeship, compared with 85 per cent of young men (Rubery and Fagan 1993). Girls experience much greater difficulties than boys in obtaining training; for example, they have to make more applications, be better qualified in the first place, accept a training place in an occupation which is not their first choice, be prepared to change their place of residence, and so forth (Bundesministerium für Bildung und Wissenschaft 1992; Westhoff 1990). All in all, two-thirds of 16–19-year-old women compared with four-fifths of 16–19-year-old men completed vocational training in the Federal Republic's dual system in 1989.

The nature of this training differs significantly between the sexes. If there is a marked degree of occupational segmentation in adult employment it is unlikely to change dramatically in the near future – if the pattern of training provided to young people is anything to go by. Table 7.1 in Chapter 7 showed the ten most popular occupations for men and women undertaking apprenticeships in (West) Germany in 1988. There is little overlap between them; only bank clerks and clerks in wholesale and export trade feature in the top ten for both sexes. The degree of "crowding" in training for "women's jobs" is loosely indicated by the observation that, whereas 36.5 per cent of young men are trained in the top ten male occupations, some 55.5 per cent of all young women trainees are in *their* top ten fields. However, as Chapter 7 indicated, the position *is* changing. In 1977, 47.1 per cent of all female trainees were in female-dominated occupational fields (where more than 80 per cent of all trainees were female). By 1990 this proportion had dropped to 38 per cent.

In the dual system, the type of firm with which training is obtained is often of considerable significance for trainees' future prospects. Women are more likely to receive training with small firms, where they are less likely to be taken on as permanent employees and there are few opportunities for internal promotion. Only about a quarter of companies providing training in Germany take on both male and female trainees. Moreover, only one-third of girls, compared to half of boys, are trained in firms with a works council (Braszeit *et al.* 1989). Such firms are likely to be larger on average, to have trade union representation and to have many of the features of internal labour markets.

Differences in initial training are also marked in the UK. Table 12.6 uses data from the Youth Cohort Study. It shows the percentage of young people in England and Wales aged 18 or 19 in 1988 and 1990 who had experienced various types of initial training by these dates.[6] There are clear gender differences: men were more likely to have received any type of training, and in particular they were much more likely to have been apprentices. Over time these differences seem to have increased, and there appears to have

Table 12.6   Gender and types of initial training, England and Wales (% of those who had ever had each category of training)

	Cohort 3[a] (to 1988)		Cohort 4[b] (to 1990)	
	M	F	M	F
Apprenticeship	28	16	31	12
Course-based	48	39	48	39
On-the-job	69	63	64	55
None	5	8	3	5

Notes
[a] Those whose compulsory education ended in 1986.
[b] Those whose compulsory education ended in 1988.
Source: Youth Cohort Study, figures derived from Ashford and Gray (1993).

been a reduction in the proportion of women receiving on-the-job training. Receipt of apprenticeship and on-the-job training is likely to be associated in later years with longer job tenure.

There is also evidence that the occupations young women enter are associated with a lower level of training (Clarke 1991). Where training is under the aegis of Youth Training or its predecessors (see Chapter 6), young women are less likely than men to have employee status. A greater proportion of women leave the programme early, and more enter part-time work (ibid.). It also appears to be the case that young women are less likely to gain employment directly on leaving the scheme (Association of London Authorities 1992; London East Training and Enterprise Council 1991).

In the very different institutional set-up of the United States, we again find marked gender differences in initial training experiences. As we noted in Chapter 5, the emphasis on school-based vocational preparation means that initial work-based training is relatively less important in the US than in most European countries. Nevertheless, it is significant that young women are less likely to receive such training than their male counterparts. As Table 12.7 shows, women are likely to get fewer of the small number of apprenticeship places available in US firms than men, and are less likely to get formal company training.

The general picture that emerges, therefore, is that young women entering the labour force are typically trained in different ways to, and for different occupations than, their male contemporaries. This cannot fail to be reflected in future career paths and earnings patterns. To take a simple example, those receiving apprenticeship training or other on-the-job general training are likely to experience somewhat depressed earnings during the

Table 12.7   Post-school training in the United States by the age of 25 (%)

	Males	Females
Formal company training	14	8
Off-the-job training	30	33
Apprenticeship	3	0.5
No post-school training[a]	58	60

Note: [a]Previous categories are not mutually exclusive.
Source: Lynch (1993).

training period, as suggested in Chapter 2, as a means of paying at least a proportion of their training costs. In order for sufficient recruits to be attracted into these fields, earnings will (other things being equal) have to be higher after successful completion of training in order to compensate. They will thus have experience–earnings profiles that are steeper than those undertaking other forms of training, and different pay rates at any particular time.

FURTHER TRAINING

Initial training, together with education, is an important predictor of further training. It is perhaps surprising that women's disadvantage in initial training does not at first glance seem to be reflected in some broad indicators of training in older age groups. In the United States in the early 1990s, 40 per cent of men and 41 per cent of women received some training (Amirault 1992). In Great Britain, Labour Force Survey data have demonstrated that since 1988, although the disadvantage of young female workers has continued, women as a whole are marginally more likely to have received some training in the previous four weeks than men. Table 12.8 illustrates this for 1992. These British figures are based on individuals' self-reporting of training. They could relate to a substantial period of formal training leading to transferable qualifications, or a viewing of a short video on how to greet customers. There is evidence that women tend to be concentrated in occupations where training is of relatively short duration, and also that they are more likely to be receiving induction training (basic familiarization with the firm by which they are employed), partly as a consequence of having shorter job tenure (Green 1991a, 1991b). There appears to be somewhat less employer commitment involved. In 1987, 42 per cent of women had to part-fund their training and education, as against only 37 per cent of males (ibid.). A

Table 12.8   Job-related training received by employees, Great Britain, 1992

	Females			Males	
Age	Thousands	% of age group	Age	Thousands	% of age group
16–19	127	20	16–19	167	27
20–24	245	19	20–24	256	19
25–34	396	15	25–34	496	16
35–49	530	14	35–49	523	14
50–59	131	8	50–64	153	7
16–59	1,429	15	16–64	1,596	14

Source: Labour Force Survey.

similar pattern is evident in the United States, where women (although slightly more likely to receive training than men) have shorter periods of training; only some 60 per cent on average of the time spent by men (Altonji and Spletzer 1991). American women are less likely than men to receive adult education from their employers, less likely to have some of their fees paid, and less likely to be given study leave (National Center for Education Statistics 1992b).

In Germany the emphasis on the dual system means that there is relatively less emphasis placed on training for adult workers. Further training in the Federal Republic is of three kinds: for the unemployed and those threatened by job losses; in plant; and paid educational leave of up to five days per year in some Länder. All tend to favour relatively young, highly qualified males. In general, women experience greater difficulty than men in obtaining training and attend shorter training programmes (Bundesministerium für Bildung und Wissenschaft 1992; Blossfeld 1987). Even those women with occupational training qualifications are under-represented on further training schemes, whether state-run or in-firm, including (for example) meister training (see Chapter 7). Only 11.6 per cent of those achieving meister qualifications in West Germany in 1989 were women; the proportion was a little higher in the former German Democratic Republic, at 17 per cent (Bundesminister für Bildung und Wissenschaft, 1992).

One reason for the low level of further training for women in Germany is that, as might be expected, many areas where women tend to be employed, such as banking, the computer industry and retailing, are those where further training is in any case rather limited. There have been some government attempts to increase further training for women, but these have been voluntary and arguably not particularly helpful for the unskilled and semi-skilled. In the early 1980s, for instance, subsidies were introduced to give women preferential treatment after it was shown that only 13 per cent of participants in additional qualification schemes were women.[7]

DISCUSSION

The picture that emerges is one where in many significant respects the education and training experiences of men and women differ quite sharply. Pay differentials reflect these disparate experiences, and although it is plausible that there remains an element of pure discrimination, either by employers or male workers (Bergmann 1989; Greenhalgh 1980), substantial changes in the pattern of education and training for women would probably be necessary if average pay levels for men and women are to be brought closer together.

Whether such changes would be desirable, and how they might be brought about, are questions which are more complicated than is sometimes thought. Some analysts may see inadequate training for women as part of a more general market failure in the creation of human capital, that is becoming more urgently in need of remedy as women's role in the economy grows. As suggested in Chapters 2 and 3, fear of "poaching" may deter firms, or inadequacies in the capital market may deter individuals, from optimal levels of training: a "low-skill equilibrium" may ensue. Men and women will both be under-trained; it is simply that women's disadvantage is rather more marked. In this view what is required may be government action, either to subsidize training directly or to place obligations on firms (and perhaps individuals) to train. However, such policies alone are unlikely to improve women's relative position in the labour market. Gender-neutral subsidies to training may indeed lead to greater increases in men's access to training than to that of women.[8]

Labour market segmentation theorists see women as being crowded into occupations where training is limited and rates of pay are low because they cannot gain access to fields where conditions are better. Two solutions often proposed are described in the US context as "affirmative action" and "comparable worth" policies. The former involve setting quotas, "numerical goals and timetables for hiring and sometimes promotion" (Bergmann 1989: 53); they are highly contentious and in extreme cases have the potential for some injustice to males rejected in favour of apparently poorer-qualified female applicants. They have not been noticeably successful in the USA, and have not generally found favour in Europe. "Comparable worth" schemes involve setting rates of pay for women in segregated occupations by reference to job evaluations which compare female jobs to those done by men. To the extent that such schemes raise female pay, they might be expected to act like minimum-wage laws and thus tend to reduce employment and, therefore, training opportunities. However, their proponents argue that such effects would be minimal.

A less controversial way of reducing gender inequality is through the provision of government-financed training programmes specifically targeted at women. As indicated earlier, there has been a big increase in such schemes in recent years, but they are expensive to run if they are of a sufficiently high quality to attract recruits and to get them into appropriate work. They also suffer from the same sort of displacement effects which most government schemes involve (see Chapter 4).

All this assumes that gender inequality in training is in itself undesirable. We have seen that human capital theorists have put forward the view that such inequality is rational, given many women's expectations of spending less time than men in the workforce. It may be pointed out that women's options are by no means as tightly constrained as is suggested by labour market segmentation theorists, and that their education, training and job choices are broadly utility-maximizing. Evidence (Hewitt 1993: 22) may be cited to show that women are on average happier in their jobs than men.[9] In this view, gender inequality is not a market failure at all: its causes lie ultimately in the socialization of boys and girls and the sexual division of labour in households, and are therefore relatively unamenable to conventional policy interventions (which regulate, or alter the costs and benefits of, economic activity).

There are difficulties with the human capital approach to this issue. As we have seen in earlier chapters, the human capital model depends on a range of assumptions which may not fully hold in practice. In simple versions of the model, for instance, something approximating to perfect foresight is assumed: young people look ahead and manage to form reasonably accurate estimates of likely returns from different types of education and training. Even if their expectations of economic variables are broadly rational, however, it could be argued that people's tastes and attitudes change over their lifecycle in a way which standard economic theory tends to ignore. A girl who quite rationally chose to be a hairdresser in the expectation of being in and out of the workforce while she has children, may feel very differently as a mature 35-year-old woman whose life did not turn out the way she had expected as a teenager. It may be argued that some interference with market forces may be justified in order to keep individuals' options open longer. For instance, this would argue in favour of requiring a broad general education for young people rather than allowing excessive specialization at school and a narrow occupational focus in vocational training.

CONCLUSIONS

We have shown that there are significant differences in men's and women's experience of education, and initial and continuing training: these differences are reflected in gender inequality in pay and other areas.

This picture, which appears common to most countries, is capable of alternative interpretations. Human capital theorists see it as a rational response to "differences in life cycle labour force participation" (Polachek and Siebert 1993: 164); because women expect to spend less time in the labour force they choose different educational paths and different occupations. In the labour market segmentation view, however, choice is not as important. Women are channelled into "women's jobs" by institutionalized discrimination.

Change is taking place; younger cohorts of women are more highly educated and are entering a wider range of occupations than their predecessors. This means that they are likely to participate in the labour force to a greater extent over their lifetimes. Seeing this, future female cohorts are likely to invest still more in education and training. Nevertheless the scale of change is not likely to be sufficient to eradicate gender inequality, as we have seen. In order to increase the convergence between men and women's human capital, policy initiatives seem necessary. Whether such an objective is desirable, and whether currently proposed policies could help to achieve it, remains controversial.

NOTES

1. It should be noted that even in those countries with a relatively small female share of employment, women's participation in the economy has been growing: over the 1980s, the increase in Spain and Greece was of the order of 25%.
2. The degree of segregation shown in Table 12.4 refers to all women. The concentration of part-time workers in "female" occupations is even greater. In the UK, for instance, the figure of 76% for all women could be broken into 67% for full-timers but 85% for part-timers.
3. These figures refer to uncompleted spells with employers.
4. Bergmann makes the valid point that emphasis on women's supposedly undesirable characteristics as employees ignores the whole range of unattractive characteristics more often associated with men than with women: alcohol and drug abuse, smoking, dangerous driving, criminal records, heart disease, and so on (Bergmann 1989: 45). The suggestion is that emphasis on inappropriate characteristics is a rationalisation of prejudice rather than a genuine profit-maximising strategy.
5. These figures relate to England only.
6. Note that it is possible to have experienced more than one of these types of training, so the figures can add up to more than 100%.
7. In Germany, as in the UK and elsewhere in the European Union, some women have benefited from the NOW (New Opportunities for Women) initiative. By 1992, 472

projects had been set up across Europe, mainly for the unemployed (70%) and self-employed (16%), and in areas of new technology. Such schemes have often included recognition of the importance of child-care provision. They have thus been especially valuable in Britain and Germany, where pre-school child-care provision is very limited compared with, say, France. The absence of adequate child-care may be of more general significance in limiting female access to continuing training.

8. This follows from analysis originally developed in a slightly different context many years ago by Gary Becker (1964).

9. An alternative way of putting this is to say that women have low expectations and therefore lack apparent ambition. See Rees (1992).

PART IV

Conclusions

13. Conclusions

This book has demonstrated the wide range of contemporary thinking and writing about training and vocational education. Our intention has been primarily one of informing the reader of the role training plays in different economies and fitting this into a broad theoretical framework. We have tried as far as possible to take a dispassionate and mildly sceptical view of some of the training orthodoxies which are currently propounded, without taking a strongly partisan line. Nevertheless, in this final chapter it is appropriate to highlight a few conclusions from the material we have surveyed.

PRODUCTIVITY, SKILLS AND QUALIFICATIONS

It is clear that throughout the developed world firms, individuals and governments are investing more and more heavily in training and education. They are probably broadly correct to do so. Although, as we have argued, training and education may not always lead to enhanced productivity, it seems intuitively likely that on average a more highly educated and trained labour force will be better equipped to meet the rapid changes in technology, tastes and organizations which are characteristic of modern economies.

However, this should not lead us into uncritical pursuit of increased training at any price. Training and education may well be "goods", things we want more of. But so are machines and equipment, roads, houses and hospitals – each of which may also have an impact on productivity. In a wider context, resources devoted to education and training have to compete with other alternative forms of spending. Whether training is quite as crucial to a country's relative economic performance as is sometimes suggested is debatable, as we have seen.

For one thing, it should have become clear that there is no single training system which is "right" for all countries. We have seen that there are a number of different models which represent adaptations to particular economic and political environments. There seems to be no *a priori* reason, for example, why the emphasis on initial training at the workplace (as in

Germany and, to a lesser extent, in the UK) should be superior to the French or American systems where there is a greater emphasis on achieving pre-entry educational qualifications. Each approach has its strengths and weaknesses, and each system is capable of improvement within its own parameters.

Moreover, there is no unique mix of skills which is a prerequisite for producing a given output; firms can often compete successfully despite having very different production techniques and types of labour. Still less, as Chapter 10 pointed out, does a given level of economic development imply a given labour force structure.

We have indicated that we should be wary of over-simplified international comparisons. There are, as we saw in Chapter 9, only limited comparative data on training. Given the catholicity of the concept of training and the fact that a large element of the costs of training are implicit rather than explicit, we cannot even say with any certainty that one country spends proportionately more or less than another. What we do have are data on qualifications. However (apart from the difficulties of comparing the standards of qualifications between countries), qualifications are only a proxy for economically relevant skills, and sometimes not a very good one.

Training can improve a worker's potential productivity. However, his or her actual productivity often depends more proximately on the machines and equipment he or she uses, the way in which work is organized and monitored, and the incentives provided to individuals to work hard and effectively. A cautionary example is the case of the former German Democratic Republic. On paper East German workers appear to have been at least as well qualified as their Western counterparts (Lange 1993a); yet we now know that their economy was badly run and their enterprises incapable of competing in a free market. Having a qualified labour force (and there is no suggestion that East German qualifications did not attest the possession of genuine skills) is not enough.

Formally recognized qualifications can improve labour force utilization by making it easier for workers to transfer between employers. However, an excessive emphasis on qualifications can introduce an element of rigidity in an economy if, for example, pay scales are tied too closely to traditional differentials associated with qualification levels. This will prevent appropriate price signals being sent when changes in the demand for and supply of different types of labour occur. There will be apparent "skill shortages" in some occupations if wages are prevented from rising to avoid upsetting relativities. Elsewhere demand for particular skills may decline, but wages may remain high, and "job queues" will form. Those who cannot obtain jobs which others with their qualifications hold may prefer to remain unemployed, waiting for vacancies to occur. Alternatively they may take lower-paid jobs where they will therefore appear to be "over-qualified".

These rigidities may be increased if qualifications can only be obtained in a particular, over-formalized manner. For example, traditional apprenticeships had a strong "time-serving" element, as does (for example) entry into the legal profession in England and Wales. Such requirements have little justification in terms of skill enhancement and primarily serve to restrict entry into occupations, artificially raising the pay of existing skilled workers or professionals. More open systems will allow alternative ways of acquiring a given qualification, and make it easier rapidly to expand the supply of skills for which there is increased demand. The emphasis on accreditation of proven competences, as in the British NVQ system, is therefore in principle a desirable development (though the British system has its weaknesses in practice, with critics arguing that the procedures for assessing competence are flawed; see Prais 1989), and we would expect similar schemes to be instituted elsewhere.

TRAINING AND SOCIAL POLICY

Despite these and the other caveats that we have noted, expanded training and the certification often associated with it clearly can in theory enhance productivity. There are other claims made for training, however, that are more debatable. It is often assumed that training and/or education are the key to overcoming a range of social problems.

As we saw in Chapter 11, it is often assumed that retraining the unemployed can make a major contribution to solving the macroeconomic problem of unemployment. Although the evidence suggests that training may (but does not always) improve the chances of particular individuals getting back into work, it is unclear whether this means a reduction in total unemployment or simply a reshuffling of job queues.

Nor can training easily redress other types of disadvantage in the labour market. We have seen that some women and people from some ethnic minorities fare badly in the labour market. Although training may again have some positive impact on their position, this is not necessarily the case. A generalized system of incentives to more training, for example, might be taken advantage of disproportionately by already privileged groups in the community, perhaps leading to yet greater disparities in employment and earnings outcomes. And emphasis on educational qualifications alone as a means of facilitating career advance ignores, as we pointed out in earlier chapters, the way in which qualifications are used as one (but only one) method of screening job applicants.

In any case, it seems likely that differential access to training is a symptom as much as it is a cause of labour market disadvantage. Human capital theory suggests that some apparent injustices – notably women's differential access to training opportunities – can be seen as a rational response to individual preferences for career and labour force participation patterns which differ between men and women. This can raise doubts over whether state involvement to redress the balance is justified. Even those who reject this analysis as a justification for the *status quo*, however, should recognize that the model is in principle an example of positive rather than normative economics. You may accept the analysis while still believing that young women's (and young men's) occupational choices often turn out to have unforeseen and undesirable long-term consequences which perhaps justify some form of policy intervention.

However, the human capital model suggests that the appropriate locus of such policy intervention may come before labour market entry – for example, by delaying subject choices at school and promoting general rather than narrowly vocational (and thus gender-specific) education. Similarly, post-entry intervention targeting and counselling women may be more effective than attempting to alter private-sector pay scales, imposing training requirements or job quotas on employers, and so forth.

HUMAN CAPITAL THEORY AND THE INDIVIDUAL

The human capital model has tended to be our guide in much of the discussion. It has its weaknesses, as Chapter 3 makes clear, and we have much to learn from other modes of thought as well. Nevertheless, as we have seen, the human capital approach has the great advantage to economists of having a wider scope than other models. Training becomes only one of a number of economic phenomena which can be made sense of, tends to reinforce the credibility of this approach. It also has the advantage of reminding us that training itself is a very broad category. The emphasis of training professionals is inevitably on formal, structured methods of skill acquisition: human capital theorists such as Becker and Mincer remind us that they are only part of the picture. Arguably, unstructured and unmeasured learning on the job is at least as important as formal training at work. Finally, the focus of human capital thinking is very much on the individual's responsibility for his or her training – again, a perspective which is often lost in other approaches.

With its emphasis on individuals rather than firms, human capital theory is clearly very different from both other theoretical traditions (such as the Labour Market Segmentation approach) and the "commonsense" view that firms are to blame for "skill shortages" and other perceived problems – with the corollary that it is their responsibility to promote higher levels of training. Similar thinking lies behind the UK government's continuing efforts to promote "employer-led" Training and Enterprise Councils.

It seems to us that a lesson which can be learnt from human capital theory is that the pattern of incentives to individuals may be of more importance than is often considered to be the case. For instance, general training may be inhibited if individuals are not able effectively to finance such training by taking lower pay during their early years in a job. Leaving aside the virtues or otherwise of the German dual system, it seems likely that a necessary condition for the high level of employer-provided training it produces is the relatively low level of youth pay in Germany. Conversely, the lower level of employer-provided youth training in the USA may be associated with minimum-wage legislation which keeps youth wages relatively high. In this analysis, those who believe training provision is inadequate should not seek to exhort firms to spend on training money which they do not expect to recoup, but should rather focus on the reasons why relative pay cannot adjust to appropriate levels.

GOVERNMENTS, TRAINING AND EDUCATION

Belief in the inadequacy of private-sector training is the ostensible motive for government intervention to regulate or subsidize. There are grounds for this belief, and we have explored them in the course of this book. Nevertheless, it is appropriate to close on a reminder of the point made in Chapter 4. Modern democratic polities have a systematic tendency to over-regulate, to tell people that what they choose to do themselves (or choose not to do) is wrong, and to use large sums of public money without adequate evaluation of the costs and benefits of alternative lines of action. In the area of education and training, perhaps more than elsewhere, these pressures are particularly strong. Training and education professionals are articulate, well-organized and often possessed of a strong sense of mission. Anybody who speaks against any particular government initiative therefore tends to be accused of ignoring the "needs" of the economy and individuals, and the chief complaints from opposition politicians tend to be that a particular initiative does not go far enough: the rules should be more prescriptive, and more funds should be made available.

So we need constantly to be aware of the large amount of special pleading which can be disguised as concern for the public interest in this field.

And we need to be sure that governments are actually competent to perform some of the tasks which they attempt to take on.

One area for which governments in the modern world probably cannot avoid taking responsibility is the secondary education system, or at least large parts of it. Within that system, the nature of the curriculum has been the centre of much attention recently. Our discussion in Chapter 10 indicates that a narrowly focused vocational education is unlikely to be desirable – particularly where it means in practice concentration on older skills and gender-stereotyped roles. We would argue that it is better to improve the general level of educational competence – reading, writing, quantitative skills (including, nowadays, basic familiarity with information technology), presentational skills and awareness of the nature of work and employment – than to seek to channel young people too early into what are believed to be employers' requirements. Employers can be very good at telling schools and colleges what they want, but less good at providing the resources and job opportunities to match. Governments would do well to bear this in mind.

FINALLY ...

Interest in training and education is likely to continue to grow. Research to inform this interest will also expand. As academics, we find it difficult to argue against this. We would insist that such research needs a strong comparative dimension, but should be informed by a general theoretical perspective which enables us to see why particular institutions and programmes emerge in different economic and political environments. A belief that governments can easily pick 'n mix from different training cultures seems to us mistaken.

Bibliography

Addison, J. (1989), "Job rights and economic dislocation", in R. Drago and R. Perlman (eds), *Microeconomic Issues in Labour Economics*, Hemel Hempstead: Harvester Wheatsheaf.

Addison, J. and W.S. Siebert (1992), "Vocational training and the European Community", paper presented at the Oxford Economic Papers Annual Conference, Oxford, mimeo.

Addison, J. and W.S. Siebert (1993), *Social Engineering in the European Community: The Social Charter, Maastricht and Beyond*, London: Institute of Economic Affairs.

Adnett, N. (1993), "The Social Charter: unnecessary regulation or prerequisite for convergence?", *British Review of Economic Issues*, 15(36): 63–79.

Ainley, P. (1990), *Training Turns to Enterprise: Vocational Education in the Market Place*, Hillcole Group Paper 4, London: Tufnell Press.

Ainley, P. and M. Corney (1990), *Training for the Future: The Rise and Fall of the Manpower Services Commission*, London: Cassell.

Altonji, J. G. and J. R. Spletzer (1991), "Worker characteristics, job characteristics, and the receipt of on-the-job training", *Industrial and Labor Relations Review*, 45(1): October 58–79.

Amirault, T. (1992), "Training to qualify for jobs and improve skills, 1991", *Monthly Labor Review*, September.

Anderson, K.H., R.V. Burkhauser and J.E. Raymond (1993), "The effect of creaming on placement rates under the Job Training Partnership Act", *Industrial and Labour Relations Review*, 46(4): 613–24.

Angrist, J. D. (1993), "The effect of veterans benefits on education and training", *Industrial and Labor Relations Review*, 46(4): 637–52.

Arbeitskreis Alternative Arbeitsmarktpolitik (1993), *Grenzen von Beschäftigungsmaßnahmen – Auf der Suche nach neuen Wegen*, Collection of seminar papers, Völklingen.

Ashford, Sheena and John Gray (1993), *Young People in Training: Towards a National Picture in the Late Eighties*, Employment Department Research Series: Youth Cohort Report no. 25, London: HMSO.

Association of London Authorities (1992), *The Great Skills Divide: The Jobs-Training Mismatch in London*.

Backhouse, R. (1985), *A History of Modern Economic Analysis*, Oxford: Basil Blackwell.

Barnett, Corelli (1986), *The Audit of War*, London: Macmillan.

Becker, G.S. (1957), *The Economics of Discrimination*, Chicago: University of Chicago Press.

Becker, G.S. (1962), "Investment in human capital: a theoretical analysis", *Journal of Political Economy*, 70 (Supplement): 9–49.

Becker, G.S. (1964), *Human Capital: A Theoretical and Empirical Analysis*, New York: Columbia University Press; 2nd edn 1975.

Becker, G.S. (1965), "A theory of the allocation of time", *Economic Journal*, 75(299): 493–517.

Becker, G.S. (1967), *Human Capital and the Personal Distribution of Income: an Analytical Approach*, Woytinsky Lecture no. 1, Institute of Public Administration, Ann Arbor, Mich.: University of Michigan Press.

Becker, G.S. (1981), *A Treatise on the Family*, Cambridge, Mass.: Harvard University Press.

Becker, G.S. and G. Stigler (1974), "Law enforcement, malfeasance and the compensation of enforcers", *Journal of Legal Studies*, 3: 1–18.

Beckett, Francis (1993), "Why sponsorship came in a trickle rather than in a flood", *The Guardian*, May 18.

Begg, I.G., A.P. Blake and B.M. Deakin (1991), "YTS and the labour market", *British Journal of Industrial Relations*, June, 223–36.

Bellmann, L. *et al.* (1992), 'The Eastern German labour market in transition: gross flow estimates from panel data', Discussion Paper no.102, London: Centre for Economic Performance.

Benner, H. (1982), 'Ordnung der staatlich anerkannten Ausbildungsberufe', *Berichte zur beruflichen Bildung*, vol. 48, Berlin: Bundesinstitut für Berufsbildung.

Bennett, R., H. Glennerster and D. Nevison (1992), *Learning Should Pay*, Poole, Dorset: BP Educational Service.

Ben-Porath, H. (1967), "The production of human capital over the life cycle", *Journal of Political Economy*, 75: 352–65.

Bergmann, Barbara R. (1989), "Does the market for women's labor need fixing?", *Journal of Economic Perspectives*, 3(1): Winter, 43–60.

Bernstein, A. (1993), 'How much good will training do?', *Business Week*, 22 February.

Berryman, S. (1991), 'Training in the US: state of play and future directions', in J. Stevens and R. Mackay (eds), *Training and Competitiveness*, London: Kogan Page/NEDO.

Betts, D. (1993), 'Britain in the doldrums', *NATFHE Journal*, Spring.

Bierhoff, H. and S.J. Prais (1993), "Britain's industrial skills and the school-teaching of practical subjects: comparisons with Germany, the Netherlands and Switzerland", *National Institute Economic Review*, 144(May): 55–73.

Bishop, J.H. (1991), 'On-the-job training of new hires', in D. Stern and J.M.M. Ritzen (eds), *Market Failure in Training? New Evidence on Training of Adult Employees*, Berlin: Springer-Verlag.

Bispinck, R. (1991), "Collective bargaining in East Germany: between economic restraints and political regulation", paper presented at the 13th Annual Conference of the International Working Party on Labour Market Segmentation, Bremen, July.

Björklund, A. (1990), "Evaluations of Swedish labor market policy", *Finnish Economic Papers*, no.3: 3–13.

Blachère, M. (1992), "The French system of vocational training", EC/US Conference Proceedings *Schools and Industry: Partners for a Quality Education*, Task Force Human Resources Education Training and Youth, EC and United States Department of Education.

Blanchard, O. and L. Summers (1986), "Hysteresis and the European unemployment problem", *NBER Macroeconomic Annual*, 1, 15–17.

Blanchard, O. and L. Summers (1988), "Hysteresis and the Eupopean unemployment problem" in R. Cross (ed.), *Unemployment, Hysteresis and the Natural Rate Hypothesis*, Oxford: Basil Blackwell.

Blanchet, D. (1993), "Does an ageing labour force call for large adjustments in training or wage policies?", in P. Johnson and K.F. Zimmermann (eds), *Labour Markets in an Ageing Europe*, Cambridge: Cambridge University Press.

Blanchflower, D. and L. Lynch (1992), 'Training at work: a comparison of US and British youths', Discussion Paper no.78, London: Centre for Economic Performance.

Blaug, M. (1972), *An Introduction to the Economics of Education*, Harmondsworth, Middx: Penguin.

Blaug, M. (1975), "The empirical status of human capital theory: a slightly jaundiced survey", *Journal of Economic Literature*, 14: 827–55.

Blaug, M. (1980), *The Methodology of Economics*, Cambridge: Cambridge University Press.

Blaug, M. (1993), "Education and the employment contract", *Education Economics*, 1(1): 21–34.

Blossfeld, H. (1987), "Labor market entry and the sexual segregation of careers in the federal republic of Germany", *American Journal of Sociology*, 93(1).

Bosworth, D., R. Wilson and A. Assefa (1994), "A human capital approach to training: second draft" in R. McNabb and K. Whitfield (eds), *The Market for Training: International Perspectives on Theory, Methodology and Policy*, Aldershot: Avebury.

Bourdet, Y. and I. Persson (1992), "Does labour market policy matter? Long-term unemployment in France and Sweden", University of Lund Working Paper Series 6/92, Lund.

Bowles, S. and H. Gintis (1975), "The problem with human capital theory – a Marxian critique", *American Economic Review*, 65: 74–82.

Boyer, R. (1986), *La théorie de la regulation: une analyse critique*, Paris: La Découverte.

Braszeit, A., U. Muller, G. Richter-Witzgall and M. Stackelbeck (1989), *Enstellungsverhalten von Arbeitgebern und Beschaftigungschancen von Frauen,*Bonn: Bundesminister fur Arbeit und Sozialordung.

Breen, R. (1991), "Education, employment and training in the youth labour market", Economic and Social Research Institute General Research Series no. 152, Dublin.

Brinkmann, C. (1985), "Zum Erfolg von Eingliederungsbeihilfen: Struktur und Verbleib der Geförderten', *Mitteilungen aus der Arbeitsmarkt- und Berufsforschung*, 18: 439.

Brown, C. (1991), "An institutional model of training", paper presented at the International Conference on the Economics of training, Cardiff Business School, September.

Brown, J.N. (1989), "Why do wages increase with tenure?", *American Economic Review*, 79: 971–91.

Buchanan, J. and G. Tullock (1962), *The Calculus of Consent*, Ann Arbor, Mich.: University of Michigan Press.

Buchanan, J., R.D. Tollinson and G. Tullock (1980), *Toward a Theory of the Rent-seeking Society*, College Station, Tx.: Texas A and M Press.

Buechtemann, C.F., J. Schupp and D. Soloff (1993), "Roads to work: school-to-work transition patterns in Germany and the United States", *Industrial Relations Journal*, 24(2).

Bundesministerium für Bildung und Wissenschaft (1992), *Grundlagen – Perspektiven: Berufsbildungsbericht 1992*, Bonn.

Cain, G. (1976), "The challenge of segmented labor market theories to orthodox theory: a survey", *Journal of Economic Literature*, 14: 1215–57.

Calmfors, L. and J. Driffill (1988), "Bargaining structure, corporatism and macroeconomic performance", *Economic Policy*, 6 (April): 13–61.

Cantor, L. (1989), *Vocational Education and Training in the Developed World: A Comparative Study*, London: Routledge.

Carl Duisberg Gesellschaft (1992), *Vocational Training: Investment for the Future. The Dual System of Vocational Training in the Federal Republic of Germany*, Leverkusen.

Carnevale, A.P. and H. Goldstein (1990), "Schooling and training for work in America: an overview", in L.A. Ferman, M. Hoyman, J. Cutcher-Gershenfeld and E.J. Savoie (eds), *New Developments in Worker Train-*

ing: A Legacy for the 1990s, Wisconsin: Industrial Relations Research Association.

Casey, B. (1986), "The dual apprenticeship system and the recruitment and retention of young persons in West Germany", *British Journal of Industrial Relations*, March.

Casey, B. (1991), "Recent developments in the German apprenticeship system", *British Journal of Industrial Relations*, June.

Cave, M. and M. Weale (1992), "Higher education: the state of play", *Oxford Review of Economic Policy*, 8(2): 1–18.

CEDEFOP (1987), *The Position of Social Partners in Vocational Training in France*, Berlin: CEDEFOP (European Centre for the Development of Vocational Training).

CEDEFOP (1990a), *The Financing of Continuing Vocational Training in France*, Berlin: CEDEFOP.

CEDEFOP (1990b), *The Role of the Social Partners in Vocational Education and Training including Continuing Education and Training*, Berlin: CEDEFOP.

Centre for Economic Policy Research (1993), "Labour markets: the skills gap" *CEPR Bulletin*, 57 (Summer): 3–5.

Chapman, P.G. (1993), *The Economics of Training*, Hemel Hempstead, Herts.: Harvester-Wheatsheaf.

Chapman, P.G. and M.J. Tooze (1987), "Some economic implications of the Youth Training Scheme", *Royal Bank of Scotland Review*, September, 14–23.

Clarke, K. (1991), *Women and Training: A Review*, Research Discussion Series no. 1, Manchester: Equal Opportunities Commission.

Clarke, L. (1992), "Training provision and wage form: the example of the construction labour process in Europe", mimeo.

Clarke, L., T. Lange, J.R. Shackleton and S. Walsh (1994), "The political economy of training: should Britain try to emulate Germany?", *Political Quarterly*, 65(1): 74–92.

Collier, P. and J.B. Knight (1985), "Seniority payments, quit rates and internal labour markets in Britain and Japan", *Oxford Bulletin of Economics and Statistics*, February.

Commission of the European Communities (1991), *Employment in Europe*, Luxembourg: Directorate-General for Employment, Industrial Relations and Social Affairs.

Commission of the European Communities (1992), Employment in Europe, Luxembourg: Directorate-General for Employment, Industrial Relations and Social Affairs.

Commission of the European Communities (1993), "Economic and labour market statistics", *Employment Observatory*, no. 8, August.

Commission on Workforce Quality and Labor Market Efficiency (1989), *Investing in People, a Strategy to Address America's Workforce Crisis*, Washington, D.C.: Department of Labor.

Confederation of British Industry (1993), *Routes for Success. Careership: a strategy for all 16–19 year old learning*.

Couch, K.A. (1992), "New evidence on the long-term effects of employment training programs", *Journal of Labor Economics*, 10(4): 380–8.

Crafts, N. (1992), "Productivity growth reconsidered", *Economic Policy*, 15: 388–426.

Crafts, N. (1993), *Can De-industrialisation Seriously Damage Your Wealth?*, Hobart Paper 120, London: Institute of Economic Affairs.

Crouch, C. (1992), "The dilemmas of vocational training policy: some comparative lessons", *Policy Studies*, 13(4), 33–48.

Deakin, B.M. and C.F. Pratten (1987), "Economic effects of YTS", *Employment Gazette*, October.

Del Valle, C. (1993), "From high school to high skills", *Business Week*, 26 April.

Denison, E.F. (1967), *Why Growth Rates Differ: Post-war Experience in Nine Western Countries*, Washington, D.C.: Brookings Institution.

Department for Education (1992), *School examinations survey 1990/91*, Statistical Bulletin, 15/92, July.

Department for Education (1993a), *Aspects of Vocational Education in France*, London: HMSO.

Department for Education (1993b), *Education: Facts and Figures, England 1993*, London: HMSO.

Department for Education (1993c), *The New Vocational A Level: A Brief Guide*, London: HMSO.

Department for Education (1993d), *International Statistical Comparisons of the Participation in Education and Training of 16 to 18 Year Olds*, Statistical Bulletin 19/93.

Department of Education and Science (1988), *Top-up Loans for Students*, London: HMSO.

Department of Employment (1989), *Training in Britain: A Survey of Funding, Activity and Attitudes*, 4 vols, London: HMSO.

Devine, T.J. and N.M. Kiefer (1991), *Empirical Labor Economics: The Search Approach*, New York and Oxford: Oxford University Press.

Disney, R., L. Bellman, A. Carruth, W. Franz, R. Jackman, R. Layard, H. Lehmann and J. Philpott (1992), *Helping the Unemployed: Active Labour Market Policies in Britain and Germany*, London: Anglo-German Foundation.

Dobb, M. (1938), *Wages*, London: Nisbet.

Doeringer, P. and M. Piore (1980), *Internal Labor Markets and Manpower Analysis*, Boston, Mass.: D. C. Heath.

Dolton, P.J., G.H. Makepeace and J.G. Treble (1992a), "Public and private sector training of young people in Britain", in L.Lynch (ed.), *International Comparisons of Private Sector Training*, New York: National Bureau for Economic Research.

Dolton, P.J., G.H. Makepeace and J.G. Treble (1992b), "The youth training scheme and the school to work transition", Labour Economics Unit Working Paper 92/3, Department of Economics, University of Hull.

Downs, A. (1957), *An Economic Theory of Democracy*, New York: Harper & Row.

Drew, David, John Gray and Nicholas Sime (1991), *Against the Odds: the Education and Labour Market Experiences of Black Young People*, Youth Cohort Study, Employment Department.

Dundas-Grant, V. (1989), "Vocational and technical education in France", *National Westminster Bank Quarterly Review*, February, 30–42.

Dunlop, J. (1957), "The task of contemporary wage theory", in G.W. Taylor and P.C. Pierson (eds), *New Concepts in Wage Determination*, New York: McGraw-Hill.

The Economist (1990), "Why can't little Taro think?", 21 April.

The Economist (1991a), "Missing bridge: job training in the US", 9 February.

The Economist (1991b), "Breaking through: obstacles for women", 26 January.

The Economist (1992a), "Coming top – a survey of education", 21 November.

The Economist (1992b), "Japan learning to change", 23 October.

The Economist (1993a), "Pain, gain and gravy train", 20 February.

The Economist (1993b), "Workers of the world unite", 23 October.

The Economist (1993c), "Getting Europe back to work", 28 August.

The Economist (1994), "Training up America", 15 January.

Education Week (1993), "Charting a course for reform: a chronology", Special Report, 10 February.

Edwards, K. (1993), Letter to the *Independent*, 16 December.

Elbaum, B. (1991), "The persistence of apprenticeship in Britain and its decline in the United States", in H. Gospel (ed.), *Industrial Training and Technological Innovation*, London: Routledge.

Employment Department (1990), *Training Statistics 1990*, London: HMSO.

Employment Department (1991), *Training Statistics 1991*, London: HMSO.

Employment Department (1992a), *People, Jobs and Opportunity*, CM 1810, London: HMSO.

Employment Department (1992b), *Training Statistics 1992*, London: HMSO.

Employment Department (1993), *Training Statistics 1993*, London: HMSO.

Employment Department (1994), "LFS help-line", *Employment Gazette*, February.

European Centre for the Development of Vocational Training, *see* CEDEFOP.

Ferber, R. and W.Z. Hirsch (1982), *Social Experimentation and Economic Policy*, Cambridge: Cambridge University Press.

FEU (1993), *Vocational Education and Training in Europe: A Four-country Study in Four Employment Sectors*, London: Further Education Unit.

Financial Times (1993), "Survey of training and enterprise councils", May.

Finegold, D. and D. Soskice (1988), "The failure of training in Britain: analysis and prescription", *Oxford Review of Economic Policy*, 4(1): 1–13.

Fogel, R.W. and S.L. Engerman (1974), *Time on the cross*, Chicago: Chicago University Press.

Foster, P.J. (1965), "The vocational school fallacy in development planning", in C.A. Anderson and M.J. Bowman (eds), *Education and Economic Development*, London: Aldine Press.

Freeman, R.B. (1988), "Labour market institutions and economic performance", *Economic Policy*, April.

Friedman, M. (1953), *Essays in Positive Economics*, Chicago: Chicago University Press.

Friedman, M. (1968), "The role of monetary policy", *American Economic Review*, March, 1–17.

Friedman, M. and S. Kuznets (1945), *Income from Independent Professional Practice*, New York: Columbia University Press.

Führ, C. (1988), *Schulen und Hochschulen in der Bundesrepublik Deutschland*, Bonn: Inter Nationes.

Gapper, J. (1992), "The high price of ignorance: American worries over competitiveness have put education and training on the political agenda", *Financial Times*, 17 August.

Garland, S.B. (1992), "90 days to learn to scrub? Sure, if Uncle Sam's paying", *Business Week*, 20 January.

Goldthorpe, J.H. and K. Hope (1974), *The Social Grading of Occupations*, Oxford: Oxford University Press.

Gospel, H.F. (1993), "Whatever happened to apprenticeship training? A British, American, Australian comparison", Working Paper 93/15, Canterbury: University of Kent.

Grasso, J. and J. Shea (1979), *Vocational Education and Training: Impact on Youth,* Washington, D.C.: Carnegie Foundation.

Green, Francis (1991a), "The determinants of training of male and female employees in Britain", The International Conference on the Economics of Training, Cardiff Business School, September.

Green, Francis (1991b), "Sex discrimination in job-related training", *British Journal of Industrial Relations*, 29: June.

Greenhalgh, C. (1980). "Male-female wage differentials in Great Britain: is marriage an equal opportunity?", *Economic Journal*, 90: 751–75.

Greenhalgh, C. and G. Mavrotas (1994), "Workforce training in the Thatcher era: market forces and market failures", in R. McNabb and K. Whitfield (eds), *The Market for Training: International Perspectives on Theory, Methodology and Policy*, Aldershot: Avebury.

Greinert, W.-D. (1992), *The Dual System of Vocational Training in the Federal Republic of Germany: Structure and Function*, Eschborn: GTZ Press.

Gritz, R.M. (1988), "The impact of training on the frequency and duration of employment", Department of Economics, University of Washington, mimeo.

Gustman, A. and T. Steinmeier (1980), "The relation between vocational training in high school and economic outcomes", Technical paper prepared for the office of Assistant Secretary for Planning and Budget, US Department of Labor.

Hacker, A. (1986), "Women at work", *New York Review of Books*, 14 August.

Haynes, P. (1991), "America, it is said, has the best business schools, Japan the best business", *The Economist*, 2 March.

Hendry, J. (1987), *Understanding Japanese Society*, Beckenham, Kent: Croom Helm.

Henley, A. and E. Tsakalotos (1992), "Corporatism and the European labour market after 1992", *British Journal of Industrial Relations*, 30(4): 567–86.

Her Majesty's Inspectorate and Department of Education and Science (1990), *Aspects of Education in the USA: Vocational and Continuing Education*, London: HMSO.

Herrlitz, H.-G., W. Hopf and H. Titze (1981), *Deutsche Schulgeschichte von 1800 bis zur Gegenwart – Eine Einführung*, Konigstein: Athenäum Verlag.

Hewitt, P. (1993), "Flexible working: asset or cost?", *Policy Studies*, 14(3): 18–28.

Hilton, M. (1991), "Shared training: learning from Germany", *Monthly Labor Review*, March.

Holzer, H.J., R.N. Block, M. Cheatham and J. Knott (1993), "Are training subsidies for firms effective? The Michigan experience", *Industrial and Labor Relations Review*, 46(4): 625–36.

Hüfner, K., J. Naumann, H. Köhler and G. Pfeffer (1986), *Hochkonjunktur und Flaute: Bildungspolitik in der Bundesrepublik Deutschland 1967–1980*, Stuttgart: Klett-Cotta.

Hughes, J.J. and R. Perlman (1984), *The Economics of Unemployment: A Comparative Analysis of Britain and the United States*, Brighton, Sussex: Wheatsheaf.

Incomes Data Services (1991), "National agreement on training concluded", *IDS European Report*, No. 356, August.

Incomes Data Services (1992), "French graduates face tough jobs market", *IDS European Report*, No. 366, June.

The Independent (1993), "Blacks 'jobless despite degrees'", 7 September.

IRIS (1992), *An Evaluation of the IRIS Network*, Report prepared (by PA Cambridge Economic Consultants) for DGV, Brussels.

Johnes, G. (1993), *The Economics of Education*, London: Macmillan.

Johnson, P. and K.F. Zimmermann (1993), "Ageing and the European labour market: public policy issues", in P. Johnson and K.F. Zimmermann (eds), *Labour Markets in an Ageing Europe*, Cambridge: Cambridge University Press.

Jovanovic, B. (1979), "Job matching and the theory of labour turnover", *Journal of Political Economy*, 87: 972–90.

Kenrick, J. (1981), "Politics and the construction of women as second-class workers" in F. Wilkinson (ed.), *The Dynamics of Labour Market Segmentation*: London: Academic Press.

Kerr, C. (1954), "The Balkanisation of Labour Markets", in E.W. Bakke (ed.), *Labour Mobility and Economic Opportunity*, Cambridge, Mass.: MIT Press.

Kirsch, I.S., A. Jungeblut and A. Campbell (1992), *Beyond the School Doors: The Literacy Needs of Job Seekers Served by the US Department of Labor*, Washington, D.C.: Employment and Training Administration, US Department of Labor.

Köditz, V. (1990), *Vocational Guidance and Counselling for Adults: Summary Report on the Services Available for the Unemployed, Especially the Long-Term Unemployed in Denmark, Federal Republic of Germany, France, Italy, the Netherlands, Portugal, Spain, United Kingdom*, Berlin: CEDEFOP.

Koretz, G. (1992), "Just how welcome is the job market to college grads?", *Business Week*, 9 November.

Korpi, T. (1992), "Employment stability following unemployment and manpower programs", Stockholm University Research Reports in Demography no. 72, Stockholm.

Krugman, P. (1994), "Competitiveness: a dangerous obsession", *Foreign Affairs*, 73(2): March/April, 28–44.

Kuttner, R. (1993), "Training programs alone can't produce $20-an-hour workers", *Business Week*, 8 March.

Lampert, H. (1989), "20 Jahre Arbeitsförderungsgesetz", *Mitteilungen aus der Arbeitsmarkt- und Berufsforschung*, no.2, Nürnberg.

Lange, T. (1993a), "Training for economic transformation: the labour market in Eastern Germany", *British Review of Economic Issues*, 15(37): 145–68.

Lange, T. (1993b), "Das Übel der falschen Rezepte – Langzeitarbeitslosigkeit in der Europäischen Gemeinschaft", *Gewerkschaftliche Bildungspolitik*, July/August, 167–70.

Lange, T. (1993c), "Langzeitarbeitslosigkeit und Aktive Arbeitsmarktpolitik – Die Bundesrepublik und Großbritannien Im Vergleich", *Wirtschaft und Berufserziehung*, April, 105–12.

Lange, T. (1994), "Training for Europe – should Britain follow the German model?", *Journal of European Industrial Training, 18: 2.*

Layard, R. (1993), "How to mend the labour market", *Financial Times*, 9 February.

Layard, R. and S. Nickell (1986), "Unemployment in Britain", *Economica*, 53 (Supplement): S121–69.

Layard, R., S. Nickell and R. Jackman (1991), *Unemployment: Macroeconomic Performance and the Labour Market*, Oxford and New York: Oxford University Press.

Layard, R., K. Mayhew and G. Owen (1992), *The Training Reform Act of 1994*, Swindon: Economic and Social Research Council.

Lazear, E. (1979), "Why is there mandatory retirement?", *Journal of Political Economy*, 87: 1261–84.

Lazear, E. (1981), "Agency, earnings profiles and hours restrictions", *American Economic Review*, 71: 606–20.

Lefresne, F. (1992), *Young People and Labour Markets: A Comparison between France and the United Kingdom*, Paris: IRES.

Levitan, S.A. and F. Gallo (1990), "Uncle Sam's helping hand: education, training, and employing the disadvantaged", in L.A. Ferman *et al.* (eds), *New Developments in Worker Training: A Legacy for the 1990s*, Madison: Industrial Relations Research Association.

Lillard, L.A. and H.W. Tan (1986), *Private Sector Training: Who Gets It and What Are Its Effects*, Rand Corporation Paper R-3331-DOL/RC.

Lindley, R.M. (1991), "Interactions in the markets for education, training and labour: a European perspective on intermediate skills", in P. Ryan (ed.), *International Comparisons of Vocational Education and Training for Intermediate Skills*, London: Falmer Press.

London East Training and Enterprise Council (1991), *LETEC Labour Market Assessment*, November.

Lucas, R.E. (1981), *Studies in Business Cycle Theory*, Cambridge, Mass.: MIT Press.

Lucas, R.E. (1988), "On the mechanics of economic development", *Journal of Monetary Economics*, 22: 3–42.

Lynch, L.M. (1991), "The role of off-the-job vs on-the-job training for the mobility of women workers", *American Economic Review*, 81(2): May, 151–6.

Lynch, L.M. (1993), "The economics of youth training policy in the U.S.", *Economic Journal*, 103(402): September, 1292–1302.

Mahnkopf, B. (1992), "The skill-oriented strategies of German trade unions", *British Journal of Industrial Relations*, 30(1): March 61–81.

Marin, A and G. Psacharopoulos (1982), "The reward for risk in the labour market: evidence from the United Kingdom and a reconciliation with other studies", *Journal of Political Economy*, 90: 827–53.

Marshall, A. (1919), *Industry and Trade*, London: Macmillan.

Marshall, A. (1920), *Principles of Economics*, 8th edn, London: Macmillan.

Mason, G., S.J. Prais and B. van Ark (1992), "Vocational education and productivity in the Netherlands and Britain", *National Institute Economic Review*, May.

Maurice, M., F. Sellier and J.J. Silvestre (1986), *The Social Foundations of Industrial Power: A Comparison between France and Germany*, Cambridge, Mass: MIT Press.

Mayhew, K. (1991), "Training: the problem of employers", *Economic Report*, 5(10) March/April, Employment Institute.

Mayhew, K. and B. Rosewell (1979), "Labour market segmentation in Britain", *Oxford Bulletin of Economics and Statistics*, May.

McNabb, R. and P. Ryan (1990), "Segmented labour markets", in D. Sapsford and Z. Tzannatos (eds), *Current Issues in Labour Economics*, London: Macmillan.

Medoff, J. and K. Abraham (1981), "Are those paid more really productive? The case of experience", *Journal of Human Resources*, 16: 186–216.

Méhaut, P. (1992), "Vocational training and the labour market: the French and German systems compared", in A. Castro, P. Méhaut and J. Rubery (eds) *International Integration and Labour Market Organisation*, London: Academic Press.

Méhaut, P. (1993), "The challenge of competence and further training policies", mimeo.

Meulders, D. (1992), "A working community: segmentation among employment relationships", paper presented at the European Labour Market Conference, Glasgow, November.

Michiels, K. (1991), "Youth unemployment in West Europe: Alternating training systems as responses to youth unemployment in five Western European countries", in K. Forrester and K. Ward (eds), *Unemployment, Education and Training: Case Studies from North America and Europe*, Caddo Gap Press Ltd.

Mill, J. S. (1909), *Principles of Political Economy*, London: Longmans Green; first published 1848.

Milner, S. (1992), "EC training policy", *European Business and Economic Development*, July, 15–21.

Mincer, J. (1958), "Investment in human capital and personal income distribution", *Journal of Political Economy*, 66: 281–302.

Mincer, J. (1962), "On-the-job training: costs, returns, and some implications", *Journal of Political Economy*, 70(2): 50–79.

Mincer, J. (1974), *Schooling, Experience and Earnings*, New York: National Bureau of Economic Research/Columbia University Press.

Mincer, J. (1979), "Human capital and earnings", in National Academy of Education, *Economic Dimensions of Education*, Washington, D.C.: NAE.

Mincer, J. (1991), "Job training: costs, returns and wage profiles',' in D. Stern and J.M.M. Ritzen, (eds), *Market Failure in Training? New Evidence on Training of Adult Employees*, Berlin: Springer Verlag.

Mincer, J. and B. Jovanovic (1981), "Labor mobility and wages", in S. Rosen (ed.), *Studies in Labor Markets*, Chicago: University of Chicago Press.

Minford, P. with D.H. Davies, M.J. Peel and A. Sprague (1983), *Unemployment: Cause and Cure*, Oxford: Basil Blackwell.

Mortensen, D.T. (1986) "Job search and labor market analysis", in O. C. Ashenfelter and R. Layard (eds), *Handbook of Labor Economics*, vol. II, Amsterdam: North-Holland.

NATFHE/Youthaid (1993), *Credit Limits*, London: National Association of Teachers in Further and Higher Education.

National Center for Education Statistics (1992a), *The Condition of Education*, Washington, D.C.: US Department of Education.

National Center for Education Statistics (1992b), *Digest of Education Statistics, 1992*, Washington, D.C.: US Department of Education.

National Center on Education and the Economy (1990), *America's Choice: High Skills or Low Wages*, Washington, D.C.: NCEE.

National Commission on Education (1993), *Learning to Succeed*, London: Heinemann.

National Council for Vocational Qualifications (1993), *The NVQ Monitor*, August, London: NCVQ.

NEDC/MSC (1984), *Competence and Competition: Training and Education in the Federal Republic of Germany, the US and Japan*, London: National Economic Development Council.

National Institute for Economic and Social Research (1990), *Productivity, Education and Training: Britain and Other Countries Compared.*

National Training Task Force (1992), *National Targets for Education and Training* (fact pack), London.

Noah, A. and B. Eckstein (1988), "Business and industry involvement with education in Britain, France and Germany", in J. Laugloi and K. Lillis (eds), *Vocationalising Education. An International Perspective*, London: Pergamon Press.

Oi, W, (1962), "Labour as a quasi-fixed factor of production", *Journal of Political Economy*, 70: 538–55.

Okun, A. (1981), *Prices and Quantities: A Macroeconomic Analysis* Oxford: Basil Blackwell.

Organization for Economic Cooperation and Development (1989), *Employment Outlook*, Paris: OECD.

Organization for Economic Cooperation and Development (1990), *Assessment and Recognition of Skills and Competencies: Developments in France*, Paris: OECD.

Organization for Economic Cooperation and Development (1991), *Employment Outlook*, Paris: OECD.

Organization for Economic Cooperation and Development (1993a), *Education at a Glance*, Paris: OECD.

Organization for Economic Cooperation and Development (1993b), *Employment Outlook*, Paris: OECD.

Osterman, P. (1975), "An empirical study of labour market segmentation", *Industrial and Labour Relations Review*, 28: 508–23.

Oulton, N. and H. Steedman (1992), "The British system of youth training: a comparison with Germany", National Institute of Economic and Social Research Discussion Paper 10, April.

Pätzold, G. (1980), *Die betriebliche Berufsbildung 1918–1945*, Cologne and Vienna.

Payne, J. (1991), "Training women: private or public responsibility?", *Policy Studies*, Summer.

Peel, D. (1990), "Rational expectations", in J. R. Shackleton, *New Thinking in Economics*, Aldershot, Hants., and Brookfield, Vt: Edward Elgar.

Perelman, L.J. (1990), *The American Learning Enterprise in Transition*, part of OECD's project on Further Education and Training of the Labour Force, Country Reports. Paris: OECD.

Phelps, E.S. (1972), "The statistical theory of racism and sexism', *American Economic Review*, September, 659–61.

Pines, M. and A. Carnevale, (1991) "Employment and training", in D.W. Hornbeck and L.M. Salamon (eds), *Human Capital and America's Future*, Baltimore, Md: Johns Hopkins University Press.

Pissarides, C.A. (1981), "Staying on at school in England and Wales", *Economica*, 48: 345–63.

Polachek, S. (1981), "Occupational self-selection: a human capital approach to sex differences in occupational structure", Review of Economics and Statistics, 58: 60–69.

Polachek, S.W. and W.S. Siebert (1993), *The Economics of Earnings*, Cambridge: Cambridge University Press.

Pollard, S. (1965), *The Genesis of Modern Management*, Harmondsworth, Middx: Penguin.

Prais, S. J. (1987), "Educating for productivity: comparisons of Japanese and English schooling and vocational preparation", *National Institute Economic Review*, February, 40–56.

Prais S.J. (1989), "How Europe would see the new British initiative for standardising vocational qualifications", *National Institute Economic Review*, August, 52–54.

Presse- und Informationsamt der Bundesregierung (1992), "Gedämpfter Herbstaufschwung auf dem Arbeitsmarkt", *Sozialpolitische Umschau*, no. 444, October.

Psacharopoulos, G. (1973), *Returns to Education: An International Comparison*, Amsterdam: Elsevier.

Psacharopoulos, G. (1985), "Returns to education: a further international update and implications", *Journal of Human Resources*, 20: 583–604.

Psacharopoulos, G. (1987), "To vocationalize or not to vocationalize? That is the curriculum question", *International Review of Education*, 33: 187–211.

Pugh, G. (1993), "Problems of economic transformation in Eastern Germany: an overview", *British Review of Economic Issues*, 15(37): 119–44.

Pujol, M.A. (1992), *Feminism and Anti-Feminism in Early Economic Thought*, Aldershot and Brookfield, Vt: Edward Elgar.

Raaum, O. (1991), "Labour market training and employment probabilities: preliminary results from Norway', memorandum from the Department of Economics, University of Oslo.

Rainbird, H. and Maguire, M. (1993), "When corporate need supersedes employee development", *Personnel Management*, February, 34–7.

Rees, Teresa (1992), *Women and the Labour Market*, London: Routledge.

Ricketts, M. (1987), *The Economics of Business Enterprise*, Brighton, Sussex: Wheatsheaf.

Ridder, G. (1986), "An event history approach to the evaluation of training, recruitment and employment programmes", *Journal of Applied Econometrics*, 1: 109–26.

Robbins, L. (1932), *An Essay on the Nature and Significance of Economic Science*, London: Macmillan.

Rose, M. (1985), "Universalism, culturalism and the Aix group: promise and problems of a societal approach to economic institutions", *European Sociological Review*, 1(1): 65–83.

Rubery, J. and C. Fagan (1993), *Occupational Segregation of Women and Men in the European Community*, Synthesis Report, Luxembourg: Commission of European Communities.

Rumberger, R.W. (1981), "The rising incidence of over-education in the US labor market", *Economics of Education Review*, 1: 293–314.

Ryan, P. (1981), "Segmentation, duality and the internal labour market", in F. Wilkinson (ed.), *The Dynamics of Labour Market Segmentation*, London: Academic Press.

Salop, J. and S. Salop (1976), "Self-selection and turnover in the labour market", *Quarterly Journal of Economics*, 91: 619–27.

Sapsford, D. and Z. Tzannatos (1993), *The Economics of the Labour Market*, London: Macmillan.

Schäfer, G. (1988), "Arbeitsmarktpolitische Maßnahmen zwischen 1980 und 1988 – Arten, Umfang und direkte Wirkungen", *RWI Mitteilungen*, 39: 353–82.

Scharpf, F.W. (1987), *Sozialdemokratische Krisenpolitik in Europa*, Frankfurt.

Schmid, G. (1988), "Labour market policy in transition: trends and effectiveness in the Federal Republic of Germany", *EFA Report no. 17*, Stockholm.

Schultz, T.W. (1960), "Capital formation in education", *Journal of Political Economy*, December.

Schultz, T.W. (1961), "Investment in human capital", *American Economic Review*, March.

Sehlstedt, K. and L. Schröder (1989), "Språngbråda till arbete? En utvärdering av beredskapsarbete, rekryteringstöd och ungdomsarbete', Document prepared for the Ministry of Labor, EFA, Stockholm.

Sengenberger, W. (1981), "Segmentation and business cycles", in F. Wilkinson (ed.), *The Dynamics of Labour Market Segmentation*, London: Academic Press.

Sengenberger, W. (1984), "West German employment policy: restoring worker competition", *Industrial Relations*, 23, Fall.

Shackleton, J.R. (1976) "Adam Smith and Education", *Higher Education Review*, 8(2): 80–90.

Shackleton, J.R. (1981), "Gary S. Becker: the economist as empire-builder" in J.R. Shackleton and G. Locksley (eds), *Twelve Contemporary Economists*, London: Macmillan.

Shackleton, J.R. (1992), *Training Too Much? A Sceptical Look at the Economics of Skill Provision in the UK*, Hobart Paper 118, London: Institute of Economic Affairs.

Shackleton, J.R. (1993), "Investing in Training: questioning the conventional wisdom", *Policy Studies*, 14(3): 29–40.

Shackleton, J.R. and T. Lange (1993), "Training in Germany: a dissident view", *Economic Affairs*, 13(4): 26–9.

Shaw, G.K. (1990), "Neo-Keynesian theories of unemployment" in J.R. Shackleton (ed.), *New Thinking in Economics*, Aldershot: Edward Elgar.

Sheldrake, J. and S. Vickerstaff (1987), *The History of Industrial Training in Britain*, Aldershot, Hants: Avebury.

Sicherman, N. (1991), "'Overeducation' in the labor market", *Journal of Labour Economics*, April, 101–22.

Siebert, W.S. and J.T. Addison (1991), "Internal labour markets: causes and consequences", *Oxford Review of Economic Policy*, 7(1): 76–92.

Smith, A. (1910), *An Enquiry into the Nature and Causes of the Wealth of Nations*, London: J.M. Dent; first published 1776.

Smithers, A. (1993), Report for *Dispatches* television programme, London: Channel Four Television.

Solow, R. (1957), "Technical change and the aggregate production function", *Review of Economics and Statistics*, 39: 312–20.

Spitznagel, E. (1989), "Zielgruppenorientierung und Eingliederungserfolg bei Allgemeinen Maßnahmen zur Arbeitsbeschaffung (ABM)", *Mitteilungen aus der Arbeitsmarkt- und Berufsforschung*, 22(4): 523–39.

Steedman, H. (1990), "Improvements in workforce qualifications: Britain and France, 1979–88", *National Institute Economic Review*, August, 50–61.

Steedman, H. (1992), "Mathematics in vocational youth training for the building trades in Britain, France and Germany", Discussion Paper no. 9, London: National Institute of Economic and Social Research.

Stevens, J. and R. MacKay (eds) (1991), *Training and Competitiveness*, London: National Economic Development Office and Kogan Page.

Stigler, G.J. (1971) "The theory of economic regulation", *Bell Journal of Economics* 2: 1.

Stiglitz, J. (1975), "The theory of screening, education and the distribution of income', *American Economic Review*, June, 283–300.

Streeck, W., J. Hilbert, K.-H. van Kevelaer, F. Maier and H. Weber (1987), *The Role of the Social Partners in Vocational Training and Further Training in the Federal Republic of Germany*, Berlin: CEDEFOP.

Tan, H., B. Chapman, C. Peterson and A. Booth (1991), *Youth Training in the United States, Britain and Australia*, Rand Corporation, Paper R-4022-ED.

Taubman, P. and M.L. Wachter (1986), "Segmented labor markets" in O. Ashenfelter and R. Layard (eds), *Handbook of Labor Economics*, Volume II, Amsterdam: North-Holland.

Taubman, P.F. and T. Wales (1973), "Higher education, mental ability and screening", *Journal of Political Economy*, Jan./Feb., S28–S55.

Thomas, G. (1992), "The Labour Force Survey in the European dimension", paper given at the European Labour Market Conference, Glasgow, November.

Thompson, P.J. (1989), "Providing a qualified society to meet the challenge", *National Westminster Bank Quarterly Review*, February.

Thurow, L.C. and R.E.B. Lucas (1972), *The American Distribution of Income: A Structural Problem*, Washington DC: Joint Economic Committee.

Turner, P., I. Dale and C. Hurst (1992), "Training: a key to the future", *Employment Gazette*, August.

Tysome, Tony (1993), "GNVQs give false hope to students", *Times Higher Education Supplement*, 19 November.

Unemployment Unit (1993) *Working Brief*, Issue 44, May.

United States Department of Education (1991), *America 2000*, Washington, D.C.: USGP.

United States Department of Education and Department of Labor (1988), *The Bottom Line: Basic Skills in the Workplace*, Washington, D.C.: USGPO.

United States Department of Labor (1992), *How Workers Get Their Training: A 1991 Update*, Bulletin 2407, Washington, D.C.: Bureau of Labor Statistics.

United States General Accounting Office (1988), *Job Training Partnership Act: Participants, Services and Outcomes*, Washington, D.C.: USGP.

Vaughan, R.J. (1989), *Public Subsidies and Private Training*, National Assessment of Vocational Education, Washington, D.C.: US Department of Education.

Verdier, E. (1994), "Training and enterprise in France", in R. McNabb and K. Whitfield (eds), *The Market for Training: International Perspectives on Theory, Methodology and Policy*, Aldershot: Avebury.

Wachter, M.L. and R.D. Wright (1990), "The economics of internal labour markets" ` D.J.B. Mitchell and M.A. Zaidi (eds), *The Economics of Human R urce Management*, Oxford: Basil Blackwell.

Walsh, Siob, an (1994), *Does Training Work?*, London: Catholic Association for Racial Justice.

West, E.G. (1965), *Education and the State*, 2nd edition, London: Institute of Economic Affairs.

West, E.G. (1971), *Education and the State*, London: Institute of Economic Affairs.

Westhoff, G. (1990), "Die Ausbildungbeteiligung von jungen Frauen im dualen system" in M. Frackman, *Ein Schritt vorwarts: Frauen in Ausbildung und Beruf*, Hamburg.

Williamson, O.E. (1980), "The organization of work", *Journal of Economic Behaviour and Organization*, 1: 5–38.

Williamson, O.E. (1985), *The Economic Institutions of Capitalism*, New York: Free Press.

Wirtschaftswoche (1993), "Zweiter Arbeitsmarkt – Geringer Anreiz", 6 August.

Wolf, A. (1992), *Mathematics for Vocational Students in France and England: Contrasting Provision and Consequences*, NIESR Discussion Paper (new series) no.23, London: National Institute of Economic and Social Research.

Ziderman, A. (1978), *Manpower Training: Theory and Policy*, London: Macmillan.

Ziderman, A. and E. Katz (1990), "Investment in general training: the role of information and labour mobility", *Economic Journal*, 100: 1147–58.

Index